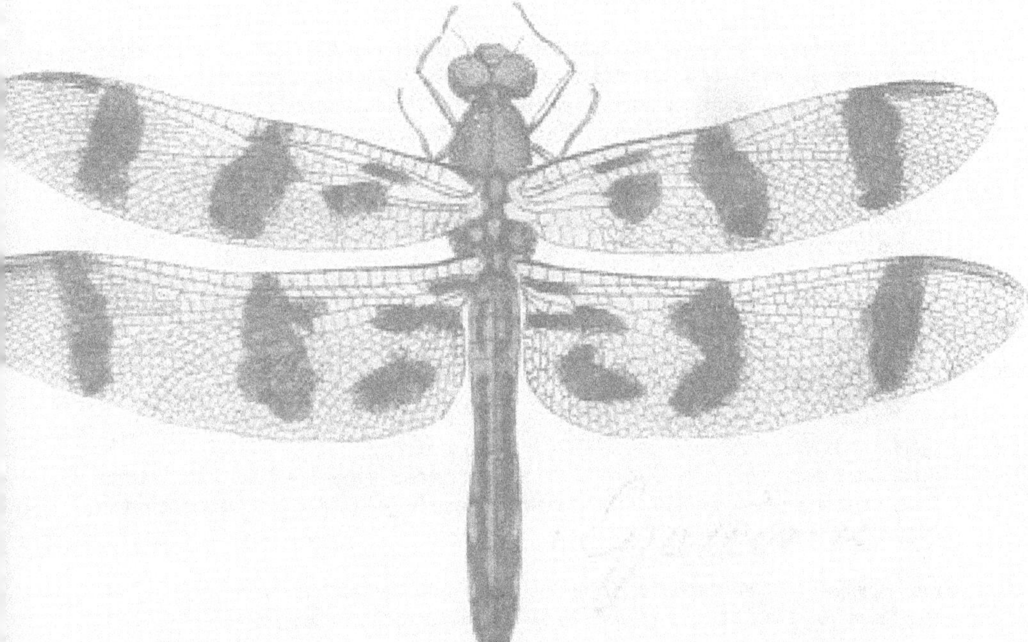

First published by Busybird Publishing 2019

Copyright © 2019 Heinrich Fliedner and Ian Endersby

ISBN 978-1-925949-08-7

Heinrich Fliedner and Ian Endersby have asserted their right under the Copyright, Designs and Patents Act 1988 to be identified as the author of this work. The information in this book is based on the author's experiences and opinions. The publisher specifically disclaims responsibility for any adverse consequences, which may result from use of the information contained herein. Permission to use information has been sought by the author. Any breaches will be rectified in further editions of the book.

All rights reserved. No part of this publication may be reproduced, stored in or introduced into a retrieval system, or transmitted in any form, or by any means (electronic, mechanical, photocopying, recording or otherwise) without the prior written permission of the author. Any person who does any unauthorised act in relation to this publication may be liable to criminal prosecution and civil claims for damages. Enquiries should be made through the publisher.

Cover design: Busybird Publishing
Layout and typesetting: Busybird Publishing

Busybird Publishing
2/118 Para Road
Montmorency, Victoria
Australia 3094
www.busybird.com.au

Front Cover: *Libellula pulchella*. One of the earliest named dragonflies from North America. Drury's specimen came from New York. Illustration from Plate XLVIII, 5 *Illustrations of Natural History* 1. Dru Drury 1770.

Frontispiece: *Celithemis eponina*. Another species described and illustrated by Dru Drury. Illustration from Plate XLVII, 5 *Illustrations of Natural History* 2. Dru Drury 1773.

Back Cover: *Cordulegaster sarracenia*. The most recent dragonfly to be named from North America by John Abbott & Troy Hibbitts in 2011. Photo by Martin Reid. http://www.martinreid.com/Odonata%20website/odonate204.html

'The Progress of Naming North American Odonata' diagram provided by Ian Endersby.

 A catalogue record for this book is available from the National Library of Australia

The Scientific Names of North American Dragonflies

**HEINRICH FLIEDNER
IAN ENDERSBY**

Contents

Preface	i
Acknowledgements	iii
Photo and Portrait Credits	v
Introduction	1
History	1
Scientific names	7
Eponyms	8
Names Concerning People	12
Toponyms	14
The Authors	17
Endnotes	83
The Etymologies	91
References	245
Resources used in eliciting etymologies	245
References containing original descriptions or explanatory matter	246
Appendix	265

Preface

While we were preparing our book *The Naming of Australia's Dragonflies*, each of us consulted the etymologies given in *A Checklist of North American Odonata: including English name, etymology, type locality, and distribution* by Dennis R. Paulson & Sidney W. Dunkle (2012). When we met for the first time at the European Congress of Odonatology (2016) in Tyringe, Sweden, amongst our many conversations we agreed that we had found some entries which could warrant a review. Also recent work by Matti Hämäläinen had shed additional light on some people commemorated with an eponym. We contacted Dennis, the senior author of the checklist, and offered to provide amendments for some of the definitions, and he readily agreed. With this encouragement a number of amendments were suggested for inclusion in the next edition of the checklist. However, our research which included perusal of the original description for every taxon, revealed much information that could not be encapsulated in the phrase or sentence to match the checklist format. When assembled, it was fast approaching the size that warranted publication as a book. If a short biography of each author was included, a book it had to be.

We have many people to thank for help in finding copies of the more obscure references. Once the etymologies were essentially complete, and we had started on the biographies, Dennis recruited Harold "Hal" White to help with sourcing photographs of American practitioners and to give a point of contact for those entomologists still, or recently, active in this field.

Publication and Distribution presented another problem. This was not the sort of work that would be snapped up by a commercial publisher who would then market and distribute it worldwide, and it was not feasible to distribute from somewhere as remote from America as Australia (or Europe). Whilst many people now prefer publications as a pdf, neither of us would be happy if that were the only medium to be made available. Busybird Publishing, who prepared the volume on the Australian taxa, introduced us to the concept of Print On Demand, and that was the solution we had been seeking.

In November 2018 a new edition of the Checklist was published which required us to include an extra four species and another author's biography.

And here you have the result of that team's work over more than two years.

      Heinrich Fliedner   Ian Endersby

                         2019

Acknowledgements

All genus and species names that are included in this work are those in current use in the *Checklist of North American Odonata: Including English Name, Etymology, Type Locality, and Distribution* by DENNIS R. PAULSON and SIDNEY W. DUNKLE (2012 and 2018 editions). Its comprehensive bibliography was an invaluable resource. The checklist was augmented with the changes to Gomphid genera (WARE ET AL. 2016) and the addition of *Coryphaeschna apeora* to the North American fauna REID & RICKARD (2018).

The Biodiversity Heritage Library – www.biodiversitylibrary.org/ – was the source of most of the original descriptions that were consulted. For those which it did not contain, we are grateful to Martin Schorr, Harold White and John Abbott for supplying copies.

The following people provided biographical details about themselves, photographs, or both: John Abbott, Paul-Michael Brunelle, Rob Cannings, Carl Cook, Jerrell Daigle, Rosser Garrison, Troy Hibbits, Ken Knopf, Ellis Laudermilk, Mike May, Dennis Paulson, Ken Tennessen, Tim Vogt.

We received valuable assistance from the following for biographical details, photographs, introductions to staff of relevant institutions and extant odonatologists, and suggested avenues of research:

John Abbott (University of Alabama); Ellen Alers (Smithsonian Institution Archives); Bo Beolens; Andres Betschart (Winterthurer Bibliotheken, for use of the portrait of Sulzer); Stephanie Conant (Department of Biology, University of Detroit Mercy); Patrick Franklin

(Bartlett Tree Research Laboratories); Matti Hämäläinen; Lisa Junker, (Entomological Society of America); Mark O'Brien (University of Michigan); Martin Reid; Dawn Roberts (Peggy Notebaert Museum, Chicago); Emily Sandall (Department of Entomology, Penn State University); Editha Schubert and Grit May (Senckenberg Deutsches Entomologisches Institut); Nick Tew; Erika Tucker (University of Michigan Museum of Zoology), Marcel Wasscher, Florian Weihrauch.

Julia Colby and Jennifer Zaspel (Milwaukee Public Museum) searched their archives on our behalf, but were unsuccessful.

To Dennis Paulson we are grateful for encouragement, advice, proof reading and recruiting Hal White to the project. Hal White's contribution included the provision of photos and references, introductions to people who could assist, proof reading and encouragement, and persisting with slow and recalcitrant contributors. These two have made the preparation of this work much easier for two authors remote from the country and its odonatological community.

And to anyone we have inadvertently overlooked, our apologies and sincere thanks.

Photo and Portrait Credits

Abbott, John: Courtesy of John Abbott

Banks, Nathan: OSBORN, H. 1937. Fragments of Entomological History, Part I. The Author. Pl. 32

Beatty, Alice (Ferguson): Courtesy of Hal White

Belle, Jean: *Guernsey Evening Press and Star.* 24 July 1978 p. 3

Bird, Ralph: http://www.mhs.mb.ca/docs/people/bird_rd.shtml

Brauer, Friedrich: https://en.wikipedia.org/wiki/Friedrich_Moritz_Brauer. In the public domain

Brittinger, Christian: From: *Oesterreichische botanische Zeitschrift* 10 (1860), facing p. 210

Bromley, Stanley: OSBORN, H. 1946. Fragments of Entomological History, Part II. The Author. Pl. 3

Brunelle, Paul-Michael: Courtesy of Paul-Michael Brunelle

Burmeister, Carl: https://upload.wikimedia.org/wikipedia/de/2/2f/Burmeister_hermann.jpg

Byers, Charles: *Odonatologica* 11 (1982) p. 245, with permission

Calvert Philip: https://en.wikipedia.org/wiki/Philip_Powell_Calvert : see website for Wikipedia justification for Fair Use

Cannings, Robert: Courtesy Rob Cannings

Carle, Frank Louis: http://rci.rutgers.edu/~carle/

Charpentier, Toussaint de: Portrait from: "*Glückauf - Berg - und Hüttenmännische Zeitschrift*" 28 (1892) p. 565

Cook, Carl: *images.peabody.yale.edu/lepsoc/nls/2010s/2011/2011_v53_n1.pdf* – *News of the Lepidopterist Society* 53 (1) (2011) p. 9

Cowley, John: University of Michigan Museum of Zoology, Insect Division Archives

Currie, Rolla: USGS Patuxent Wildlife Research Center, with permission

Daigle, Jerrell: Hal White Collection

Davis, William: OSBORN, H. 1937. Fragments of Entomological History, Part I. The Author. Pl. 21

Donnelly, Thomas: Courtesy of John Abbott

Drury, Dru: Engraving by W.H. Lizars for the *Memoir of Dru Drury* by C.H. Smith, published in Jardine's Naturalist's Library in 1842

Dunkle, Sidney: Hal White Collection

Erichson, Wilhelm: *Entomologische Zeitung, Stettin* 17/1856, pl. 1 (copyright expired)

Fabricius, Johan: https://en.wikipedia.org/wiki/Johan_Christian_Fabricius. In the public domain

Förster, Friedrich: University of Michigan Museum of Zoology, Insect Division Archives

Fraser, Frederic: *Entomologists' Monthly Magazine* 99 (1963): 97

Garrison, Rosser: Image courtesy of Rosser Garrison

Gloyd, Leonora: From the Beatty collection, Pennsylvania State University

Photo and Portrait Credits

González-Soriano, Enrique: http://www.ib.unam.mx/directorio/70, with the permission of the author

Gundlach, Juan: https://en.wikipedia.org/wiki/Juan_Gundlach. In the public domain

Hagen, Hermann: https://en.wikipedia.org/wiki/Hermann_August_Hagen. In the public domain

Harvey, Francis: OSBORN, H. 1937. Fragments of Entomological History, Part I. The Author. Pl. 19

Hibbitts, Troy: Courtesy of Troy Hibbitts

Hine, James: *The Ohio Journal of Science.* 31 (6) (November, 1931), opposite p. 511

Hodges, Robert (in pith helmet)**:** Alabama Museum of Natural History/Alabama Geological Survey

Karsch, Ferdinand: Senckenberg Deutsches Entomologisches Institut

Kellicott, David: *Transactions of the American Microscopical Society* Vol. 20, Twenty-First Annual Meeting (1898), facing p. 21 ex JSTOR

Kennedy, Clarence: *Annals of the Entomological Society of America*, Volume 40, Issue 2, 1 June 1947, facing p. 168

Kirby, William: *The Entomologist's Record and Journal of Variation* 24 (1912) pl. XVI

Knopf, Kenneth: http://www.millhopperfamilydentistry.com/meet-the-staff/

Laudermilk, Ellis: Courtesy of Ellis Laudermilk

Linnaeus, Carl: https://en.wikipedia.org/wiki/Carl_Linnaeus, Alexander Roslin, 1775 (oil on canvas, Gripsholm Castle)

Martin, René: *Entomological News* 38 (1927): pl. IV facing page 197

May, Michael: Courtesy of Leslie May

McLachlan, Robert: *Entomological News* 15 (1904) pl. XVI

Montgomery, Basil: *Odonatologica* 12 (1983) p. 1, with permission

Morse, Albert: *Psyche* Volume 44 (1937), Issue 1-2, pl. I between pp. 2 and 5

Muttkowski, Richard: 1930 yearbook for University of Detroit p.120

Navás, Longinos: Senckenberg Deutsches Entomologisches Institut

Needham, James: Hal White collection

Newman, Edward: *Zoologist* ser. II, 11 (1876) preceding title page

Packard, Alpheus: *Entomological News* 16/1905, pl. IV

Palisot, Ambroise: https://commons.wikimedia.org/wiki/File:Palisot_de_Beauvois_Ambroise_1752-1820.jpg. In the public domain

Paulson, Dennis: Courtesy Dennis R. Paulson

Pritchard, Arthur: *Journal of Economic Entomology*, Volume 58, Issue 4, 1 August 1965, Page 807, with permission

Provancher, Léon: *Entomological News* 6/1895 Pl. IX

Rambur, Jules: OBERTHÜR, C. 1914. Portraits de Lépidoptérologistes. Première Série. Études de Lépidoptérologie comparée. Fasc. IX (2). Rennes, Oberthür

Robert, Adrien: http://www.sbl.umontreal.ca/batiments/index.html#robert

Root, Francis: *American Journal of Epidemiology*, Volume 21, Issue 1, 1 January 1935, Pages 1–2, https://academic.oup.com/aje/article-abstract/21/1/1/182414/FRANCIS-METCALF-ROOT

Say, Thomas: *Entomological News* 6/1895, pl. I

Scudder, Samuel: *Entomological News* 22/1911, pl. VIII

Selys, Baron Michel: *Journal für Ornithology*, Vol. 49 (1901), preceding p. 361

Sulzer, Johann: © Winterthurer Bibliotheken, Sammlung Winterthur

Photo and Portrait Credits

Tennessen, Kenneth: Courtesy of Kenneth Tennessen

Trybom, Filip: AURIVILLIUS, C. 1914. Filip Trybom †. Med poträtt. *Entomologisk tidskrift* 35: 81-86

Uhler, Philip: *Entomological News* 24 (1913) pl. XV preceding p. 433

Vogt, Timothy: Courtesy Timothy Vogt

Walker, Edmund: *Annals of the Entomological Society of America*, Volume 63, Issue 2, 16 March 1970, Pages 631–632, with permission

Walsh, Benjamin: OSBORN, H. 1937. Fragments of Entomological History, Part I. The Author. Pl. 8

Westfall, Minter: *Odonatologica* 15 (1986) p. 2, with permission

Westwood, John: *Entomologist's Monthly Magazine* 29 (1893) following p. 50

Williamson, Edward: *Entomological News* 46 (1935) preceding p. 1

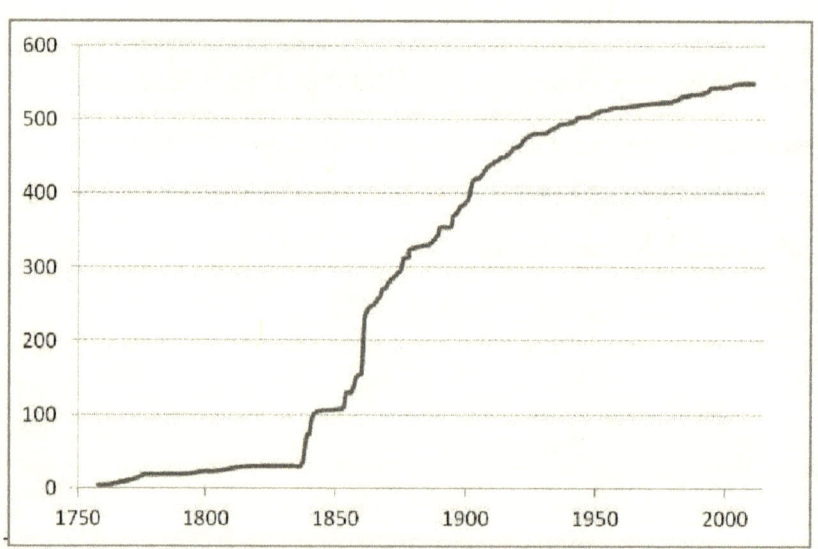
The Progress of Naming North American Odonata

Introduction

History

The North American Odonata Checklist 2012, with a new edition in 2018 (after augmentation by WARE ET AL. 2016 and REID & RICKARD 2018) comprises 88 genera and 469 species. Linnaeus named the first five taxa in two publications (1758, 1763). *Libellula* was the genus name which he used for all Odonata and that still persists in *Libellula quadrimaculata*. *Erythrodiplax umbrata* and *Tramea carolina* are North American endemics while *Aeshna juncea* and *Libellula quadrimaculata* have a much wider distribution.

The specimens on which he based his descriptions for these last two were from Europe. *Cordulegaster sarracenia* is the most recent to be named, in 2011. The first American entomologist to name a local specimen was Thomas Say whose paper[*], published posthumously in 1839, named 25 species, five of which are retained in his original genus.

Between LINNAEUS in 1758 and ABBOTT & HIBBITS in 2011, 74 authors and co-authors, in 196 scientific papers or books, named the North American odonates. The progress of this naming can be seen in the figure on the opposite page.

---

[*]. *Journal of the Academy of Natural Sciences of Philadelphia.* 8: 9–46

Prior to the publication of Say's "*Descriptions of new North American neuropterous insects, and observations on some already described*", European specialists had been the source of new taxonomy. Between them, Linnaeus, Drury, Fabricius, Leach, and Burmeister had described just under 9% of the 550 taxa recognised today.

The chart shows two periods of intense activity: one about 1840 and the other about 1860. Much of the first period was due to Thomas Say with his posthumous 1839 publication, but Carl Burmeister, also in 1839, published his *Handbuch der Entomologie*, which contained descriptions of 16 taxa from North America. Also in this time frame, Jules Rambur, a French physician and entomologist, produced *Histoire naturelle des insectes* (part of the Suites à Buffon, 1842) in which he attempted to catalog the Neuroptera (*sensu* Linné) on a world wide scale. It includes more than 350 Odonata, amounting to more than half of the known described species at the time, including 28 taxa known from North America. The second peak is due primarily to Hermann Hagen and Baron Michel Edmond de Selys Longchamps, who often collaborated. When the Smithsonian Institution wanted a compendium of the North American Neuroptera, the German Baltic entomologist C. R. von Osten-Sacken, then a Russian diplomat in the U.S., recommended Hagen for the task and arranged for more than 1500 specimens to be sent to Königsberg for his use. In 1867 Hagen accepted an invitation by L. Agassiz to curate the collection of Harvard University, where he remained until his death. European entomologists were still the primary sources for the taxonomy of North American Odonata until about 1890. By this time 65% of the taxa currently known from North America had been described. The most prolific of the describers had been Hagen and Selys, with 126 and 73 taxa respectively.

As previously mentioned, Thomas Say, in 1839, was the first North American odonatologist to name local species. It wasn't until 1857 that Philip Uhler described four species prior to the Smithsonian Institution publishing his translation from the Latin of Hagen's *Catalogue of the Neuroptera of North America*. In all, 53 authors from the Americas have named species or genera currently on the North American checklist.

Thirty-six of these sole or senior authors named only one species. Calvert (48 taxa); Say (25); Williamson (19); Needham (18); Walker (13); Kennedy (11); Walsh (11) and Morse (7) produced the highest totals. Philip Calvert, initially encouraged by Hagen, produced over 300 publications and spent most of his teaching life at the University of Pennsylvania. Bruce Williamson held the position of Associate Curator of Entomology in the Museum of Zoology, University of Michigan, moving to Ann Arbor after his retirement. He was in contact with, and mentor to, many odonatologists. Working predominantly from Cornell University, James George Needham was a pioneer in the studies of larval stages of the Odonata and was internationally recognised for his studies of wing venation with John Henry Comstock. His handbook, followed by his manual to the dragonflies of North America, were extremely influential. As well as lecturing at the University of Toronto, Edmund Walker was the first honorary curator of Entomology at the Royal Ontario Museum and the author of the three volume work *The Odonata of Canada and Alaska* (Philip Corbet completed volume 3). Clarence Kennedy, influenced by E.B. Williamson, completed a thesis on the phylogeny of damselflies and was one of the finest illustrators of Odonata. Benjamin Walsh, originally from England, had been Charles Darwin's classmate at Cambridge. He was involved in the founding of the Illinois Natural History Society and was the editor of scientific journals including *American Entomologist*. The insect collection of Albert Morse, comprising more than fifty thousand specimens, was acquired by the Harvard Museum of Comparative Zoology in 1920-22.

From the table below, the breadth and depth of the publications and taxonomic effort of those who named North American Odonata can be judged. Following that are some remarks on scientific names in general, on eponyms and toponyms, and finally short biographies of most of the authors. The headings in parantheses indicate species that have been synonymised or subspecies raised to full species rank.

	Publications	First	Last	Genus	Species	(Species)	(Subspecies)	TOTAL
Abbott & Hibbitts	1	2011			1			1
Banks	1	1896			1			1
Belle	3	1970	1987	1	2			3
Bird	1	1933			1			1
Brauer	2	1868	1900	5	1	2		8
Brittinger	1	1850		1				1
Bromley	1	1924			1			1
Brunelle	1	2000			1			1
Burmeister	1	1839		1	5	10		16
Byers	2	1927	1939		2			2
Calvert	14	1890	1952	2	34	6	7	49
Cannings & Garrison	1	1991			1			1
Carle	6	1979	1992		7	1		8
Carle & May	1	1987			1			1
Charpentier	1	1840		2				2
Cook & Daigle	1	1985			1			1
Cook & Laudermilk	1	2004			1			1
Cowley	1	1934		1				1
Currie, B.P.	1	1917			1			1
Currie, R.P.	1	1903			1			1
Daigle	1	1995			1			1
Davis	4	1913	1927	1	3			4
Donnelly	4	1961	1967		3	1		4
Drury	1	1773			1	7		8
Dunkle	1	1992			1			1
Erichson	1	1848			1			1

Introduction

	Publications	First	Last	Genus	Species	(Species)	(Subspecies)	TOTAL
Fabricius	3	1775	1798	1	2	5		8
Ferguson	1	1950				1		1
Förster	2	1900	1909	1				1
Fraser	1	1922		1				1
Garrison	4	1986	1996		6			6
Gloyd	4	1933	1943		4	2		6
González Soriano	1	2002			1			1
Gundlach	1	1888				1		1
Hagen	13	1856	1890	12	46	68		126
Harvey	1	1898			1			1
Hine	1	1901			1			1
Hodges	1	1955			1			1
Karsch	1	1890		1	2			3
Kellicott	1	1895			1			1
Kennedy	5	1915	1920	3	7	1		11
Kirby	3	1889	1894	8	5			13
Knopf & Tennessen	1	1980			1			1
Leach	1	1815		5				5
Linnaeus	2	1758	1763	1	1	3		5
Martin	1	1907			1			1
McLachlan	4	1883	1896	1	5	1		7
Montgomery	1	1943			1			1
Morse	1	1895			7			7
Muttkowski	2	1910	1911	1	1	1		3
Navás	1	1911		1				1
Needham	7	1897	1955	8	7	3	1	19

	Publications	First	Last	Genus	Species	(Species)	(Subspecies)	TOTAL
Needham, Westfall & May	1	2000	2000	1				1
Newman	1	1833		1				1
Packard	1	1863			1			1
Palisot de Beauvois	1	1805				1		1
Paulson	2	1983	1994		2			2
Pritchard	1	1935			2			2
Provancher	1	1875				1		1
Rambur	1	1842		4	9	15		28
Robert	1	1954			1			1
Root	2	1923	1924		2			2
Say	1	1839			5	20		25
Scudder	2	1866	1866		2	4		6
Selys	23	1850	1883	23	22	27	1	73
Sulzer	1	1776				1		1
Tennessen	2	1983	2004		2			2
Tennessen & Vogt	1	2004			1			1
Tough	1	1900				1		1
Trybom	1	1889			1			1
Uhler	1	1857		1	1	2		4
Vogt & Smith	1	1993			1			1
Walker	7	1907	1952		12		1	13
Walsh	2	1862	1863		6	5		11
Westfall	6	1943	1975		6			6
Westwood	1	1837			1			1
Williamson	15	1898	1932	1	15	3		19
Williamson & Gloyd	1	1933			1			1

Scientific names

We are used to the Linnean binomial system which specifies each species by just two names, one for the genus, which it normally shares with closely related organisms, and the other one, which identifies the species itself. The great improvement that was achieved by Linnaeus' brilliant idea can be seen by how the English scientist John Ray (1627-1705), about 50 years before Linnaeus, tried to hallmark different species of dragonflies, for instance: 2. *Libella maxima, abdomine longo tenuiore, alis fulvescentibus* † [2. very large dragonfly with a long, rather slim abdomen and tawny wings]. If the tawny wings had not been mentioned, it would be nearly impossible to recognize by this description the Eurasian species *Aeshna grandis*. Others of his names are even longer so it can readily be seen what was achieved by Linnaeus' system to identify each species by two names in Latin (or latinized Greek). That also solved the problem of the different native languages of scientists around the world thus allowing for international communication. The importance of a distinctive nomenclature was well known to Linnaeus. So in his Philosophia Botanica he declares: "*Nomina si nescis, perit et scientia rerum*" ‡ [If you are unaquainted with the names, the knowledge of matters is lost also].

But scientific names may have an additional meaning besides labeling organisms unmistakably for taxonomists. Fabricius, Linnaeus' disciple, who specialized in entomology, wrote: "*Nomina ... Optima sunt, quae omnino nil significant*" §[Best are the names which do not signify anything at all]. From the context it can be seen that he has only generic names in mind, which – if referring to a special character of the taxon – might very well be falsified by a newly detected species which does not share the typical feature conveyed by the generic name. However, most authors have not followed his advice but chosen names which have an additional meaning. That may be information on the appearance of the respective species like morphology, coloration, pattern, similarities, size, or on their provenance, distribution or typical environment. This information may be helpful for recognizing the species either in collections or in their natural habitat. If a species is named for a person

---

†. Raius, J. 1710. Historia insectorum. Opus postumum. London, A.&J. Churchill, pp. 48 + 140.
‡. Linnaeus, C. 1755. Philosophia Botanica (Editio secunda). Vindobonae, Trattner, p. 158
§. Fabricius, J.C. 1792. Entomologia Systematica, Emendata et Aucta. Vol. I, Copenhagen, C.G. Proft, p. X

this may show a special relation between the author and the person honored by the dedication of the species.

As the scientific names have to be Latin (or latinized from other languages, especially ancient Greek), this book endeavors to assist those who are less knowledgeable in these languages to understand the meaning of the names.

But there are limits as before the middle of the last century it was not customary to explain the etymology of the names. And so often one can only guess what an author had in mind when choosing a name. That applies for many of the names Hagen gave in 1861, even though they are unmistakable Latin words. Why did he call an *Enallagma* by the adjective *civile* [= civil, of citizens]? That is not a quality one would associate with a damselfly. Probably he decided repeatedly to use an unmistakable name without any connotation, as he had to find so many for that publication. Difficulties for the interpretation also arise when names from Hagen's collection or manuscripts were published later by Calvert (e.g. *Argia munda*) or Gundlach (*Brachymesia herbida*).

In the explanation of the names the following methodology has been observed:
- If the etymology is explained in the original description, it has been directly quoted.
- If there is no explanation, but the Greek or Latin roots are obvious (*bi-line-ata* = with two stripes), the best match of these roots in the original description has been chosen.
- If no obvious characters are apparent, the probable derivations are given with some speculation as to how they might apply.

Eponyms

Considering only odonates known from North America, among its 557 taxa 103 refer to people (or gods). Of these, seven are what we might call 'typological' as they do not denote certain individuals, but types. The first names of this kind in modern odonatological nomenclature are the names Linnaeus gave to his first two species of damselflies in 1758, namely *virgo* (virgin) and *puella* (girl, maid) certainly in reference to the French name of *demoiselles*, which also is at the base of *damselflies*. North American taxa of this kind are Fabricius' species name *heros* (hero), Leach's genus names *Anax* (Lord of the house) and *Lestes* (robber, pirate),

Hagen's *Hetairina* (like a courtesan), *princeps* (chief), *vidua* (widow) and Calvert's *domina* (mistress, dame), which name he says is from a letter of Hagen.

Then there are ficticious persons at the base of names, that is from mythology or literature. Of the latter kind there are only Burmeister's *amazili* after an Inca heroine from a French novel and Selys' *attala*, which might reflect the main character from another French novel, or might be prompted by a saint of the seventh or eighth century. Drury's seven names from history also are inspired by literature of his time.

Of the seven names from mythology, most refer to classical antiquity. Only one, Calvert's *tezpi*, a survivor of the Deluge, is from a Mexican tradition. But this name at the same time is a reference to the range of the species. So it is to be seen, that besides being names there may be some additional information intended. This may also be an allusion to appearance like in Sulzer's *danae*, which probably refers to the goldish sparks of the thorax in young individuals. Donnelly named his *Aeshna* species *persephone* after the Queen of the netherworld to evoke the habitat with its regular change of light and shadow. Then there are Selys' genus names *Nehalennia* after a goddess from Belgian Gaul inspired by archeological excavations of that time, the compound name *Amphiagrion*, formed according to his habit when splitting a new genus from an existing genus to combine a name of a representative species of the new genus with the old genus name; in this case the species *A.amphion*, named after a Theban hero, which as a younger synonym is no longer in use. Then there is Hagen's *irene*, which may denote the Greek goddess of peace, but may also refer to some unknown woman of his time, and last Kirby's *dryas* (tree nymph), which name replaced the preoccupied name *Lestes nympha* Selys by another demi-goddess from antiquity.

The names ending in *–themis* shall not be treated individually here, whereas *Themis* certainly was a goddess in ancient Greece, because Hagen used this element exclusively in compound names as a formal indication, that these were libellulid genera. (Later *–themis* names may also pertain to Corduliidae and Synthemistidae).

The other names of this category refer to real persons, either from history or from the time of the author. Of the eight taxa described by Drury seven are named after women, whose names come from classical antiquity, but he does not explain his choice. So we are not able to assign these names to individuals in particular with certainty. Also for Uhler's *julia* there may be several women from Roman antiquity or an unknown woman of his time, as he does not give any explanation. The species name *lais*, which goes back to a collection name at Vienna chosen by Brauer, is not an indication of his enthusiasm for the famous courtesan, but it is to indicate a similarity to the calopterygid genus *Lais* established by Selys some twenty years before. The Selysian name *marcella* (and perhaps also *attala*) probably refers to a saint from antiquity (as may Drury's *lydia*). There is one name by Selys, for which it is not clear to whom it refers, for *Triacanthagyna septima* must reflect a female name (see below p. 219), but as the author does not explain who he had in mind, we cannot be certain about her identity: if ficticious, from history or an aquaintance.

There remain 76 eponyms, which refer to contemporaries of the respective authors. Not all of these will be mentioned here explicitly, but some will be treated to give an idea why taxa can be dedicated to persons. Normally they show esteem or, that in some kind of way, the author owes something to that person or wants to show close bonds to someone, with the effect of a lasting tribute of the eponym.

Twenty-eight of this kind of name refer to the person from whom the authors got their typological material or some of it. In the table below they are summarized as 'collectors'. Two of the names in this category are special, because they do not name the collector himself, because he is not known. One of these is Hagen's (*Tachopteryx*) *thoreyi*, because G. Thorey was the dealer, from whom Hagen had got this American species even before he published his 'Synopsis' in 1861. The other one by Selys comes from an historical person generating this kind of name: the species name *S. franklini* is a tribute to the famous Arctic explorer John Franklin, who at the time of the dedication was lost in the Arctic region already for more than thirty years. But at the same time there is a special reason for the dedication of the species, because Franklin was in charge of the expedition by which the type specimen was secured. All other names from this category refer to the actual collectors like Selys' (*Enallagma*) *doubledayi*. Because of the collector's special relation to the species named after him in the table below all these are to be found in this category, also, if like S.H. Scudder, to whom Selys dedicated *S. scudderi*, the collector was a distinguished odonatologist himself, or if he was a near relative of the author, like the eponym of Williamson's *L.*

jesseana, who was a cousin. Some of the collectors even accompanied the author when securing the type material, like Ivy and Laura Ditzler, who took part in Williamson's collecting trip in 1931.

The largest group of eponyms comprises other odonatologists (31 names). Incorporated into this group are all entomologists who have described at least one taxon from North America. The odonatologist, to whom most taxa from North America are dedicated, was H.A. Hagen, two of them by his colleague and friend Selys (to whom he dedicated one species himself), one by B.D. Walsh, and one by W.F. Kirby; three taxa are dedicated to E.B. Williamson (*Williamsonia* Davis, *Somatochlora williamsoni* Walker and *Aphylla williamsoni* (Gloyd)), two have P. Calvert as eponym (*Tramea calverti* Muttkowski and *Somatochlora calverti* Williamson & Gloyd) and just as many, M.J. Westfall (Cook & Daigle 1985; Carle & May 1987). Among these names are some from former students or assistants for their teachers, like *Ischnura kellicotti* Willamson, *Aphylla williamsoni* (Gloyd), *Argia leonorae* Garrison, *Libellula needhami* Westfall, *Phanogomphus westfalli* (Carle & May), some in admiration of outstanding publications like *Ophiogomphus howei* Bromley, *Progomphus bellei* Knopf & Tennessen, *Aeshna walkeri* Kennedy, *Telebasis byersi* Westfall, *Gomphurus gonzalezi* (Dunkle), *Ophiogomphus westfalli* Cook & Daigle.

Some of the dedications may have been prompted by a special anniversary of the honored, like Hagen's *H. selysii* by the 65th birthday of his friend and Westfall's *L. needhami* by the 75th birthday or his *G. septima* for the 65th birthday of Septima Smith.

The next group are 7 species named for other scientists, mostly entomologists. But Calvert dedicated one species to the Swedish-American polymath Gustav Eisen, especially known by his studies of worms, and one to the mycologist H.W. Harkness, who both had been helpful in Calvert's expedition to Baja California. *Somatchlora sahlbergi* was dedicated by Trybom to another entomologist of the expedition to the Yenisei river, where the species was detected, Williamson, following the collector's suggestion, named a species detected in Canada after the renowned entomologist J. Fletcher, and Leonora Gloyd named one species after J.S. Rogers, who had donated many specimens to UMMZ, and another one to F.M. Gaige, director and curator of entomology at the same museum.

The last group of eponyms are relatives (9). Of these, two are the mother and the father of C.H. Kennedy, the son of M. Brunelle, a grandson of J.G. Needham, the others the wifes of Hagen, Calvert, Williamson (before marriage), Westfall and Tennessen, so that four generations fall into this category.

Legend: (each name is found in the table only once, whereas it may also pertain to other categories)
? - assignment not certain
r - replacement name
x - special case, see text

Names Concerning People

Author	Number	When	Typological	From Literature	Mythological	From History	Saints	Collector	Odonatologists	Other Scientists	Relatives	Uncertain
Drury	7	1773				7						
Sulzer	1	1776			1							
Fabricius	1	1798	1									
Leach	2	1815	2									
Burmeister	1	1839		1								
Rambur	1	1842	1									
Selys	15	1850-1878		1?	2	1	1	4+1^x	4			1
Hagen	8	1858-1878	3		1?			1^x	1	1	1	
Walsh	1	1863							1			
Scudder	2	1866						1	1			
McLachlan	2	1883-1896						1	1^r			
Uhler	1	1887				1?						
Kirby	2	1889			1^r				1			
Trybom	1	1889								1		

Introduction

Author	Number	When	Typological	From Literature	Mythological	From History	Saints	Collector	Odonatologists	Other Scientists	Relatives	Uncertain
Calvert	10	1895-1905	1		1			5		2	1	
Williamson	11	1898-1932						6	3	1	1	
Currie, R.P.	1	1903						1				
Walker	3	1907-1925						1	2			
Muttkowski	1	1910						1				
Navás	1	1911						1				
Davis	1	1913						1				
Kennedy	4	1915-1918						2			2	
Bromley	1	1924						1				
Williamson & Gloyd	1	1933							1			
Gloyd	4	1936-1938						1	1	2		
Westfall	5	1943-1957						1	3		1	
Ferguson	1	1950						1				
Needham	3	1950-1951						2			1	
Donnelly	2	1961-1962			1			1				
Knopf & Tennessen	1	1980							1			
Paulson	1	1983						1				
Tennessen	1	1983									1	
Cook & Daigle	1	1985							1			
Carle & May	1	1987							1			
Dunkle	1	1992							1			
Garrison	1	1994							1			
Daigle	1	1995							1			
Brunelle	1	2000									1	
Tennessen & Vogt	1	2004							1			
	103		7	2	7	9	1	28	32	7	9	1

Toponyms

A relativly large group of names refers to localities. Some of them give a hint to the environment that the taxon prefers. As an example, the former genus name *Agrion* (= living in the fields), which is now the second part of six actual genus names, evokes the environment. But the environment may also be suggested by mentioning a plant which is typical for the biotope, like *juncea* (= of the rushes), one of the oldest names given by Linnaeus, or the youngest name in North American Odonata, *sarracenia* named after a genus of pitcher plants from the type locality. Similarly Kirby created a genus *Cannaphila* = reed loving. More special are *Helocordulia* (= *Cordulia* of marsh meadows or backwaters) and *amnicola* (= river dweller). Hagen described the adaption of two *Leucorrhinia* species to a temperate climate by the names *frigida* (= cold) and *glacialis* (= icy), which cannot refer to the animals themselves, which certainly are poikilothermic, but only to their northern distribution. That construction leads to names which refer to the geographical direction of North America in which the species is found, like *australis* (= southern) from the southern states or the Caribbean, *borealis, -e* or *septentrionalis* (= northern) or *subarctica* (= somewhat arctic) from northern regions, *eurinus* (= eastern), which Say knew only from Massachusetts, *occidentis* (= of the west) from Oregon and Washington and *Hesperagrion* (*Agrion* of the west), which has its easternmost range in western Texas.

Besides these names evoking the geographic direction, others indicate a geographical position. So Kennedy established the genus **Neo**erythromma (= new redeye) to show, that it is not identical with the Old World genus *Erythromma*, but restricted to the New World. Of the *ca.* 50 remaining names referring to localities in a broad sense 15 are formed with the Latin suffix *–ensis –is –e,* which indicates the place of origin, as in *alabamensis* (= from Alabama), *cubensis* (= from Cuba) and so on. Another adjectival morpheme found in such names is *–anus –a –um* (= belonging to) [which in English is shortened to –an], as in *georgiana* (= belonging to Georgia) or *mexicana* (= Mexican).

Often the type locality is referred to by the name; but type locality may not be a very distinct term, as in earlier times of nomenclature even the whole continent might be used for denomination. In a proper sense it would be the place, where the type material has been secured. The first species with an American type locality is *Tramea carolina* described by Linnaeus in 1763, the second one *Hetaerina americana* named by Fabricius in 1798. Probably from a European point of view the reference to the (north and south) continent might have seemed a sufficient statement of place, when less than a total of 80 species around the world had been described, and only about a quarter of them from the Americas. But to be informative a name should cover an obviously more restricted area, and this requirement has been observed since then.

Names referring to type localities in the proper sense are, for instance, *Aeshna eremita* from Hermit Lake or *Neurocordulia yamaskensis* from the Canadian Yamaska River. Many of the names give not the type locality itself, but the region or the state where it is situated. So the type locality of *Macromia alleghaniensis* is Ohiopyle, a borough within the Alleghenies, or that of *Ophiogomphus arizonicus* are the Huachuca Mountains in that state. Often also the main area of distribution of a species is at the base of the name, for instance in *Aeshna canadensis* or *Triacanthagyna carribbea*. Calvert had a special way of indicating regions where the species are found: he named them from indigenous tribes like *azteca, comanche, maya, nahuana, tarascana, tonto*. This practice was followed by Garrison, when naming his *Argia pima*. This tradition may also have been observed in *Ophiogomphus susbehcha*, named with the denomination of dragonflies in Lakota Sioux.

Why Needham's *Stylurus potulentus* (= tipsy *Stylurus*) falls into the category of names that indicate a place may be seen on page 206.

The Authors

Abbott, John C. (*December 13, 1972 Beaufort, South Carolina)
[1]

John Abbott grew up in Texas where his interest in entomology was encouraged by his parents, while living on a small farm with lots of opportunity to explore. He was fascinated by all living things and spent a great deal of time raising numerous reptiles, amphibians and fish as well as arthropods. He built an insect collection starting at age five and took a particular interest in beetles. He attended the Texas Academy of Mathematics and Science at the University of North Texas (UNT) for the last two years of high school and planned on a career as an engineer. While at UNT he met Ken Stewart, a well known plecopterologist and started doing research in his lab. He was the primary author for his first publication on the male search behaviour of *Pteronarcella badia* in 1993. He published three additional papers on stonefly drumming. It was during this time when he worked with Steve Moulton, one of Stewart's Ph.D. students, who introduced him to George Harp at Arkansas State University and his interest in odonates became serious. He started avidly collecting and studying the group. He completed the last two years of his bachelor's degree in Zoology and Entomology at Texas A&M University. While at A&M he worked in the TAMU Insect Collection and was mentored by Ed Riley, a noted beetle expert. Abbott's long interest in beetles grew during this time, but his passion stayed with odonates. He curated the Odonata collection at TAMU. He returned to UNT and Ken Stewart's lab in 1993 where he earned his Ph.D. studying the biogeography of south-central U.S. Odonata. He graduated from UNT with a Ph.D. in biology in 1999 and did a short post-doc at Stroud Water Research Center in Avondale, Pennsylvania, before moving back to Texas to take a faculty and curator of entomology position at the University of Texas at Austin in 1999. While at UT Abbott taught entomology, aquatic entomology and field biology courses and mentored numerous students. While at UT he also met Kendra Bauer, an ecologist, who he married in 2010. John and Kendra enjoy traveling the world, learning about and photographing nature and have worked together on numerous research projects together. In 2014 he took a position at St. Edward's University, in Austin, as the Director of Wild Basin Wilderness Preserve and then in 2016 left Texas accepting a position as Chief Curator and Director of Collections and Research for the University of Alabama Museums at the University of Alabama in Tuscaloosa. Abbott has so far published three books, five atlases and 15 papers on odonates. Abbott has named one species of Odonata, *Cordulegaster sarracenia*, named for the pitcher plants that it often occurs with. His collection of Odonata which is particularly strong in both nymphal and adult material from North America is housed at the University of Alabama. Abbott is an avid nature photographer and runs Abbott Nature Photography, LLC with his wife.

Banks, Nathan (*April 13, 1868 Roslyn, New York – †January 24, 1953 Holliston, Mass.) [2] [3]

After graduate studies at Cornell University under the supervision of J.H. Comstock, which resulted in a M.Sc. in 1890, Banks was appointed to a position in the Bureau of Entomology of the United States Department of Agriculture in Washington, which he held until 1916, with an intermission from 1892 to 1896, when due to a reduction of appropriations government employees were retrenched. Banks used this time to carry on with his entomological studies, to enlarge his collection and to publish. In 1904 he applied for a position at the Museum of Comparative Zoology, but did not succeed until twelve years later. There he remained until his retirement in 1945, being appointed Associate Professor of Zoology in 1928 and in 1941 being designated Head Curator of Insects. His informal instruction by research courses is said to have been invaluable to advanced students. His collection of more than one hundred twenty thousand specimens with about eighteen hundred types and his large library had been presented to MCZ in 1916. Banks was an expert in systematic entomology noted for his work on Neuroptera, Megaloptera, Hymenoptera, and Acarina.

Belle, Jean (*1920 Sukabumi, West Java – †2001) [4]

When Belle was 14 his family moved from what then was the Dutch East Indies (now Indonesia) to the Netherlands. Even though he loved biology, Jean chose to study maths and science at the University of Amsterdam. In 1947 Belle started his career as a Secondary School maths and science teacher. In 1950 he finished his studies which had been partly delayed by World War II. He and his wife, in 1953, decided to migrate to the tropics, choosing Suriname.

In Paramaribo, Jean was impressed by a large collection of dragonflies in the newly opened Suriname Museum. They had been collected by its director Dirk Geijskes, a Dutch entomologist based in Suriname since 1938. It was Geijskes who stimulated Jean to start collecting dragonflies. He started collecting in 1955 and somewhat later he began corresponding with North American odonatologists. His specialization in neotropical Gomphidae came from their suggestions as well as that from Geijskes. Although James Needham was at that time unable to have had an extensive correspondence with him (being already blind) he, together with Philip Calvert, may well have been the stimulus that cemented this choice.

Belle's excursions can be deduced from the data on his collected specimens. They included the interior of Suriname, either by train (e.g. to Kabel or Gansee), or sometimes by boat (visiting the Corantijn River in 1956, the Tapahoni River in 1958, the Upper Suriname River in 1959, the Lawa and Litanie Rivers in 1960, the Coppename River in 1961, the Nickerie River in 1962 and the Kabalebo River in 1963 and 1964).

Belle started publishing on dragonflies in 1963 prior to returning to the Netherlands in 1965, where he continued as a Secondary School science teacher. Altogether he described a total of 124 new species of Odonata with the genus *Progomphus* (sanddragons) as his ultimate specialization. His publication "Revision of the New World genus *Progomphus* Selys, 1854 (Anisoptera: Gomphidae)" published in *Odonatologica* in 1973, served as his Ph.D. thesis which was awarded in 1974.

After the death of his wife, Belle visited Costa Rica for seven months during the period 1986-1989, and he was appointed as honorary curator in Panama in 1986. However, he decided to remain living in the Netherlands.

In 1987 Belle sold his personal odonate collections to RMNH (now Naturalis, Biodiversity Center) in Leiden, The Netherlands, but he kept on working in their rich Odonata collection as a volunteer. Together with Marcel Wasscher, he worked on a checklist of the Odonata of Suriname. Finally he did publish the paper as sole author in 2001, though sadly he died of a heart attack while it was in proof.

Bird, Ralph Durham (*May 20, 1901 Arrow River – †March 1, 1972 Ganges, British Columbia) [5] Entomologist, naturalist.

After his early education at Blenheim School, Thoona School, and Birtle School, he then moved to Winnipeg to study Botany, Zoology, and Entomology at the University of Manitoba, receiving B.Sc. (1924) and M.Sc. (1926) degrees.

Work at Aweme during summers of 1924 to 1926, under the guidance of entomologist Norman Criddle, had a profound impact on his subsequent career. He obtained a Ph.D. in 1929 from the University of Illinois, then took a teaching position at the University of Oklahoma, from 1929 to 1933.

During the summers of 1931 to 1933, he conducted research on insects at Vernon and Hat Creek, British Columbia. Following Criddle's death Bird returned to Canada permanently in 1933 as Officer-in-charge of the Federal Entomology Laboratory at Aweme. Later that year the facility was moved to the Brandon Post Office building and he remained in the position until 1957. Although his work from 1933 to

1942 was focussed on grasshoppers, it expanded after 1942 to include other insect pests on agricultural crops. When the laboratory was closed in 1957 its staff were transferred to Winnipeg as part of the newly-formed Canada Department of Agriculture Research Station at the Fort Garry Campus of the University of Manitoba. Bird was Head of its Entomology Section and, from 1963, Head of the Crop Protection Section until his retirement in 1966 when he moved to Saltspring Island, British Columbia.

Bird was a Life Member of the Entomological Society of Canada and the Natural History Society of Manitoba (from which he received its Bronze Medal, in 1927, for his research on the insect life of the Treesbank area). He served as President of the Natural History Society (1960-1961), and of the Entomological Society (1964-1965). He was also a member of the Scientific Club of Winnipeg.

Bird's broad interests as a naturalist were shown in his writing about birds, vascular plants, and lichens and as an active amateur taxidermist. He wrote the book *Ecology of the Aspen Parkland of Western Canada in Relation to Land Use* (1961). Fascinated by archeology, he carried out investigations of the Stott Site near Brandon.

Brauer, Friedrich Moritz (*May 12, 1832 Vienna – † December 29, 1904 Vienna) [6] was an Austrian entomologist who was Director of the Zoological Department of the Naturhistorisches Hofmusem, Vienna, at the time of his death.

Brauer probably was the most significant entomologist of his time in Austria. His main subjects were Neuroptera sensu Linné and Diptera, especially Oestridae. From his research into metamorphosis he was able to split the Linnean class Insecta into 17 orders and the Neuroptera into seven.

At a young age Brauer, whose parents had migrated to Vienna from Northern Germany, was inspired to dedicate himself to entomology by a tutor. His ability for scientific work was so great that, by 1851, a treatise by him on the development of *Panorpa communis* L. was published in the proceedings of the Viennese Academy. In 1853 he began to study medicine at the university of his native town. In 1861 he accepted a post at the 'Naturalienkabinett' (which later on became the 'Naturhistorisches Hofmuseum'), however not an entomological one, which would have been more amenable to him, but a conchological one as, for 16 years, there was no vacancy in his special field of interest. In 1857-1859 the Austrian frigate *Novara* had been sent around the world to collect botanical, zoological and ethnological material. Subsequently Brauer was assigned to the description of the Neuroptera by the Academy of Science. By his excellent publication of these, other collectors were induced to ask him to determine their findings. So Brauer gained a distinctive knowledge of 'Neuroptera' from around the world, which in 1868 led to his '*Verzeichnis der bis jetzt bekannten Neuropteren in Sinne Linnés* (Catalogue of the neuropteres sensu Linné known until now)'. The advantage of this publication was that its key better allowed those families of Odonata which were not covered by a synopsis from Selys and Hagen to be distinguished. Brauer was an honorary member of 12 entomological societies, among these those of Berlin, Brussels, London, Paris, Washington and Saint Petersburg. Of Brauer's 24 genus names 3 are synonyms, of his 111 species group names 8 are now recognised as subspecies, 25 are synonyms and 1 is a homonym.

Brittinger, Christian Casimir (*April 30, 1795 Friedberg, Hassia – †January 11, 1869 Steyr, Austria) [7] [8] was a botanist, entomologist and ornithologist.

After a pharmaceutical apprenticeship in the Austrian monastery at Schlägl, Brittinger found employment at Linz, from where he explored the flora of that region. In 1818 he went to Vienna to study pharmacology at the university and in 1827 he established himself as an apothecary at Steyr, a town in Lower Austria, where he lived until his death. There he studied the flora of that region, but also attended to the lepidopteran and odonate fauna, which studies led to several publications, among others a synopsis of the Austrian dragonfly fauna in 1850. Brittinger was a member of the Stettiner entomologischer Verein, through which he was in contact with Hermann August Hagen. Later on he also turned to ornithological studies.

Bromley, Stanley Willard (*December 7, 1899 near Charlton, Worcester County, Mass. – †February 16, 1954 Stamford, Conn.) [9] [10]

Already at a young age Bromley through contact with the dipterologist C.W. Johnson, whom he met at the museum of the Boston Society of Natural History, was won over to entomology. His first publication, on Asilidae, which he wrote aged 13, was still referred to in 1946 appreciatively. He achieved his M.Sc. at the Massachusetts Agricultural College and later in 1934 a Ph.D. at Ohio State University. Professionally he engaged in insect pest control, at first employed at the American Cyanid Company, later at the Bartlett Tree Research Laboratories at Stamford, Connecticut. In this context he built up a collection of tree and shrub insects with examples of the injury they caused. In 1951 he had to retire due to bad health. Many of his publications deal with Diptera, most of them with Asilidae, for which Bromley was an authority. Bromley has described just one odonate species.

Brunelle, Paul-Michael (*1952) [11]

Brunelle received a degree as a graphic designer in his twenties, practicing for two decades before becoming interested in Odonata in the Maritime Provinces of Canada. An autodidact in entomology, he learned principally through the major continental publications, and the generous guidance of senior workers in the order, most notably Dr. Robert Cannings, Dr. Thomas W. Donnelly, Dr. Sidney Dunkle, and others. His interest in the order expanded with his establishment of two volunteer surveys, the Atlantic Dragonfly Inventory Program (ADIP, 1992), and the Maine Damselfly and Dragonfly Survey (MDDS, 1997, supported by the Maine Department of Inland Fisheries and Wildlife), which together attracted hundreds of citizen scientists to the interest, and guided their contributions. In addition to his contributions of some 12,500 records, the volunteers tendered a further 32,700. The voucher specimens of most of these records have been deposited with the New Brunswick

Museum, resulting in one of the largest collections of the order in the country. Brunelle specializes in survey, documentation, and analysis of geopolitical, geofaunal, and ecological distribution, and phenology. He has published on these subjects and described one species new to science (*Neurocordulia michaeli* Brunelle, 2000). He is a Research Associate of the New Brunswick Museum, and in 1996 was awarded the Norman Criddle Award by the Entomological Society of Canada, the award being for notable non-professional contributions to entomology.

Burmeister, Carl Hermann Conrad (*January 15, 1807 Stralsund – †May 2, 1892 Buenos Aires) [12] [13] [14] was a German Argentine zoologist, entomologist, herpetologist, and botanist.

Born in Stralsund, Burmeister studied medicine at Greifswald and natural science at Halle. At both universities he achieved a doctorate degree, a medical and a philosophical one in 1829. One of his theses dealt with the systematics of insects. As he was not successful in getting an appointment as a doctor in the Dutch colony in Indonesia, he abandoned his medical profession and devoted himself to teaching natural history. In 1932 he published the first volume of his '*Handbuch der Entomologie* (Manual of Entomology)', which won him some renown, also because it initiated a new kind of systematics based on the types of metamorphosis. In 1837 he was appointed to a professorship in Halle, at the same time becoming responsible for the Zoological Museum founded only two years before, to the collections of which he contributed very much. In 1848, during the revolution in some German states, he was sent as deputy to the National Assembly and to the Prussian 'Herrenhaus'. But in 1850 he resigned, disappointed at the course of events. By recommendation of the famous explorer Alexander von Humboldt he was allowed an expedition to Brazil and subsequently, in 1856, an expedition to Argentina and the La Plata States, which lasted until 1860, returning home via Panama and Cuba. In 1861 he accepted an invitation to Buenos Aires to take the direction of the Natural History Museum, which he did with great success. He enlarged the collections by further expeditions throughout Argentina and published not only on zoological, but also on botanical, paleontological, geological and meteorological subjects, mostly concerning findings from his travels. He also became head of the scientific faculty of the University of Córdoba and eventually of the Academy of Science. He met his death aged eighty five by an accident in 'his' museum. His description of 168 Odonata in the second volume of his '*Handbuch der Entomologie*' in 1839 was the first attempt to sum up the species already known on a world-wide scale. This catalogue, while being by no means complete, provided a good basis for further research.

Byers, Charles Francis (*November 18, 1902 Johnstown, Pennsylvania – †October 27, 1982 Williston, Florida) [15]

After graduating at his home town in 1921, Byers studied at the University of Michigan. These studies were interrupted by periods at the University of Florida in 1924 and at Cornell University in 1926-27. While at Cornell he contributed to the *Handbook of the Dragonflies of North America* by J.G. Needham and H.B. Heywood before returning to Florida as Assistant Professor of Biology in 1927 and then in 1928-29 to Michigan to complete his Ph.D. with a thesis on the Odonata of Florida. After that he continued to teach in Florida in several advanced positions until 1959. During this time he developed recommendations for the reorganization of the biology curriculum for secondary and high schools. After this he taught at the University of Idaho, at Elmira College (New York), Ripon College (Wisconsin), Winter Park (Florida), before retiring to Gainesville. During his teaching years he conducted courses in General Biology or Zoology, Invertebrate Zoology, Parasitology, Evolution, Genetics, Geography and Geology. Among the many honors awarded to him was a Fulbright Fellowship to India in 1957-58. Byers was a member and officer in many learned societies. His collection is now part of the Florida State Collection of Arthropods at Gainesville.

Calvert Philip Powell (*January 29, 1871 Philadelphia – †August 23, 1961 Philadelphia) [16] [17] [18]

Calvert's life was centered at his home town and he was closely connected with the American Entomological Society which was based there. He served in several functions, especially as assistant editor or editor of the *Entomological News* from 1893 until 1943. Like many of the outstanding biologists Calvert already in his young years developed an interest in nature, encouraged by his parents. During his time at high school with others he founded a group of the Agassiz Association, the members of which were to study "nature, not books". He was persuaded by the entomologist of the insect collections of the Academy of Natural Sciences not to specialize in Lepidoptera or Coleoptera, as did many entomologists, but in Odonata. So Calvert in 1888 contacted H.A. Hagen, who was the leading authority of this order, and was encouraged by him. So in 1890 he was entrusted to edit Hagen's synopsis of the genus *Leucorrhinia*. Calvert studied at the University of Pennsylvania completing his Ph.D. in 1895. He then continued his studies for one year in Germany at the universities of Berlin and Jena. Before his doctorate he had begun to teach at his home university sucessively from 1892 as assistant instructor, instructor (1897), assistant professor (1907) and professor (1912) until his retirement in 1939. [On this occasion Calvert described his successful teaching as to have been by trying to stimulate the students to learn by themselves.] Shortly after this he was paralysed by a stroke, but he recovered, so that he was able to continue his scientific work. His over 300 publications, the last of which appeared only weeks before his death, for a great part deal with the taxonomy of North, Central and South America, but Calvert was a leading authority on Odonata world wide, and he published also on anatomy, distribution and paleontology. His collection was given to the Academy of Natural Sciences at Philadelphia.

Cannings, Robert Alexander (*August 12, 1948, Summerland, British Columbia, Canada) [19]

Robert Cannings grew up in the Okanagan Valley in British Columbia in a family known across Canada for its contributions to natural history and conservation. In his early career he was a biologist and nature interpreter for BC Parks and the Canadian Wildlife Service and in the 1970s served as a lecturer in the Zoology Department and curator of the Spencer Entomological Museum at the University of BC in Vancouver. At the Royal British Columbia Museum in Victoria, from 1980 until his retirement in 2013, he was Curator of Entomology and, from 1987 to 1996, managed the museum's Natural History Section. He is now Curator Emeritus there. Cannings has been active in many organisations, including the Scientific Committee of the Biological Survey of Canada (Terrestrial Arthropods), the Arthropod Subcommittee of COSEWIC (Committee on the Status of Endangered Wildlife in Canada), and the executives of the Societas Internationalis Odonatologica and the Dragonfly Society of the Americas. His B.Sc. and M.Sc. are from the University of BC; his Ph.D. comes from the University of Guelph. Although he has published on many insect orders, Cannings' main interests are in the Odonata and Asilidae (Diptera). His Odonata studies focus on systematics, larval descriptions, faunistics and conservation issues while his major robber fly research is the evolution of the genus *Lasiopogon* around the Northern Hemisphere. He has a strong interest in popularizing insects and insect identification through handbooks, keys and the internet. He is the author or co-author of several books, including *The Dragonflies of British Columbia* (1977), *The World of Fresh Water* (1998), *Introducing the Dragonflies of British Columbia and the Yukon* (2002) and *The Systematics of Lasiopogon (Diptera: Asilidae)* (2002). Robert and his brothers, Sydney and Richard, were made Honorary Fellows of Okanagan College in 2008 for their work in biology, public education and nature conservation in BC. In 2009 Cannings won the Bruce Naylor Award from the Alliance of Natural History Museums of Canada for outstanding contributions to museum-based natural history studies in Canada. On his retirement from the RBCM he received the museum's Lifetime Achievement Award and was made an Honorary Member of the Entomological Society of BC.

Carle, Frank Louis [20]

Professor Frank Louis Carle is Curator of the Rutgers Entomological Museum and Director of The New Jersey Aquatic Insect Survey with interests in systematics, biodiversity, phylogenetics, aquatic entomology, palaeontology and biogeography. His research efforts have been devoted toward the conservation of biodiversity and environmental protection.

Early in his career he invented the circular depletion benthic sampler, developed Maximum Weighted Likelihood estimation, proposed a system for ranking rare and endangered species, and established rare and endangered rankings for North American dragonflies, mayflies, stoneflies, and caddisflies. Carle has described several species of Odonata and Ephemeroptera new to science, described many fossil Odonata, named several new genera. He has completed revisions of Austropetaliidae, Gomphoidea, and Libelluloidea. Carle teaches several courses including: The World of Insects, Insect Structure and Function, Aquatic Entomology, Advanced Aquatic Entomology, Insect Systematics, Entomology for Anglers, and Molecular Phylogenetic Methods.

Charpentier, Toussaint de (*November 22, 1779 Freiberg, Saxony – † March 4, 1847 Brieg, Silesia). [21] [22]

Charpentier, son of a teacher at the mining Academy at Freiberg who later became the head of the mining inspectorate there, studied mining at Freiberg and, later, law at Leipzig. In1802 he went to Prussia where he accepted a post in the Silesian upper mining authority. Later in 1828 he transferred to Westphalia and sucessively advanced to become Mining Administrator at Dortmund

with responsibility for controlling mining throughout that province, and five years later was made chief of all Silesian mining based at Brieg.

Besides his professional responsibilities he was a keen hobby entomologist, whose odonatological publications of 1825 and especially of 1840 described the European dragonflies known to him. The latter included engravings of all 60 species, which were praised by Hagen as the best of that time. Charpentier says he did not edit these books as Publications of an Academy but to reach a wider public. However, as they were written in an excellent Latin, his hope might have been a little optimistic.

Cook, Carl (* December 24, 1925 Green County, Kentucky) [23] [24] [25] [26]

Cook's great grandfather came to Indiana from Ireland during the Great Famine of the 1840s. His grandfather successsfully established a large tobacco farm in Kentucky about 1900, of which Cook's father took over the management in the 1920s, but also had his own business of maintaining roads for the county. From his childhood Cook was a collector of natural history objects and Indian arrow heads as well, and he developed a propensity for entomology. His special interest in Odonata and Lepidoptera was spurred by Harrison Garman, an authority on North American dragonflies, who met Cook while collecting butterflies for a 4-H project and offered a reward of ten cents per specimen. Cook graduated from the University of Louisville during the Second World War and subsequently served in the US Air Force during the Korean War. Back home he supplemented his farming operations with heavy contracting (roads, bridge building, earth moving) and later also purchased an insurance agency. Following his liking of stock car racing in addition he took a partnership in a racetrack near Glasgow, Ky.

In 1989 Cook was one of the founding members of the Dragonfly Society of (the) America(s) and acted as its first president until 1991and also as the editor of its newsletter *Argia* until 1992. In 1993 he was one of the founders and first director of the International Scientific Collectors Association, the purpose of which is to support collectors by legal advice on difficulties which might arise abroad and providing contacts for requests and exchange of material. For his merits he received the annual Kentucky Biodiversity Protection Award in 1999 and he became an honorary member of the DSA in 2005 and of the Lepidopterist's Society in 2011. His collections contain more than 100,000 specimens of Odonata and more than 30,000 of Lepidoptera.

Cowley, John (*1909 in Albourne, Essex – †June, 1967 in Essex) [27] was a British amateur entomologist.

After completing his studies at Cambridge, during which he also achieved a thorough education in the classical languages, Cowley spent his life dedicated to his studies in natural science, his special interests being Odonata and Diptera. He achieved his large collection (now at the British Museum) not only by travelling extensively, but also supported by his correspondents all over the world. Largely he engaged in systematics, and at the early age of twenty five he was elected a Fellow of the Royal Entomological Society, which shows the high degree of his knowledge.

Currie, Bertha Pauline (*April 3, 1886 Grand Forks, North Dakota – † March 23, 1966) [28] [29] [30] [31]

The early years of Bertha were overshadowed by the accidental death of her and her brother Rolla's father and their sister in a river in 1891 [32]. As a teenager Bertha followed her brother to the National Museum of Natural History in Washington, where Rolla was employed then; WARD (1976) mentions that the museum's Odonata collection "received its first major impetus from the efforts of *Rolla P. Currie*, who was employed at the Museum from 1894 to 1904 and was ably assisted by his sister, *Bertha P. Currie*." In the 1910 census she is listed as working as Matron of Boys at the Curtis Home, a social institution for widows and orphans at Meriden, CT. Later she joined her brother at the Entomological Bureau of the Department of Agriculture, where she was working as a clerk when she described *Gomphus parvidens* in 1917. She also took charge of the dragonfly collection at the USNM, for in 1922 Williamson mentions her as "Miss Bertha P. Currie, of the Bureau of Entomology, U.S. Department of Agriculture, efficient and obliging custodian of dragonflies in the National Museum". According to the census of 1920 she lived with her brother's family. EDMUNDS & MUESEBECK (1961) mention that she survived her brother.

Currie, Rolla Patteson (*March 25, 1875 Preemption, Illinois – †Sept. 20, 1960 Washington?) [33] [34] [35]

Currie achieved his B.A. from the University of North Dakota in 1893, to which state the family had moved, and in 1894 was hired as aide at the Museum for Natural History, which post he held until 1904, when he transferred to the Bureau of Entomology at the U.S. Department of Agriculture, where he stayed until his retirement in 1944 at the age of 69. After that he began a second career, entering the Theological Seminary in Alexandria, Virginia. Having been ordained as an episcopal priest two years later he became curate of a Washington church, which he served until he became ill four years before his death. During his time at the National Museum Currie with his sister Bertha brought together a large collection of Odonata, Mymeleontidae and Hemerobiidae. He was active with the Columbian Exposition in Chicago in 1893, and in 1898 he was sent to Liberia under O.F. Cook to collect zoological and ethnological material. In 1903 with H.G. Dyar he spent the summer collecting in British Columbia. Soon after entering the Department of Agriculture he was placed in the Entomological Bureau's editorial office, where he helped other authors to prepare their publications until his retirement.

He was elected to membership in the Washington Biologists' Field Club in 1901 and terminated his membership in 1930. Rolla served as secretary/treasurer from 1904 to 1905.

Daigle, Jerrell James (*December 13, 1950 Oceanside, California) [36]

Daigle received his Biology/Limnology B.Sc. Degree from Florida Technological University in Orlando in 1978. He was employed by Orange County Pollution Dept. in Orlando from 1971-1980 and worked for Florida Dept. of Environmental Protection in Tallahassee, Florida from 1980 until retirement in 2001. Daigle became interested in Odonata after meeting Dr. Minter J. Westfall and students Ken Knopf, Sid Dunkle, Bill Mauffray, and Ken Tennessen at the University of Florida in Gainesville. He was former treasurer of the Dragonfly Society of the Americas (DSA) and is currently [2018] organizer of their National and SE regional meetings. He has described many new species of Odonata from Hawaii, USA, Mexico, Dominican Republic, Guadeloupe, Bolivia, and Ecuador, mostly in the journal, *Odonatologica*. Daigle currently resides in Tallahassee, Florida and travels frequently to cloud forests in the Caribbean, Central and South America with his friends looking for rare dragonflies and damselflies.

Davis, William Thompson (*October 12, 1862 Staten Island – †January 22, 1945 Staten Island) [37] [38] [39] [40] [41]

Davis was born into a prosperous family on Staten Island, where he remained as resident for all his life. He was interested in his surroundings and their nature, and so in 1879 he joined the Brooklyn and the New York Entomological Societies together with his friend Charles W. Leng, who was to become a renowned coleopterologist, and with whom Davis later authored a five volume work on the history of Staten Island from 1609 to 1933. Two years later, together with twelve other enthusiasts, he founded the 'Staten Island Institute of Arts and Sciences' and it is to be noted that Davis gained his extensive knowledge mostly by mutual communication and his own observations. He had no academic education after graduating from school. Due to the family tradition that one has to earn one's own living, he became a clerk in a New York business, but retired at the age of forty six to devote his life totally to his interest in natural history. As an entomologist he expended most efforts on Cicadidae, which had won his attention from his schooldays. Of the approximately 170 North American species, he has described more than hundred. In appreciation of his vast knowledge and scientific proficiency, in 1910 Davis was made fellow of the New York Academy of Sciences and the American Association for the Advancement of Science. In 1917 he became a fellow of the American Entomological Society. After his death the type specimens of the species he described were left to the American Museum of Natural History.

Donnelly, Thomas Wallace (*December 23, 1932 Detroit, Michigan) [42]

Due to his father's military profession the Donnelly family moved to Washington D.C. After his sophomore year at High School, Thomas attended a summer camp of the Audubon Society in Maine where he met Donald J. Borror, who aroused an interest in dragonflies in the teenage boy (as another counselor in that camp interested him in ferns, for which Donnelly now is a specialist as well). For study Donnelly went to Cornell, where he chose geology, not entomology, but he made good use of the entomological facilities there, where J.G. Needham was still teaching. After B.Sc., Donnelly continued his studies at Caltech and later at Princeton, where he did his Ph.D. in1959. Until 1965 he was Assistant Professor at Rice University in Houston, Texas, before he served a term as chair in geology at the State University of New York at Binghamton. His geological special research interests are Central American geology, marine geology and chemistry of sediments. But all the time he also has published on Odonata, especially from Central America and the Caribbean, but also from his travels around the world, e.g. the Fijis and India. He attended the first International Colloquium on Odonata at Purdue in 1963 and was one of the founders of the DSA in 1989, acting as president elect and holding presidency 1991-92. He also edited the society's *Bulletin of American Odonatology* from the beginning and *Argia* from 1992, when he took over from Carl Cook, until 2006. In *Argia* his articles were mostly signed as Nick Donelly. In 2012 the 'Nick and Ailsa Donnelly Fellowship' was founded, the purpose of which is "to promote and facilitate the attendance of colleagues to the annual Dragonfly Society of the America's meetings by paying ... for travel and travel-related expenses" and to support research and education for promoting the knowledge of Odonata. [43]

Drury, Dru (*February 4, 1724 London – †December 15, 1803 Turnham Green) [44] was a British entomologist.

Drury, a silversmith by profession, turned to entomology aged about twenty five. His wealth allowed him to spend much money on assembling the biggest entomological collection of his time, for he was said to have paid sixpence for any insect bigger than a honeybee. He also gave instructions to passengers and crews of many ships on how to collect and preserve insects for him. So he got insects from around the world, a part of which he published in three volumes (1770, 1773, 1782) with colored plates, most of them made by Moses Harris. For naming dragonflies he chose almost without exception female names from Roman antiquity.

Drury was in contact with Linnaeus and Fabricius. He met the latter often, when he stayed in London for the winters 1772-1775. He also presided over the Society of Entomologists of London from 1780 to 1782. His collection, amounting to some 11,000 species, was sold by auction after his death, many of his specimens were bought by friends like William Kirby and Edward Donovan.

Dunkle, Sidney Warren (*September 27, 1940 Cleveland, Ohio) [45]

Genetically interested in animals from the start. First in the family to attend college, he attended Baldwin-Wallace College (now B-W University) in Berea, Ohio, majoring in Biology and graduating in 1962. He then attended the University of Wyoming, Laramie, majoring in Zoology, graduating in 1965 with a thesis on the ecology of Swainson's Hawk. His final degree was a Ph.D. at the University of Florida, Gainesville, majoring in Entomology and graduating in 1980, with a dissertation on Second Instar Anisoptera.

Dr. Dunkle has taught a variety of subjects in biology at Cuyahoga Community College, Cleveland, Ohio; Orange Coast Community College, Costa Mesa, California; Santa Fe Community College, Gainesville, Florida; Fresno City College, Fresno, California; the University of Florida, Gainesville; and he retired from Collin University, Plano, Texas in 2006.

He has also worked as a Trailside Naturalist for Cleveland Metro Parks; as a Ranger-Naturalist, Grand Teton National Park; on Grizzly Bear and Wapiti in Yellowstone National Park; on the Purple-backed Jay in Sinaloa, Mexico; on bioacoustics at the Florida Museum of Natural History; on katydid ecology for Earthwatch in Peru; and as a consultant on benthic macroinvertebrates in Florida.

He has published three books: *Dragonflies of the Florida Peninsula, Bermuda and the Bahamas* (1989); *Damselflies of Florida, Bermuda and the Bahamas* (1990); and *Dragonflies through Binoculars, a Field Guide to Dragonflies of North America* (2000). He has published a great variety of interesting papers on odonates as well as describing 14 species of Odonata.

Erichson, Wilhelm Ferdinand (*November 26, 1808, Stralsund – †November 18, 1849, Berlin) [46] was a German entomologist specialising in Coleoptera.

Having passed his final examination at the Gymnasium of his home town, Erichson, the oldest son of an influential family, went to the University of Berlin to study medicine. He completed a Dr. med. in 1832 with a thesis on Dytiscidae, a family of diving beetles. In due course he achieved the license to practice medicine in 1834, but all the time he worked also as volunteer at the entomological department of the Natural History Museum and took care of the entomological collections. After having been granted an annual remuneration for this activity in 1836 he acquired a D. phil. from the University of Jena in 1837, his habilitation (a graduation which was normally a precondition for being appointed as a professor) at Berlin in 1938 led to teaching duties at the university in entomology and helminthology. In 1842 he was appointed to an associate professorship there. In 1843 he was installed as curator of the Coleopteran collection. While his main interest was Coleoptera, he was well-informed also in other orders. From the first volume of the periodical *Archiv für Naturgeschichte* in 1835 he contributed among other articles the annual reports on the progress of entomology, and after the death of the founder in 1841 he became its editor until the last year before his death, when tuberculosis impaired him so much, that he could continue neither his editorial nor his teaching duties. But he still managed to edit publications on the insects caught by the botanist M.R. Schomburgk on a British-Prussian expedition to British Guiana in 1840-44, which were given to the Natural History Museum. Among the insects described by him were eight new dragonfly species, one of which has been observed in the US in recent years.

Fabricius, Johan Christian (*January 7, 1745 Tønder, Duchy of Schleswig – †March 3, 1808 Kiel, Holstein) [47] [48] was a Danish zoologist.

Fabricius, son of a doctor, began his studies in Copenhagen with medicine, then in 1762 went for two years to Uppsala as a student of natural history with Linnaeus, where he directed his special attention to 'Insecta', which at that time included all arthropods. Later, in 1775, he went to Leipzig for economical and botanical studies and 1766 to Leiden for chemical and physical studies, at the same time visiting the large entomological collections in the Netherlands. During 1767, while travelling through England to London, he became acquainted with many naturalists, such as Joseph Banks and Dru Drury. In 1770 he was appointed professor in Copenhagen lecturing on economics in winter and travelling in summer to amplify his knowledge, in the first years mostly to England, later to Paris. This habit he also continued after he had been transferred to the University of Kiel (Germany) in 1776, which was then under Danish rule, where he stayed as a professor of natural history and economics until his death. While Fabricius published on various subjects, his importance lies in the fact, that he established entomological systematics, which remains at the basis of insect classification today.

Ferguson, Alice Howard [since 1956 Ferguson Beatty] (*March 5, 1915 Dallas, Texas - † November 22, 1987 State College, PA) [49] [50]

After receiving her M.Sc. in 1939 with an odonatological thesis from the Southern Methodist University in Dallas, Texas, she became an assistant professor of biology at the East Texas State Teachers College in Commerce, Texas. Subsequently, she moved to Louisiana State University, where she completed her doctor's degree in 1955 with the description of taxonomically relevant features of the proventriculus of anisopteran larvae. In 1956 she married George H. Beatty, who was also engaged in odonatological research, and began to teach biology and entomology at the Pennsylvania State University, where she remained until her retirement in 1980. With her husband she explored the odonate fauna of Pennsylvania, but they also undertook seven expeditions to Mexico, which resulted in a collection of >30,000 odonate specimens. In the late 70's the Beattys gave their odonate collection to the Frost Entomological Museum at Penn State and served for some time as associate curators. Following her botanical interests in her last two years, she traced plant distribution in Sweden. It is to be noted, that the Beattys did not publish any odonatological paper after 1971; so the *ca* 20 undescribed species they had collected in Mexico were not described by themselves.

Förster, Johann Friedrich Nepomuk (*February 5, 1865 Kehl – †December 2, 1918 Offenburg) [51] [52] was a German odonatologist.

After his studies of natural history at the university of Heidelberg, Förster, the son of a customs officer, became a teacher of biology, physics and chemistry at secondary schools in the grand duchy of Baden. The first sign of his interest in dragonflies is a letter by him to Selys in 1895, asking him for some of his publications he had not been able to buy in Germany. That was the beginning of an animated correspondence, of which more than 60 of Förster's letters are preserved in the Selysian archives (M. Wasscher, in litt.), and a cooperation, which had its basis in their common interest in Odonata from the Indomalayan region. Later odonatological publications of Förster focus on Africa, Madagascar and the neotropics. Other odonatologists with whom he was in contact, were E.B. Williamson, F.F. Laidlaw, R. McLachlan, G. Severin and S. Uchidai. As Förster died some days after the armistice of World War I, no obituary was published in any international periodical. Besides his odonatological papers there are some publications covering botany, New Guinea marsupials and palaeontology.

Fraser, Frederic Charles (*February 15, 1880 Woolwich †March, 2 1963 Linwood) [53] [54] [55]

Fraser graduated from Guy's Medical School, London in 1903 and obtained his M.D. from Brussels in the following year. After two years in general practice in London he joined the Indian Medical Service. He saw active military service in Mesopotamia during the 1914-18 war when he was in charge of field hospitals and hospital ships. Appointments with the Indian Medical Service included posts of Superintendent of the Central Jail, Rangoon, and the jail at Hyderabad, Sind, Professor of Surgery at Vizagapatam Medical College, and Professor and Lecturer in Obstetrics and Gynaecology at Madras University Medical School. For some part of his service he was stationed in the Nilgiri Hills, south of Mysore. He made many contributions on the dragonfly fauna of this area to the Bombay Natural History Society.

During 1933, Colonel Fraser was asked to become Acting Surgeon-General at the Madras Medical School; however as this appointment would have interfered with his entomological pursuits, he resigned from the Service and returned to England to live in Bournemouth.

Although Fraser was a good all-round naturalist, his main interests were in the field of entomology but it is his many works dealing with the dragonflies for which his name is remembered; he studied the Odonata of the world.

By 1955, 255 of his papers on this Order had been published by various societies and periodicals, and this had grown to more than 300 by 1962. He was, in consequence, recognised as one of the leading authorities, and he received a constant flow of material from all over the world for identification. He was responsible for the Royal Entomological Society of London's Handbooks dealing with the Odonata, Mecoptera, Megaloptera and Neuroptera. Major works include the three volumes on Odonata in the *Fauna of British India* series; a monograph on the Fissilaboidea [56]; the reclassification of the order Odonata, left incomplete by Dr. R.J. Tillyard at his death, and published 17 years later (1957) by the Royal Zoological Society of NSW as a completely revised edition. His collections were given to the British Museum (Natural History), while his library, one of the most complete on the Odonata in existence at the time, is now in the Manchester Museum.

Garrison, Rosser William (*August 29, 1948 Hagerstown Maryland) [57]

Garrison, who has been interested in dragonflies from an early age, received his Bachelor of Science Degree at Northern Arizona University, Flagstaff, Arizona, in 1971, his Masters at the University of California, Berkeley in 1974 and his Ph.D. at the same institution in 1979. From February 1981 to June 1982, he worked as a terrestrial invertebrate ecologist for the Center of Energy and Environment Research where he conducted ecological research in a tropical rain forest at the El Verde Field Station in Luquillo Forest, Puerto Rico. From 1984-2004, he was Senior Biologist/Entomologist for Los Angeles County before becoming a Senior Insect Biosystematist with the Plant Pest Diagnostics Branch, California Department of Food & Agriculture, in Sacramento where since 2004 he identified orthopteroid, heteropteroid, other groups of invertebrates including mollusks. He retired on 1 August, 2017 and currently lives in Sacramento. Garrison's main interest has always been the systematics of Odonata with a strong emphasis on the Neotropical fauna. He and his wife Natalia von Ellenrieder, a Senior Insect Biosystematist with CDFA, have worked intensively with the Odonata fauna of the Neotropical region. Rosser is the author or co-author of over 90 scientific papers including two books, several book chapters, and several monographs.

Gloyd, Leonora Katherine (*August 29, 1902 near Larned, Kansas – †June 2, 1993 Plano, Texas) [58]

The family of Leonora "Dolly" Gloyd (née Doll) moved a number of times, disrupting her schooling, until they settled down in Kirksville, Missouri. There she soon caught up with her age group. In 1924 she received the degree of B.Sc. at the Kansas State Agricultural College (now Kansas State University) and a M.Sc. with a major in vertebrate embryology and a minor in chemistry in 1925. In the same year she married a young herpetologist, Howard K. Gloyd, and assisted him in his work.

Leonora's introduction to dragonflies was in the summer of 1924, when she attended a course in entomology taught by Professor H.B. Hungerford at the Biological Station of the University of Michigan. Although members of the class were asked to give all specimens of Odonata to C. Francis Byers who was then writing his paper on "Odonata collected in Cheboygan and Emmet Counties" Leonora kept samples of a few common species for her own collection.

A major advance occurred in 1929 when Mrs. Gloyd was offered the job of assistant to E.B. Williamson, who was giving his library and collection of Odonata to the Museum of Zoology, University of Michigan (Ann Arbor). The first task for Mrs. Gloyd was to add references on index cards which introduced her to the classification of Odonata and scientific names. When his huge collection arrived, by comparison it revealed misidentifications in the museum collection, necessitating a checking of all the Odonata. Mrs. Gloyd sorted all *Enallagma* specimens correctly and associated all but two specimens in the museum collection with species in the Williamson collection. Mr. Williamson decided that these two specimens, taken in early spring at a lake four miles west of Ann Arbor, were of a new species. He encouraged her to try to collect more of them, subsequently named *Enallagma vernale*. Although she did not describe it until 1943, Mr. Williamson was responsible for Leonora Gloyd's first paper published in 1932, and a second one in 1933, a few months after his death.

Upon his coming to the University of Michigan, Mr. Williamson had hoped to persuade, and to make it possible for Friedrich Ris and Philip Calvert to join him at the museum to monograph the genus *Argia*. First,

Dr. Calvert declined as he wished to devote all his available time to finishing his Neotropical *Aeshna* study. The deaths of Dr. Ris, in 1931, and of Mr. Williamson himself, in 1933, left this task to Leonora Gloyd. In 1935 Mrs. Gloyd was given a grant by the Men's Senior Research Club of the University of Michigan to visit eastern museums and study types of *Argia* species. From 1936 to 1965 domestic circumstances allowed her only little time to spend on this study.

After moving to the Chicago area, where Dr. H.K. Gloyd had accepted the position of Director of the Museum of Chicago Academy of Sciences, the dragonfly work was continued at home, with occasional trips back to Ann Arbor, in an effort to keep the Williamson collection and library up to date. In 1947 Mrs. Gloyd obtained a half-time position as a laboratory-assistant at the Illinois State Natural History Division in Urbana and she and the children moved to Champaign. In the mean time the Williamson collection at the museum in Michigan continued to be enlarged by numerous collecting expeditions in which Leonora Gloyd also took part and she did the identifying and labeling work on approximately 25,000 newly added specimens, making a total of close to 75,000 specimens in the collection.

In 1954 Mrs. Gloyd was again employed for two months of the summer to work on the Williamson collection and also on the Kennedy collection which had recently been acquired. From December 1965 to mid 1968 she was awarded a National Science Foundation grant to support her study in *Argia*. Dr. Minter J. Westfall invited her to spend some months in 1970, 1976 and 1977 at the University of Florida examining the large number of specimens of *Argia* in the Florida State Collection of Arthropods.

The International Odonatological Society appointed her a Member of Honour at the Fourth International Symposium of Odonatology (Gainesville, Florida, August 1-5, 1977).

González Soriano, Enrique (*1951) [59]

Dr González Soriano is a Mexican odontologist. The Faculty of Sciences, National Autonomous University of Mexico, awarded his B.Sc. (1977) and M.Sc. (1982). He is a Professor at the Departmento de Zoologia, Instituto de Biologia, Universidad Nacional Autonoma Mexico, Distrito Federal, Mexico, and the Curator of the National Odonata Collection. He has conducted entomological research throughout his career (1979-present), writing around seventy scientific papers, book chapters and books. He has described nearly 20 new Odonata species. His publications include: A *synopsis of the genus Amphipteryx Selys 1853* (*Odonata: Amphipterygidae*) (2010), *A biodiversity hotspot for odonates in Mexico: the Huasteca Potosina, San Luis Potosi* (2011) and *Biodiversidad de Odonata en Mexico* (2014). His research focus is the taxonomy and reproductive biology of neotropical Odonata. He has edited three books. An eponymous species was named after him because he discovered a small isolated population in northeastern Mexico in the state of San Luis Potosi and part of the type series was collected by him.

Gundlach, Juan Cristóbal (*July 17, 1810 Marburg – †March 14, 1896 Havana), [60] born **Johannes Christoph Gundlach**, was a Cuban naturalist and taxonomist.

After completing his zoological studies in his native town with a Ph.D., Gundlach went to Cuba in 1838 intending to do research on the fauna there. It might be noted that his journey was financed by the Society of Natural History Cassel, that meant Gundlach was expected to send 'natural products', zoological, botanical or geological items back in compensation for his legacy. In addition to sending collected material to Museums abroad he built up a collection of his own from all parts of Cuba, for which he founded a zoological museum at Havana in 1864. When the first insurrection against Spanish rule made it too difficult to collect in Cuba he resorted to Puerto Rico, where he continued his studies in 1873 and 1875/76. His publications included birds, mammals, reptiles, molluscs and insects. In his last years he worked almost daily at his museum, where he died. He was a member of several learned societies, among others the Entomological Society of Philadelphia. Due to his merits he was honored as eponym of a number of zoological and botanical taxa. Gundlach's information on the dragonflies of Cuba was adopted verbatim into Hagen's related publications of 1867/68.

Hagen, Hermann August (*May 30, 1817 Königsberg, Prussia {now Kaliningrad/ Russia} – †November 9, 1893 Cambridge, Massachusetts) [61] [62] [63] [64]

Hagen was born as a son, grandson and nephew of professors at the University of Königsberg. Inspired by the collection of his grandfather and the encouragement from his father he turned to entomology whilst in his youth. He studied medicine in his hometown and, before his final examinations, he accompanied his professor M. H. Rathke on a journey to Sweden, Norway and Denmark to study the entomological collections there. His thesis, by which in 1840 he achieved the M.D., was a synonymy of the European Odonata described until then. In the following years he continued his medical and zoological studies at Berlin, Vienna and Paris, after which he settled as a doctor at Königsberg. But during that time he also published entomological papers, by which he became renowned. So, when the Smithsonian Institution wanted a compendium of the North American Neuroptera, Hagen was entrusted with this task, on the recommendation of the German Baltic entomologist C. R. von Osten-Sacken, then a Russian diplomat in the U.S., who also arranged for more than 1500 specimens to be sent to Königsberg to enable Hagen to meet that challenge [65]. This publication, as it contained more than seventy new odonate taxa in addition to an English description of all taxa known until then from that region, and also a list of the South American Neuroptera, provided a sound footing for all further studies. In 1862/63 Hagen edited his outstanding *Bibliotheca Entomologica,* by which he tried to sum up all entomological literature published until then, and which was to be an indispensible tool for further entomological studies, although papers in Russian were not included. As the living provided by his medical profession was scarce and several times his hope to become head of some major entomological collection in Germany had failed, in 1867 Hagen accepted an invitation from L. Agassiz to curate the entomological collection of Harvard University, where he remained until his death. In 1870 he was the first to be appointed to an entomological professorship in the U.S. Disabled by a stroke in 1890, he was devotedly cared for by his wife Johanna, née Gerhards, who after his death remigrated to Königsberg.

Hagen was one of the most prolific entomologists of his time, his main field being the Neuroptera and Odonata, but also he contributed important publications on termites, psocids and insects enclosed in amber. With Selys, the cooperation with whom dated from 1841, he provided a solid basis of the taxonomy of Odonata. In the organization of the Harvard collection he took care to incorporate the diverse stages of development. He was in contact with all major entomologists of his time and said to have been very helpful to others who requested his aid. Hagen gave his library and his collection to Harvard University.

Harvey, Francis Leroy (*1850 near Ithaca, N.Y. – †March 6, 1900 Orono, Maine) [66] [67]

Harvey's first education was in the city schools of Ithaca, N.Y., but later his parents moved to Independence, Iowa, and so Harvey entered Iowa Agricultural College at Ames (now Iowa State University) in 1868, where he received his B.Sc. in 1872 and fourteen years later received the M.Sc. degree. In 1873 he became principal of a graded school in Iowa and the year following was made professor of natural science in Humboldt College. He continued in this capacity until 1875 when he was elected to the chair of theoretical and applied chemistry and natural history in the Arkansas Industrial University. In 1881 the chair was divided and he was given that of biology and geology, which position he held until 1885.

During his time in Arkansas he discovered many plants and fossils new to science and collected widely of the flora and minerals of the State. His special studies encompassed insect depredations, plant diseases, forestry problems, botanical subjects and the more practical branches of agriculture and horticulture. He discovered about fifty taxa new to science and described a number of new insects and algae.

In 1886 he assumed charge of the natural history establishment of Dr. A. E. Foote in Philadelphia, but after a year's service here he accepted the call to the chair of natural history in the University of Maine at Orono, additionally being botanist and entomologist to the Maine State Experiment Station, which was connected with the University. The Arkansas University in 1890 conferred a Ph.D. upon him.

These positions he held until his untimely death, which is said to have been due to overwork. Harvey published on the Odonata of Maine from 1890. Other publications were on Thysanura, Collembola and on economic entomology.

Harvey was a corresponding member of the Academy of Natural Science of Philadelphia, an honorary member of the American Association of Forestry, a member of Torrey Botanical Club of New York, of the Washington Entomological Society, the Portland Natural History Society and an active member of the American Association of Economics, Botanists and Entomologists.

Hibbitts, Troy D. (*April 3, 1970, Bryan, Texas) [68]

Hibbitts received a Bachelor's of Science in Wildlife and Fisheries Sciences from Texas A&M University in May of 1992 and a Master's of Science in Biology from the University of Texas at Arlington in July of 1994. His primary research focus was on reptile and amphibian evolutionary biology. After graduate school, he has worked as a secondary science teacher with the Fort Worth Independent School District (1994-1995), the Arlington ISD (1996-2004), the Uvalde ISD (2004-2009), and the Brackett ISD (2009-present), teaching primarily biology and Advanced Placement Biology. He is a long-standing member and Past President of the Texas Herpetological Society and a co-author of three herpetological field guides for Texas: Texas Amphibians, Texas Lizards, and Texas Turtles and Crocodilians. Although much of his focus has been on the study of herpetology, he considers himself to be an all-around naturalist with diverse interests ranging from arachnids (tarantulas & scorpions), insects (odonates, lepidopterans, and coleopterans), and birds to cacti, succulents, cycads, and orchids. He is an avid outdoor photographer, with a particular interest in photographing reptiles, amphibians, odonates, and lepidopterans. His photographs have been published widely in many natural history guides.

Hine, James Stewart (* June 13, 1866 near Wauseon, Ohio – †December 22, 1930 Columbus, Ohio) [69] [70] was an Ohio entomologist with special interests in Diptera (Tabanidae) and Odonata.

Hine, who grew up on a farm, went to Ohio State University, where he studied under D.S. Kellicott and received his B.Sc. in 1893. For his whole life he stayed in connection with his alma mater, at first in teaching positions, from 1902 to 1925 as Associate Professor of Entomolgy. After that he was entrusted to organize and direct the Division of Natural History of the Ohio State Archaeological and Historical Museum. From this position he was carried off by a stroke during Christmas preparations. Hine had a considerable knowledge of the insect fauna of North America and the Caribbean, gained by collecting trips throughout Ohio, but also to the Gulf Coast (1903), Central America (1905, with E.B. Williamson), California, Arizona and Mexico (1907), Alaska (1917 + 1919), Florida and Cuba (1923). Of his *ca* 90 publications more than 50 are concerned with Diptera, 10 with Odonata.

Hodges, Robert Shattuck (* September 28, 1875 – † May 15, 1964) [71] [72] [73] [74]

Hodges is mentioned as a special student of chemistry and biology at the University of Alabama, Tuscaloosa in 1899. Later he was a chemist at the Geological Survey of Alabama and was also a chemistry professor at the University of Alabama. He collected in Alabama for the Alabama Museum of Natural History, collecting nymphs and raising them to adults. Amongst his publications was *Alabama Dragonflies (Odonata)* (1937). Hodges is buried in Tuscaloosa Memorial Park. It might be mentioned, that he was a keen photographer and in 1920 took the first known color photograph in Alabama. His odonate collection probably is now at the University of Alabama. [75]

Karsch, Ferdinand Anton Franz or **Karsch-Haack** (*September 2, 1853 Münster, Germany – † December 20, 1936 Berlin) [76] was a German arachnologist, entomologist and anthropologist.

While still at school, under a pseudonym, he published a catalogue of spiders found in Westphalia, his native region. His systematic interest and skills were probably due to the influence of his father, a doctor, botanist and entomologist who, in the year when Ferdinand was born, was appointed to a professorship of Natural Science at the Royal Academy at Münster. After four years of study in his home town Karsch went to Berlin to complete his Dr. phil. in 1877. There he was employed as an assistant at the Berlin Zoological Museum in the department of arthropods. After his habilitation in 1881 (a graduation which was normally a precondition for being appointed as a professor) Karsch taught at the agricultural college Berlin. In 1899 he became curator at the Zoological Museum being responsible for the entomological collections. More than 250 publications by him deal with entomological or arachnological themes, most of them being on systematics. From 1884 until 1900 he edited the periodical *Entomologische Nachrichten* and from 1895 also the *Berliner Entomolgische Zeitschrift*.

After 1903 he made a change in his subject. Since then his publications dwelled on homosexuality in animals and in mankind and after 1905 he mostly used the name Karsch-Haack, adding his mother's maiden name to his own. After the Nazis had come to power he had difficulties because of his sexual orientation, and his scientific merits were no longer valued, when he died in 1936.

Kellicott, **David Simons** (*January 28, 1842 Hastings Center, N. Y. – †April 13, 1898 Columbus, Ohio) [77] [78]

After a preliminary education in the elementary schools and the academy of his hometown Kellicott, who is said to have spent much of his boyhood out of doors due to delicate health, in 1865 went to Genesee College (at Lima, N.Y., which in 1870 was transferred into Syracuse University), from which he graduated in 1869 with a B.Sc. (Later he received from his alma mater a B.Ph. in 1874 and a Ph.D. in 1881). In 1871 he moved to Buffalo, where he taught natural science firstly at the State Normal School, later at the University, being Dean of the College of Pharmacy and Professor of Botany and Microscopy. In 1888 he was appointed to a professorship of Zoology and Comparative Anatomy at Ohio State University, from which in 1891 he switched to a chair of Zoology and Entomology, which he held until his premature death. In his research Kellicott specialized in rotifers and infusorians, but also in Lepidoptera and Odonata.

Kennedy, Clarence Hamilton (*June 25, 1879 Rockport, Indiana – †June 6, 1952 Columbus, Ohio) [79] [80] [81]

When Kennedy graduated from the University of Indiana (A.M. 1903), he had already been in contact with E.B. Williamson, who seems to have greatly influenced his interest in Odonata. Not much is known about his next years except that he suffered from ill health and for some time lived in Texas. Between 1909 and 1914 Kennedy collected Odonata in Oregon and Washington, for some time being employed by the U.S. Bureau of fisheries and briefly acting as collector for the herbarium of Mt. Holyoke College. From this, as well as from ornithological publications in his earlier times, is to be seen that he was an all-round naturalist. During the summer of 1914 Kennedy made collecting trips through central California and Nevada, sometimes earning his living with illustrations of fish, birds and insects. Having received an A.M. from Stanford University in 1915, Kennedy went to Cornell University where he acted as instructor in zoology and got his Ph.D. in 1919 with a thesis on phylogeny of damselflies. He then joined the staff of Ohio State University, first as instructor in entomology, later being promoted to a full professorship in 1933, which he held until his retirement in 1949. He was a member of many learned societies, among which was then the Entomological Society of America, which he served as editor of the *Annals* from 1929 to 1945 and as president in 1935. Kennedy is said to have been an outstanding teacher for advanced and graduate students as well as one of the finest illustrators of Odonata.

Kirby, William Forsell (*January 14, 1844 Leicester, England – † November 20, 1912 Chiswick) [82] [83] [84] was an English entomologist and folklorist.

Kirby, who had an extensive private education, already in his youth was keen on entomology, so much so that in 1861 he became a fellow of the Entomological Society of London, which he served as secretary from 1863 to 1885. In 1879 he was appointed curator at the British Museum of Natural History, having held a similar post at the Museum of the Royal Dublin Society (later: National Museum of Science and Art) for twelve years. His entomological publications include a wide range of orders: Lepidoptera, Tenthredinidae, Hymenoptera, Orthoptera. His *Synonymic Catalogue of Neuroptera Odonata* was the first relativly complete summing up of the dragonflies from around the world; he also contributed much to the taxonomy of the Libellulinae. But his entomological work is only one part of his broad field of interest. Having learned many languages, and being interested in mythology and folktales, he also made an English translation of the Finnish national epic *Kalevala* and gave annotations to a translation of the *Arabian Nights*. In addition he published on philosophical and theological subjects.

Knopf, Kenneth William (*1950) [85] [86]

While working on his Ph.D., "Protein variation in *Gomphus* (Odonata: Gomphidae)" at the University of Florida Ken Knopf saw his odonatologist classmates having major difficulties finding professional positions that didn't require some significant sacrifices, either financial or geographic in nature. As he wanted to stay in Gainesville he enrolled in dental insurance school in July of 1977 and continued at the same time in Entomology, finishing his degree in December of 1977. Minter J. Westfall, Jr. was the person who got him interested in Odonata. However, Westfall was not his thesis advisor. Rather, Westfall was a member of the dissertation committee. In his dissertation Knopf concludes that *Arigomphus* and *Plathemis* should be considered as separate genera from

Gomphus and *Libellula* respectively. He also synonymized two species based on patterns of starch gel electrophoresis of a large number of proteins.

His intention was to continue to work on odonates in his spare time. Starting a family, establishing a dental practice, and a new intense interest in hunting and fishing came to interfere with that plan. However, on most of his vacations to other parts of the world he has collected adults. Upon turning 68 Knopf realized he needed to make plans to donate his collection, probably about 12,000 specimens in about 1000 species. Probably half of his specimens are in triangles and many are labeled to site and date in batches, needing final curation to make the collection complete for donation. He still keeps up with the regular publications that apply to North America and Neotropics.

Laudermilk, Ellis Lee (*September 8, 1964 Springfield, Ohio) [87]
After moving with his family from Ohio to a rural Kentucky farm at age seven, Laudermilk was first attracted to dragonflies while fishing at a pond and hearing neighbors refer to the insects by the mysterious name of "snake feeders". Upon entering Eastern Kentucky University (EKU) to pursue a planned career in fisheries, he was soon influenced by Dr. Guenter  Schuster, a friend, mentor, and ultimately his graduate advisor, to focus his studies on invertebrates. He received a B.Sc. degree in Environmental Resources and a M.Sc. degree in Biology from EKU in 1990 and 1993, respectively. Immediately after graduation he took a job with the Kentucky Natural Heritage Program (KNHP) and was responsible for conducting aquatic surveys and implementing conservation strategies for rare, threatened, and endangered invertebrates across the Commonwealth. His supervisor, friend, and mentor, Mr. Ronald Cicerello, encouraged studies on additional species groups not typically covered by the KNHP during annual surveys. It was during this period that Laudermilk began to study the Kentucky odonate fauna. This effort led to a fortuitous meeting with Mr. Carl Cook, Kentucky's foremost authority on dragonflies and damselflies. Their collaboration resulted in the formal description of *Stylogomphus sigmastylus* in 2004. Cook's

friendship and mentorship was a driving force in Laudermilk's interest in odonates; they still collect dragonflies together and remain good friends. During his 25-year career with the KNHP, Laudermilk also coauthored papers on fishes, freshwater mussels, tiger beetles, butterflies, and moths, and he is a co-author and co-editor of *Kentucky's Natural Heritage: An Illustrated Guide to Biodiversity*.

Leach, **William Elford** MD, FRS (*February 2, 1791 Plymouth – † August 25, 1836 San Sebastiano Curone near Tortona, Italy) [88] [89] [90] was an English zoologist and marine biologist.

Leach, descended from a well-to-do family, as a boy began to collect marine animals from Plymouth Sound and the Devon coast. After a medical apprenticeship at Exeter, begun at the age of twelve, he studied medicine at a London hospital and Edinburgh university, completing his M.D. at St. Andrews in 1812. But Leach did not practise medicine, he got employment at the Natural History Department of the British Museum, where he rearranged the zoological collection, inspired by the French zoologists Cuvier and Latreille. So he erected many new genera; in the dragonflies he added six genera found in the Northern hemisphere and an Australian one to the three established by Linnaeus and Fabricius. He mainly worked on crustaceans and molluscs, but also separated the myriapods from the insects and published on amphibians, reptiles, mammals and birds. In 1817 he was elected Fellow of the Royal Society. Probably due to overworking, he had a nervous breakdown in 1821; so he retired and was accompanied by his caring sister to the continent, where he spent the following years in Italy, corresponding with his friends in England and France, until his sudden death from cholera in 1836.

Although there is a photograph on the internet under http://www.fromthemuddybanksofthedee.com/2012/09/william-elford-leach-and-his-eternal.html it is not likely to be correct, as Leach died in 1836, when photography had not yet developed so far.

Linnaeus, Carl (*May 23, 1707 Råshult/Småland, Sweden – † January 10, 1778 Uppsala, Sweden) [91] [92] [93], also known after his ennoblement as **Carl von Linné,** was a Swedish botanist, physician, and zoologist, who formalised the modern system of naming organisms called binomial nomenclature.

Linnaeus named one genus (*Libellula*) and three species of the dragonflies known from America in Edition 10 of his *System Naturae* (1758) and another species in 1763. Of the four species, three have been moved to different genera.

Although the son and grandson of parsons, he did not want to follow their vocation. After studying medicine and natural sciences in Lund and Uppsala he was sent on an expedition to Lapland to explore that then rather unknown region. Subsequently he travelled to the Netherlands, England and France to complete his studies. Afterwards for some time he settled in Stockholm as a physician; there in 1739 he initiated the foundation of the Swedish Academy, of which he became the first president. In 1741 he was given a professorship of medicine and anatomy at Uppsala and in the following year he was transferred to a chair of botany which included being Director of the botanical garden. He was appointed personal physician of the king in 1747. He instituted the classification of plants by their stamens and pistils, but also wrote a *Fauna Sueciae*. On this basis he generated his *Systema Naturae,* which he divides into three 'kingdoms', the animals, the plants and the minerals. Within these he founded the binominal system of nomenclature: each species is distinguished by a unique combination of two names: a genus name, which it may share with related species, and a specific name of its own. Whereas Linnaeus was convinced that there were unchangeable species instituted by the Creator, his system subsequently allowed adaptation to an evolutionary concept. So it is still in use today.

Martin, René (*June 5, 1846 Châtellerault, France – † August 20, 1925 Villa Alemana, Chile) [94] was a French odonatologist.

Martin, after attending the Lycée of Versailles, studied law in Paris from 1866 to 1870. After being married in 1872 he moved to Le Blanc in the department of Indre, where his wife's property was situated. There he practised as a solicitor until 1907, but at the same time expended much time in the study of vertebrates, Lepidoptera, Neuroptera (in the sense of Linnaeus), especially of Odonata. So he came in contact with Selys, McLachlan and Calvert, with whom he had an extensive correspondance, later also with E.B. Williamson, D.S. Kellicott and J.G. Needham. When Selys died in 1900 Martin accepted the task of composing the Catalogue of the corduliids and the aeshnids of Selys' collection, while Ris took the libellulids and Förster the agrionids (which task was never was finished). In the following years Martin also prepared a manuscript on the calopterygids, but it was never printed. In 1908 Martin moved to Paris. About 1912 he announced that he wanted to sell his collection of Odonata, which contained many types and more than 1600 specimens, but he did not succeed. After World War I in 1920 Martin's daughter, married to a Frenchman established in Chile, wanted to join him, and Martin decided to accompany her for at least a year, for the opportunity to study the fauna there. He gave his collection to the Paris Museum, except his lestids and the dragonflies from Chile. In Chile he took part in founding an entomological society in Santiago de Chile, where he had found congenial collectors in the Fathers of the Sacred Heart. But in 1923 Martin was stricken with cerebral congestion [a term no longer in medical use], followed by two later attacks. So he was not able to continue his studies, and he died in 1925.

Martin's entomological papers on Trichoptera, Lepidoptera and Perlidae (Plecoptera) refer to France, the odonatological papers are concerned with the indopacific region, Australia, the Seychelles, Turkey and Cyprus, diverse parts of Africa and of South America, mostly descriptive or taxonomic. Calvert mentions that Martin played a great role in the exchange of specimens around the world.

May, Michael Love (* 1946) [95] [96] [97] [98]

Growing up in Gainesville, Florida Michael May was an enthusiastic collector of insects and had accumulated an extensive butterfly collection by the time he left high school. His neighbour, and father of a school friend, was Dr Minter Westfall III, a university professor at the University of Florida. Westfall hired him as an assistant to help him in the field with Odonata. After graduating from Gainesville High School in 1964, May went to Davidson College (N.C.) then came back to the University of Florida for a Ph.D. He worked on projects including thermoregulation in Odonata, with Dr. Brian McNab, a physiological ecologist, as his advisor, gaining his Ph.D. in 1974. After graduating, he was a postdoctoral fellow at the University of Illinois and from January to September 1974 at the Smithsonian Tropical Research Institute (STRI) on Barro Colorado Island in Panama.

He started at Rutgers University's School of Environmental & Biological Sciences, New Brunswick, in 1978, initially focusing on behavior in the Colorado Potato Beetle but dragonflies and damselflies became his main research area, where he published seminal works on thermoregulation, phylogeny, morphology and identification. May was well known at Rutgers as an enthusiastic professor of insect behavior and insect morphology and physiology. He advised graduate students working on ants, mantises, grasshoppers, dung beetles, and dragonflies. After retiring in 2012 he continues to be a research associate.

The principal focus of his current research is on the taxonomy and phylogeny of Odonata and the implications of phylogeny for the interpretation of the evolution of their morphology and behaviour. On a regional level, he maintains a strong interest in the distribution and conservation of dragonflies in North America. He co-authored two handbooks on North American dragonfly species with Dr. Westfall. After encountering large swarms of *Anax junius* in New Jersey and again in Florida he started projects on dragonfly migration which have since been taken on by others.

Nationally, May was and is an active member of the Dragonfly Society of the Americas, a society of which he has been president. Internationally, he was one of the founding members of the World Dragonfly Association, of which he was president in 2003–2004 and he served time as the principal editor of the *International Journal of Odonatology*.

McLachlan, Robert (or **M'Lachlan** or **Mac Lachlan**) (*April 10, 1837 near Ongar, Essex – †May 23, 1904 Lewisham) [99] [100] [101] [102] [103] [104] [105] [106] was an English entomologist who specialised in 'Neuroptera' in the broad sense.

Already at a young age McLachlan had developed an interest in nature, firstly in botany. Soon afer his father's death, which left him with independent means, aged 18 he travelled for 13 months to New South Wales and Shanghai, were he collected an impressive number of plants. But soon he transferred his interest to insects. He had joined the Entomological Society at the age of 21, which he later served in several leading positions. His special interest in 'Neuroptera' (in the broad sense) was inspired by publications on that group concerning Great Britain in the years 1857 to 1861by H.A. Hagen, as whose pupil McLachlan describes himself [107]. In particular he dedicated himself to the study of the European species of Trichoptera [caddisflies], on which order he wrote a large monograph. Also the Odonata constituted a major part of his scientific work. For some time he travelled through Europe every year collecting, often together with his friend de Selys, and with special attention to the insect fauna of mountainous regions. He brought together the largest collection of 'Neuroptera' in England not only by collecting, but also by exchange and purchase. So he was able to contribute generously to the completeness of the odonate part of the *Biologia Centrali Americana* by sending a number of his unique types across the Atlantic. (In addition to his friendship with Selys and Hagen he was in contact with some other odonatologists, among these were Martin, Ris and Förster.) When Selys died he wanted McLachlan to review and catalog his collection, but due to bad health McLachlan had to decline.

Besides his studies and his work on the boards of the Entomological Society of London and the Linnean Society McLachlan also was one of the editors of the *Entomologist's Monthly Magazine* from its beginning, and for the last two years of his life also its proprietor. He was a fellow of many learned societies, among these the Entomological, Linnean, Royal, Zoological and Horticultural Societies of London, but also corresponding or honorary member of numerous entomological societies, among these that of Philadelphia.

Montgomery, Basil Elwood (*October 10, 1899 Posey County, Indiana – †January 19, 1983) [108] [109] [110]

In Montgomery's life one may observe certain traces of continuity: being linked to the state where he had been born, his proclivity for teaching, and his commitment for odonatology internationally. After graduation from Poseyville College in 1918 he was employed as teacher of science, history and Latin in diverse regions of Indiana until 1928. But from 1920 he also studied biology and mathematics at Oakland City College until his B.Sc. in 1922, at the same time being a teacher in history and mathematics there. In the next years he was in contact with E.B. Williamson, who encouraged his odonatological interests, lending specimens and manuscripts for study. In 1925 he completed his M.Sc. in entomology and education at Purdue University, at which time he was also a teaching assistant there. In the summer of 1927 he went to Iowa State University (Iowa City) for studies in parasitology and in 1928-29 became a Graduate Teaching Assistant in Entomology and Zoology at ISU (Ames). Following that he taught at Purdue University for 39 years, beginning as instructor for entomology. While teaching there he achieved his Ph.D. from Iowa State University in 1936. His teaching duties at Purdue spanned the whole field of entomology and during World War II from 1939 to 1943 he had to teach mathematics also. Nevertheless in addition to his academic duties he also engaged in public lectures for a variety of audiences, from preschoolers to retired groups to popularize science. One field of research in which he excelled was honeybees, and so he spent an academic year in New Zealand in 1949-50 and two summers in Alaska in 1955 and 1956. But all the time he also published on Odonatology, and in the 1960s he visited major collections in Europe, as he already had studied the collections of MCZ at Harvard in 1942. Even more important was his initiative to issue invitations for the first ever International Colloquium on Odonatology at his university in 1963. At the same time, to consolidate the contacts and communication initiated there, he founded the newsletter *Selysia*, which he edited for 17 years. These efforts resulted in the foundation of the *Societas Internationalis Odonatologica* in 1971. Due to poor health in the last years of his life he was less active in the business of that Society, but he had agreed to accept the responsibility of the Presidency for the period from 1983-87. From that he was prevented by death. His collection of some 20,000 specimens is now at the Smithsonian Institution as is his odonatological library of 18,000 titles.

Morse, Albert Pitts (*February 10, 1863 Sherborn, Massachusetts – †April 29, 1936 Wellesley, Mass.) [111] was an entomologist who specialised in Orthoptera and Odonata.

After graduating from the Sawin Academy of Sherborn in 1879 Morse could not continue his education as he had to help at home. But from his boyhood he was interested in natural history, collected specimens and studied taxidermy. In this he was encouraged by local naturalists. In 1888 he became an assistant at the zoological department of Wellesley College, where he stayed connected in different capacities until 1933. He acted as collector and instructor, developed the museum, and taught elementary and systematic zoology and entomology. In the first years he attended the summer school of the Marine Biological Labaratory at Woods Hole, and took a summer course in entomology under J.H. Comstock at Cornell University. He made extensive collections of insects in New England and in 1897, encouraged by S.H. Scudder, at the West Coast. In 1903 and 1905 as a Research Assistant at the Carnegie Institution of Washington he studied the Orthoptera of the Southern United States. In 1911 Morse was appointed Curator of Natural History with the Peabody Museum of Salem, and in 1926 he also became trustee of the Ropes Mansion at Salem, in which capacity he also had to arrange botanical lectures. Because of failing health he had to give up his regular work at the Peabody Museum in 1935. His collection of more than fifty thousand specimens was acquired by the Harvard Museum of Comparative Zoology in 1920-22. Morse was member of some learned societies, among which was the Cambridge Entomological Club.

Muttkowski, Richard Anthony von (*March 4, 1887 Milwaukee, Wisconsin – †April 15, 1943) [112] [113] [114] was an American Entomologist who made his most important publications in the field of experimental biology and the physiology of insects.

After obtaining a Bachelor of Arts in 1904 at St. Lawrence College, Colorado, and again from the University of Wisconsin in 1913, and a Ph.D. from the latter institution in 1916, he worked as an assistant in the department of invertebrate zoology at the Milwaukee Public Museum from 1906 to 1912. Subsequent to his doctor's degree, he worked for a year in the zoological department of the University of Missouri. In 1917 he took a position at Kansas State College for a year, then he spent the years from 1919 to 1922 at the University of Idaho. He moved to the University of Detroit in 1922, becoming head of the department of Biology in 1925, a position he held until his death. Muttkowski served as an instructor in the American Expeditionary Forces in France in 1919.

During his time in Wisconsin, he gave much attention to insects and especially Odonata, publishing his Catalogue of the Odonata of North America as the first Bulletin of the Public Museum of the City of Milwaukee in 1910. Other than his Catalogue, Muttkowski's work on Odonata dealt mainly with the Wisconsin fauna and a study of the genus *Tetragoneuria*, all published before gaining his doctorate. Also while in Idaho he assembled material for 'Food of trout in Yellowstone National Park' and 'Ecology of trout streams in Yellowstone National Park', each of which included ecological aspects of Odonata. He was also author of 'Idaho' in *Naturalists' Guide*.

Navás, Longinos (*March 7, 1858 Cabacés, Tarragona – †December 31, 1938 Girona) [115] [116] was a Spanish entomologist and Jesuit priest.

Navás, who was born as the fourth child of twelve to a Catalan peasant family, began studying law at Barcelona, but soon joined the Jesuit order. Due to political turmoil he had to spend his novitiate in France. In 1878 he was able to return to Spain, where he was educated in humanities, theology and natural science. His ordination to priesthood took place in 1890. In 1892 he began to teach Natural History at the Jesuit High School 'Colegio del Salvador' at Zaragoza, which he continued for about 40 years. In addition to his teaching he studied Natural Science at Madrid from 1900 to 1901, acquiring a M.Sc. When the Spanish Republican Government banned his order by law in 1932 Navás took refuge in Piedmont, at first undertaking entomological field research on behalf of the museum of Turin. Later he arranged its collection of Neuroptera and those of museums at Rome, Naples and Genoa. Eventually he taught at a Jesuit institution for training teachers in the Aosta Valley, before returning to Spain, because circumstances had changed there. In 1936, as he prepared to leave Barcelona for an expedition to the Pyrenées, he was restricted by the civil war. After the failed coup of the Falange, many priests were assassinated due to anticlerical excesses. Navás found shelter with a former pupil of his near Girona; but after his host had been arrested, he relocated to a monastery where he died.

Scentifically Navás first studied lichens from the Iberian peninsula, later those from South America, but then he turned to zoological matters, with most of his more than 600 publications concerning 'Neuroptera' in Linnean sense, on the taxonomy of which he specialised. Among the species named by him there are 131 odonate taxa, but of his 11 genus group names only 4 are still valid (one a subgenus), 7 being synonyms and one a homonym, of his 120 species group names according to the world Odonata list there remain less than 50, for as a critic says: "Most of his studies lack the precise information required for an accurate diagnosis, because he seldom provided information on genital structures which is essential for the identification of most species. For this reason, careful and continuous revision of material studied by him is required" [117]. Additionally a great part of his collections was destroyed; at Barcelona there only exist deplorable remains. Among the entomological correspondents of Navás were Selys and McLachlan.

Needham, James George (*March 16, 1868 Virginia, Illinois – †July 24, 1957 Ithaca, N.Y.) [118] [119] [120]

After graduating from Knox College (B.Sc. and M.Sc.) he taught there from 1894 to 1896. During that time he published his *Elementary Lessons in Zoology*, which attracted J.H. Comstock's attention, who arranged for a scholarship to Cornell for him. Whilst at Cornell Needham achieved his Ph.D. and coauthored a work with Comstock on the wings of insects, which had a great influence. After teaching biology at Forest Lake University, Illinois, from 1898 to 1907, the summers of which years were spent with research on aquatic invertebrates for the New York State Conservation Department in the Adirondacks, Needham was appointed to a newly erected chair of limnology at Cornell, and upon the retirement of Comstock in 1914 was appointed head of the Department of Entomolgy, which position he held until his own retirement in 1934. But he remained active in research, and he spent the last winters of his life at Archbold Biological Station, Florida. Needham is said to have been able to excite the enthusiasm of his students for interrelationships in nature. In odonatology he was a pioneer in the studies of larval stages and he was able to popularize dragonflies with his '*Handbook of Dragonflies of N.A.*' (1929, with Hortense Butler Heywood) and his '*Manual of the Dragonflies of N.A.*' (1955, with Minter J. Westfall Jr.).

Newman, Edward (*May 13, 1801 Hampstead – †June 12, 1876 Peckham) [121] [122] [123] was an English entomologist, botanist and writer.

Newman was the eldest of four sons born to a Quaker family. As well as his parents encouraging his love for nature, also teachers at the public school at Painswick in Gloucestershire stimulated this aspiration. So Newman throughout his later life tried to give others access to naturalist studies by his publications. When he was sixteen his father, who then settled at Godalming (Surrey) as a wool stapler, wanted him to join him in business. In 1826 Newman moved to Deptford, to take over a rope making business. But as this did not leave him sufficient time to follow his naturalist avocation and his journalistic impulse he abandoned it in 1837. In Deptford he met like-minded people, with whom he founded an entomological club with regular meetings, the first entomological society in Britain. In 1832 the members of the club founded the periodical '*The Entomological Magazine*' entrusting Newman to edit it. This was the first of several journals edited by him. It amounted only to 5 editions. In 1833 the Entomological Society of London had been started with Newman playing a large role in it. His magazine had not secured the right to publish the memoirs read at the meetings, which was left to special *Transactions* of the society. In 1840 Newman became a partner in a firm of London printers, which he took over two years afterwards. In this new position he founded a new periodical, the *Entomologist*, which after two years was merged with the *Zoologist*, a paper edited by Newman for the following 34 years. In 1864 he revived the *Entomologist*, which journal continues until the present. Newman published on many fields of natural history: books on ferns, birds and bird's nests, butterflies, moths, but he demonstrated an all-round knowledge in his papers. His aim was to publish in well readable English and his publications – partly also written under pseudonyms – had a comparatively wide distribution. So his impact on the younger generation of his time must not be underestimated.

Packard, Alpheus Spring Jr., LL.D. (*February 19, 1839 Brunswick, Maine – † February 14, 1905 Providence, Rhode Island) [124] [125] [126]

From his youth Packard was interested in natural history. Even before he entered Bowdoin College in 1857 to study geology and entomology, he made extensive use of its library, to which he was conceded access because his father was one of Bowdoin's professors. During study with a professor of Williams College, who concurrently taught natural history at Bowdoin, he came into contact with S.H. Scudder, which was the beginning of a lifelong friendship. After graduating in the fall of 1861, Packard went to the Lawrence Scientific School at Harvard to study under L. Aggassiz, working at the MCZ as well. In 1864 he received his B.Sc. there and an M.D. from the Maine Medical School at Bowdoin as well. He served in the civil war as assistant surgeon until 1865. In the following years he acted as librarian and custodian of the Boston Society of Natural History, as curator of the Peabody Academy of Science at Salem, lectured on economic entomology at Maine State Agricultural College and at the Massachusetts Agricultural College at Amherst, and on entomology and comparative anatomy at Bowdoin. In 1867 he was one of the founders of the journal *The American Naturalist*, for which he acted as coeditor from 1878 to 1887. In 1869 he published his *Guide to the Study of Insects*, a volume of some seven hundred pages illustrated copiously. In 1872 during his first journey to Europe he met many of the outstanding entomologists there. In 1874 he went to investigate the Mammoth and other caves on behalf of the Kentucky Geological Survey and in 1875-76 he worked for the U.S. Geological Survey in the region of the Great Salt Lake and in Colorado. In 1876 his *Monograph of the Geometrid Moths* appeared, a publication as complete as possible at that time. In 1877 he was appointed one of the three members of the U.S. Entomological Commission to find a solution for the plague of the Rocky Mountains Locust and other noxious insects, the last report of which commission was published in 1890. In 1878 Packard became Professor of Zoology and Geology at Brown University, Providence, Rhode Island, where he stayed until his death. In his last years he was more interested in structures, growth and evolution according to Lamarck's theories than in identifying new taxa. Packard was a prolific writer: with more than five hundred publications and the description of more than 500 new genera and species. As well, he has contributed much to entomological knowledge, not only by his influential introductions to entomology but also by his works on moths. However, his only contribution to Odonatology is a description of one species in a publication of B. Walsh.

Palisot, Ambroise Marie François Joseph, Baron de Beauvois
(*July 27, 1752 Arras – †January 21, 1820 Paris) [127] was a French naturalist.

After his study of law Palisot, not content with a juridical career, turned to natural history, especially to botany. In 1781 he was appointed corresponding member of the Académie des Sciences. In 1786 he was commissioned to establish a French settlement in Oware (in today's Nigeria). From there he sent home plants and insects. An attempt to cross Africa to the Abyssinia failed; his brother in law and his servant died from fever. He himself affected by yellow fever was sent to Haiti by ship with some of his collections, the main part remaining at the French colony, where it was destroyed when the British conquered the place. In Haiti Palisot began to collect anew. When a revolution of the slaves impeded his activities, Palisot went to the United States seeking support for the repression of the revolt, but in vain. Back in Haiti in 1793 he was imprisoned by the victorious slaves, but then allowed to return to the United States. His collections were destroyed and he was robbed of all his valuables. In the United States he had a hard living, some time forced to earn his living in the orchestra of a circus at Philadelphia. He thought of going home to France, but in the mean time the French Revolution had taken place, and being an aristocrat abroad, his citizenship was deemed to have expired. But he found sponsors who allowed him to renew his collection trips, in which he visited also the country of the Creeks and the Cherokees. Finally in 1798 his French citizenship was restored and he planned to go back home. But the ship, in which he had stored most of his collections, was wrecked, so only very few of his collections survived. Back in France he began to publish the outcome of his long-lasting studies, but died before finishing this task. Palisot was among the first who described species from western Africa, the Caribbean and the

United States.

Paulson, Dennis R. (*November 29, 1937 Chicago, Illinois) [128] American zoologist who focuses on biodiversity and biology of dragonflies and birds.

Director, Slater Museum of Natural History 1990-2004 (presently Director Emeritus).

Dennis Paulson grew up in Miami, exposed to subtropical nature in all its glory while southern Florida was still largely unspoiled. When in high school he began his long history of collecting, first with butterflies and beetles. Odonates were added in graduate school when he discovered that almost nothing was known about them in Southern Florida. He received his Ph.D. in Zoology from the University of Miami in 1966 with a study of the dragonflies of southern Florida, and shortly thereafter he moved to Seattle, where he has lived ever since. After a post-doctoral position there, he was on the faculty of the University of Washington from 1969-1974. After that, he worked part-time for an architecture/landscape architecture firm and was heavily evolved in designing zoos. He then became the Director of the Slater Museum of Natural History at the University of Puget Sound, where he also taught in the Biology Department. Dennis has taught at three universities and continues to teach adult-education courses in many venues. He has studied dragonflies and birds worldwide and published nine books and over 90 scientific papers on these taxa, including describing six new species of odonates. Over a half century, he has amassed a collection of over 60,000 odonate specimens, all intended for the International Odonata Research Institute at the University of Florida. While carrying out field research, he also collected thousands of fishes, amphibians, reptiles and birds, all of which are in museums. After retirement, he continues to work at the Slater Museum, write books, and lead nature tours and travel with his wife Netta Smith to all continents. He is also an avid nature photographer, with many photos published in magazines, books and interpretive displays.

Pritchard, Arthur Earl (*July 13, 1915 Dallas, Texas – †February 28, 1965 Torrence, California) [129] [130]

Pritchard spent most of his early years in Oklahoma but, after three years at Oklahoma State University, he transferred to the University of Minnesota where he received his B.Sc. degree in 1936, his M.Sc. degree in entomology in 1940, and his Ph.D. degree in 1942.

While at the University of Minnesota he came under the guidance of Dr. C. E. Mickel, Dr. W. A. Riley and Professor A. G. Ruggles, studying theoretical and applied phases of entomology. During his graduate studies he served as a Research Assistant in entomology, and during the summer months he was associated with State of Minnesota and U. S. Department of Agriculture insect control projects.

After graduating with his doctorate he served with the U. S. Public Health Service as Supervisor of Malaria Control in Jamaica and Puerto Rico, as Medical Entomologist in Florida, and later as Principal Entomologist for typhus control. In 1946 he accepted a position as Assistant Professor of Entomology and Assistant Entomologist in the Experiment Station at the University of California, Berkeley. From 1952 until his resignation because of ill health in 1961 he served as Associate Professor of Entomology.

Soon after Dr. Pritchard came to the University of California he organized a course and research program centered on the insects associated with ornamental plants and, later in 1952, the first course in Acarology taught at the University of California. Pritchard's systematic work focused primarily on the Acari, in particular the Tetranychoidea, and he was also interested in the taxonomy of several groups of Diptera, publishing numerous papers on Asilidae, Culicidae, and Cecidomyiidae. His broad interests in entomology are reflected by the diversity of his more than eighty publications. His first scientific paper, "Two New Dragonflies from Oklahoma" was published while he was still a student at Oklahoma State University.

Dr. Pritchard joined the Entomological Society of America in 1933, became a Fellow in 1943, and a Life Member in 1947. He was a member of the Entomological Society of Washington, Pacific Coast Entomological Society, Entomological Society of Florida, and the Society of Systematic Zoology. The Pritchard Acari Collection is integrated into the general

Acari collection in the Essig Museum. It numbers approximately 6000 slide-mounted specimens, including numerous paratypes, the majority of his holotypes having been deposited in the Smithsonian Institution.

Provancher, Léon Abel, Abbé (*March 10, 1820 Bécancour, Nicolet County, Quebec – †March 23, 1892 Cap-Rouge, Quebec) [131] [132] was one of the pioneers of Canadian natural history.

Provancher was educated for the Catholic priesthood; in 1844 he was ordained at Quebec and, after having served in several other parishes, in 1862 he became Curé of Portneuf but, tired of parish ministry, he submitted his resignation in 1869, and after some time at St. Roch he settled at Cape Rouge near Quebec, where he devoted himself to natural studies. From 1868 to 1891 he published the *Naturaliste Canadien* endeavoring to disseminate knowledge of the natural history of his home country. His other publications covered botany and horticulture, conchology, but mostly entomology, where he described hundreds of species, including many Hemiptera and more than a thousand Hymenoptera from Canada. While promoting science by these contributions he disapproved of Darwin's theory of evolution. He was a fellow of the Royal Society of Canada, an honorary or active member of other societies and received an honorary doctorate from the Laval University, Quebec. Most of Provancher's collections are preserved in the department of biology at Laval. Among the new species he described is just one dragonfly.

Rambur, Jules Pierre (*July 21, 1801 near Chinon – †August 10, 1870 Geneva) [133] was a French physician and entomologist.

Rambur became interested in entomology during his education at a boarding school in Tours. After studying medicine at Tours and Montpellier he received his degree as a doctor in Paris in 1827. He then went on a collecting trip to the Alpine region and to Corsica for more than a year, focussing on Lepidoptera and Coleoptera. Back in Paris in 1832 he helped to found the Societé Entomologique de France, published an opus on the butterflies of Corsica, and began to edit a major publication on European caterpillars with his school friends A. de Graslin and J.-B. A. Dechauffour de Boisduval. The last volume of it was issued in 1843. An expedition to Andalusia in 1834-35 (partly with de Graslin) resulted in further publications on the entomological fauna (1837-40) and a catalogue of the butterflies (1858-1866) of that region. In 1841 after having married, Rambur settled as a doctor in the department Maine et Loire. In the following year Rambur's epoch making publication was printed, in which he catalogued the Neuroptera (sensu Linné) on a world wide scale. In this book there are more than 350 Odonata amounting to greater than half of the already described species, among them are many first descriptions. The material, on which this compendium was based, had been available in the collections of the many members of the Société entomologique living in or around Paris at that time with whom he was in contact. It is to be noted that Rambur, in his preface, confessed that the Neuroptera were his least favorite group among the insects. That is by no means to be seen from the diligent and meticulous descriptions in that work. From that time Neuroptera was finished for Rambur; the specimens of his own collection he gave away or donated. In a similar way he seems to have avoided habitual routine, for every few years he changed his place of residence, but also the favourite subjects of his studies. So among others he studied recent and fossil molluscs. By the time he finally moved to Geneva he had given up his medical profession.

Robert, Brother Adrien (*1906, Ange-Gardien, near Saint-Hyacinthe, Quebec – †August 15, 1964) [134]

Adrien Robert entered the teaching order the Clerics of Saint-Viateur, and was assigned to teaching at the age of 18. He practised in particular at the Montreal Institute for the Deaf and Mute, and completed his studies for general education (B.A. at Bourget College, 1939, Lic.Ped. at the University of Montreal, 1942). A strong influence on his later life was Brother Joseph Ouellet (1869-1952), a passionate amateur entomologist, whom Robert befriended at the Institute.

Brother Ouellet had long been in contact with a group of amateur-professional entomologists (Gustave Chagnon, Father Ovila Fournier and Lionel Daviault). Adrien Robert aspired to become a professional entomologist and that is why he associated himself with the only professional of the group, Lionel Daviault, a specialist in forest entomology. Daviault was responsible for the Berthierville nursery of the Quebec Ministry of Lands and Forests, and it was here that Robert began his thesis work in 1946, culminating in a doctorate in 1953. His work is entitled "Elm insects of the bark and wood and their relation to Dutch disease." In 1946, Adrien Robert had become a lecturer in entomology at the University of Montreal, while pursuing his Ph.D. research. After completing his thesis, he became an assistant professor in 1951 and an associate professor in 1954.

Brother Robert was, by inclination and training, a specialist in the taxonomy of Coleoptera. He established a catalogue of Quebec species for his own use, but also for updating "The principal beetles of the province of Quebec". However, the group closest to his heart was the Odonata. As early as 1935, he collected odonates at Nominingue where his community had a summer house and he wrote a review in the *Canadian Naturalist* in 1939, his first scientific publication. He continued his work with explorations to Abitibi (1944), at Mont-Tremblant Park (1953, 1962) and in the Mistassini area (1956).

From 1952 to 1961, at the Mont-Tremblant Biological Station at Lake Monroe, where he spent his summers he became interested in other insects in lakes and streams. Already passionate about dragonflies, there was a new group which particularly attracted him, from 1957, the Trichoptera.

Adrien Robert died on August 15, 1964, on the Feast of the Assumption, due to cancer at the age of 58.

An important legacy that Adrien Robert left to the scientific community is his collection of insects. Thanks to the generosity and vision of the Clerics of Saint-Viateur it has been combined with that of Brother Ouellet to form the Ouellet-Robert Collection at the University of Montreal, the ensemble thus forming a rich collection of insects from Quebec.

Root, Francis Metcalf (*September 24, 1889 Oberlin, Ohio – †October 21, 1934 Baltimore) [135]

After graduating from the college of his hometown (A.B. 1911, A.M. 1912) Root received a Ph.D. at Johns Hopkins University in 1917. There he taught in the School of Hygiene subsequently as a teaching fellow, associate and from 1926 as assistant professor. In his research he worked mainly on anopheline and other mosquitoes, for the study of which group he was sent to Brasilia for half a year in 1925 by the International Health Board of the Rockefeller Foundation. Root died from heart disease at the hospital of his university. Two species of *Enallagma* were described by him, which he encountered during research trips on mosquitoes in Maryland and Georgia.

Say, Thomas (*June 27, 1787 Philadelphia – †October 10, 1834 New Harmony, Indiana) [136] [137] [138] [139] was one of the first North American descriptive zoologists, his main publications being on entomolgy, conchology and herpetology.

Say was born into a prominent family of Quakers at Philadelphia. After an education at Westtown School for some years he helped in the apothecary of his father, but in 1812 he decided to follow his love for natural history. He then helped to found the Academy of Natural Sciences and took care of its collections. He took part in several expeditions, in 1818 to the coast islands of Georgia and Florida, in 1819-20 alongside the Missouri River up to the Rocky Mountains and in 1823 to the headwaters of the Mississippi River, all of which led to publications not only on the fauna of the newly explored regions, but also on fossil molluscs and on the languages and traditions of the Indian tribes living there. In 1822 Say was appointed professor of natural history at the University of Pennsylvania. In 1825 he was persuaded by William Maclure, president of the Academy of Natural Sciences and Say's friend and promoter, to join the community of New Harmony at the Wabash River, where the social and educational ideas of Maclure and of the British social reformer Richard Owen were to be put into practice. There Say remained, even after Owen and Maclure had fallen out and the utopian community had failed in 1828, continuing with his publications, which won him a reputation even in Europe, so that he became foreign fellow of the Linnean and the Zoological Societies of London. After his death from typhoid fever in 1834 many papers prepared by him were published posthumously, among these Say's publication of 37 dragonfly species, eleven being synonyms or homonyms.

Scudder, Samuel Hubbard (*April 13, 1837 Boston – †May 17, 1911 Cambridge, Mass.) [140] [141] was a most prolific lepidopterologist, orthopterologist and palaeoentomologist.

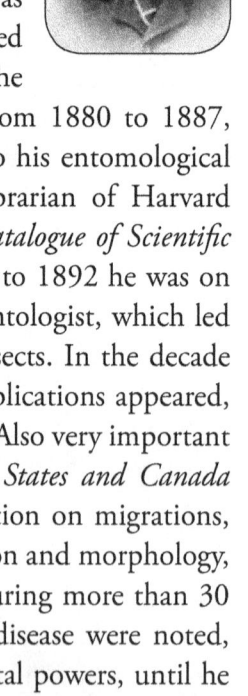

Scudder was born into a Puritan New England family. In 1857, after graduating from Williams College, where he had developed a great interest in natural history, he went to Lawrence Scientific School to study under L. Agassiz, achieving his B.Sc. in 1862. For two more years he remained there acting as assistant to Agassiz. At the same time he was associated with the Boston Society of Natural Science, which he served in various capacities, finally as president from 1880 to 1887, when he decided to dedicate himself completely to his entomological studies. From 1879 to 1882 he was assistant librarian of Harvard University, as a result of which he prepared his *Catalogue of Scientific Serials* and his *Nomenclator Zoologicus*. From 1886 to 1892 he was on the staff of the U.S. Geological Survey as a palaeontologist, which led to his description of more than thousand fossil insects. In the decade from 1891 until 1901 most of his orthopteran publications appeared, with the description of 106 genera and 630 species. Also very important was his opus *The butterflies of the eastern United States and Canada* published in 1889 in three volumes with information on migrations, feeding habits, life histories, geographical distribution and morphology, which summed up his expert knowledge gained during more than 30 years. In 1896 the first symptoms of Parkinson's disease were noted, which gradually undermined his physical and mental powers, until he was no longer able to continue his work (his last paper was published in 1902). Aware of this Scudder gave his collections to the Museum of Comparative Zoology at Harvard, his library to the Boston Society of

Natural History. He was a member or fellow of many learned societies in the U.S. and abroad. To give an impression of his productivity: by him there are 791 publications, 168 of which deal with Lepidoptera, 180 with Orthoptera, 122 with fossil insects.

Selys Longchamps, Baron **Michel Edmond de** (*May 25, 1813 Paris – †December 11, 1900 Liège) [142] [143] [144] was a Belgian liberal politician and scientist.

Selys came from a wealthy family of aristocrats, members of which in the last centuries had officiated as church or political dignitaries in the region of Liège. According to this tradition he engaged himself in politics, first on regional scale, later for many years he was a member of the senate, the second chamber of the Belgian parliament, and acted as its president for one period of legislation from 1880 to 1884. After his first nine years at Paris in the care of his grandmother he was educated privately on the family estate Longchamps near Waremme. Already then he engaged in studying the fauna and flora of his home district, an inclination he would follow for his lifetime, but on a wider scale. By this he came across Odonata, which were to become the main focus in his scientific work. In the first period from about 1831 to 1851, as Calvert puts it, there were his publications on European species, culminating in his *Revue des Odonates ou Libellules d' Europe* (1850), which work was completed with the collaboration of H.A. Hagen, with whom Selys was in contact from 1841. The second period, lasting from 1853 to 1886, brought about the monographic revisions of the Odonata of the world, again in collaboration with Hagen, especially for the monographs on calopterygids and gomphids. The only subfamily not covered was the difficult libellulids. The third group of odonatological publications comprise faunal papers, which commenced as early as 1853, but after 1878 were somewhat more extensive, and in the main were related to Asia. The relevance of the odonatological publications of Selys is due to the fact that he established wing venation as an essential tool of taxonomy. He described more than 700 species and constituted 134 valid genera, more than any other odonatologist. He amassed the largest odonate collection of his time, copiously collecting himself, but at the same time he bought extensively, not only specimens, but also the whole collections, among others those of the eminent French entomologists Latreille, Audinet-Serville, Rambur, Guerin-Meneville. Moreover he was sent material from around the world by odonatological colleagues. He had a special relationship not only with Hagen, but also with R. McLachlan. American correspondents of his were E.B. Williamson and Philip Calvert. The latter also visited him once in Longchamps. In his last will and testament Selys wanted the description of his collection to be completed by others; he hoped, that his friend McLachlan would see to this task, for which he provided a generous sum, but due to bad health McLachlan had to decline. Finally G. Severin took the coordination, F. Ris wrote on the libellulines, R. Martin on the cordulines and aeshnines; he also prepared a manuscript on the calopterygines that never was published. The part on the agrionines, which F. Förster should have prepared, and on the gomphids, which had been attributed to K. Grünberg seem never to have been written. His collections are now preserved at the Royal Belgian Institute of Natural Science in Brussels.

Smith, William Arthur [*1947] [145]

William Smith is an American entomologist who worked at the Wisconsin Department of Natural Resources. He compiled a *Checklist of Wisconsin Dragonflies* (1993) with Timothy Vogt and Karen Gaines. He collected the type for his eponymous species, and has co-written a paper with Vogt, describing a new dragonfly species: *Ophiogomphus susbehcha* (1993).

Sulzer, Johann Heinrich (*September 18, 1735, Winterthur – †August 14, 1813, Winterthur) [146] [147] was a Swiss physician and entomologist.

Sulzer, descended from an influential family of his hometown, studied medicine at Tübingen (Germany) and natural science at Strasbourg. Back at his home town, where he settled as a physician, he was entrusted with some official functions, e.g. in the school administration. He was open minded to innovations; so he was the first to introduce vaccination against smallpox. There are two entomological publications from him in which he tried to popularize the Linnean system.

Tennessen, Kenneth Joseph (*June 10, 1946 Ladysmith, Wisconsin) [148]

After he completed high school in 1964 in Phillips, Wisconsin, his parents told him they would pay for his first year of college (instead of his joining the military), an offer he accepted mainly because of his interest in biology, especially insect diversity. He majored in entomology at the University of Wisconsin, obtaining a Bachelor of Science degree in 1968. While at Wisconsin, under the tutelage of William Hilsenhoff, he focused his interest on Odonata, the group of insects that had most fascinated him in his boyhood. He advanced to graduate study at the University of Florida in the fall of 1968 where he began taxonomic studies under the direction of Minter J. Westfall, Jr. His graduate program was interrupted when he was drafted into the United States Army in 1969, and he served one year in combat in the Vietnam War. He came home in February, 1971, shortly thereafter returning to the University of Florida and earning a Ph.D. degree in entomology in 1975. The subject of his dissertation was the reproductive isolation of two sibling species of damselflies in the genus *Enallagma*. Academic positions were at a premium at the time he graduated, and having a wife and two young boys, he accepted employment with the Division of Water Quality, Tennessee Valley Authority (TVA), based in Muscle Shoals, Alabama. Throughout the Tennessee Valley he conducted research on the effects of heated water effluents and other environmental problems created by damming of the Tennessee River, mainly involving aquatic insects and other fish food organisms, for several years. He later became involved in ecological research on mosquitoes and their control before becoming lead researcher on detection of arboviruses in mosquitoes in the Tennessee Valley. On his own time, he continued to conduct systematic research on adult and nymphal dragonflies, including taking trips to the Neotropics. Tennessen served as Secretary General of the Societas Internationalis Odonatologica from 1978 to 1987, and as President of the Dragonfly Society of the Americas (1995-1996); he was a founding member of the latter society. Tennessen has described 22 new species of Odonata from North and South America. He retired from the TVA in 2004 and he and Sandi moved back to Wisconsin to take care of aging parents. He has recently published an identification guide to the Anisoptera (dragonfly) nymphs of North America, as well as doing faunistic and taxonomic studies in several South American countries.

Tough, James [* probably before 1872, † before 1941] [149] [150] [151]

There is scarce information on this author. In 1892 in the *Entomological News* he wrote a plea for a Manual of North American Lepidoptera to be compiled by the leading Lepidopterologists. His place of residence then was Chicago, as it was in 1900, when he published his *Gomphus cornutus* in the first fascicle of the *Occasional Memoirs of the Chicago Entomological Society*, to which organization he had a special connection, as in 1897 he had been one of its 16 founding members. In a publication about that society in 1941, another founding member reports that he himself is the only one still living of these sixteen. [In his 1900 publication Tough mentions J.S. Hine (1866-1930) then assistant professor of zoology and entomology at Columbus, Ohio, after whom Calvert, Kennedy and Williamson have named odonate species.

Trybom, Filip Arvid (*December 24, 1850 Fivelstad parish (Östergötland) – †February 15, 1913 Stockholm) [152] [153] was a Swedish biologist and officer in the administration of fisheries.

After studying biology in Uppsala Trybom took part in several exploring expeditions, including the Swedish expedition to Yenisei in 1876, for which he undertook the entomological studies of Lepidoptera and Odonata. In entomology his main interest was Thysanoptera. Professionally he became an officer in the administration of fishery, in which function he tried to improve breeding of fish and crawfishes, to  modernise fishing with nets and he initiated a method for monitoring fish populations. To learn more about these subjects he travelled to several European countries and in 1885-86 to the United States and Canada. Whereas in his profession he was engaged in a different field of science he maintained his interest for entomology and from 1880 was member of the Swedish entomological society until his death, serving for many years on its board.

Uhler, Philip Reese (*June 3, 1835 Baltimore – †October 21, 1913) [154] [155] [156] was an American entomologist who later specialised in Heteroptera.

Uhler began to collect insects at a young age. Having finished college he was placed into the family business by his father, a wealthy merchant, but Philip spent most of his time studying geology, botany, zoology and insects. Having published on Neuroptera in 1857 and 1858 he was asked to translate the Latin text of Hagen's Catalogue of the Neuroptera of North America, which was published by the Smithsonian Institution in 1861. Probably due to this publication Uhler, who had been appointed assistant librarian at Peabody Institute in 1863 under his long time entomological mentor J.G. Morris, was asked by L. Agassiz to take charge of the entomological collection and the library at the Harvard Museum of Comparative Zoology, which post he held for three years. During this time he also attended the Lawrence School of Science and taught entomology to some undergraduate students. After this he returned to Peabody in 1867 and became librarian there in 1870. In this capacity he perfected its cataloging system. At the same time he continued his entomological activities, becoming America's foremost authority on Hemiptera, in which order he described about 600 species. But he also published some geological papers. He was involved in the foundation of the Johns Hopkins University and became its first associate professor. In 1880 he was made provost of Peabody which post he held until his retirement in 1911. However his increased professional duties combined with failing eyesight prevented him from publishing his findings. His types of Odonata and Orthoptera are at the MCZ at Harvard, the greater part of his other collections came to the U.S. National Museum at Washington.

Vogt, Timothy Edward (*25 August 1956, Alton, Illinois) [157]

As a toddler, Vogt was terrified of insects. His grandmother taught him to track ants to their "anthill home" using bread crumbs. He was enthralled and fascinated. The following summer he was collecting butterflies. His father made his first aerial net for him when he was age four. Both parents supported and encouraged his nascent entomological interests. An unsolicited phone call by his grandmother to the Illinois State Museum (ISM) introduced him to Everett (Tim) Cashatt. At sixteen he became a summer volunteer at ISM. Cashatt taught him taxonomy, the importance of museum collections, and curatorial practices. After graduating in 1986 with a M.Sc., he spent most of his career as a conservation biologist. Much of this time he was employed for his botanical expertise. Vogt worked under Cashatt as a Research Associate at ISM (1996-2000). From 1988-2013 they conducted distribution, habitat, and ecological research for the federally listed *Somatochlora hineana*. He also was employed as the Wisconsin Natural Heritage Zoologist and the Missouri State Parks Scientist at those particular Departments of Natural Resources. *Somatochlora brevicincta* and *Ophiogomphus edmundo* were known only from the original descriptions until Vogt rediscovered them in 1990 and 1994, respectively. He was a charter member of the Dragonfly Society of the Americas.

Walker, Edmund Murton (*October 5, 1877 Windsor, Ontario – †February 14, 1969 Toronto) [158] [159] [160] [161] [162] was a Canadian entomologist.

Walker was son of a banker, who acted as a patron of the science. So during his time at school and university he had the opportunity to meet the leading Canadian entomologists of that time. He graduated in medicine from the University of Toronto in 1903 and practised for one year at the Toronto General Hospital. However as the medical profession did not satisfy him, during the next two years he studied biology at the universities of Toronto and of Berlin. After returning to Toronto in 1906 he took up the position of a lecturer in invertebrate zoology at the university. From then he focussed on entomology, especially the Orthoptera and Odonata. In the years 1910-1920 he edited the journal *The Canadian Entomologist*. From 1934 until his retirement in 1948 he was head of the Department of Zoology. After that he became the first honorary curator of Entomology at the Royal Ontario Museum, for the invertebrate collection of which he had taken responsibility when the museum had been established in 1914 and had served as its assistant director from 1918 to 1931. Walker's publications are praised because of their outstanding qualities. In odonatology, besides papers treating the larval stages of numerous taxa, there are the monographs on the North American species of the genus *Aeshna* in 1912, undertaken on the encourageemt of E.B. Williamson, and a similar work on the genus *Somatochlora* in 1925, and especially his comprehensive work *The Odonata of Canada and Alaska* (vol. I: 1953; vol II: 1959), the third volume of which was completed and edited by Philip Corbet in 1975.

Walsh, Benjamin Dann (*September 21, 1808 Hackney near London, England – †November 18, 1869 Rock Island, Illinois) [163] was a pioneer of North American economic entomology.

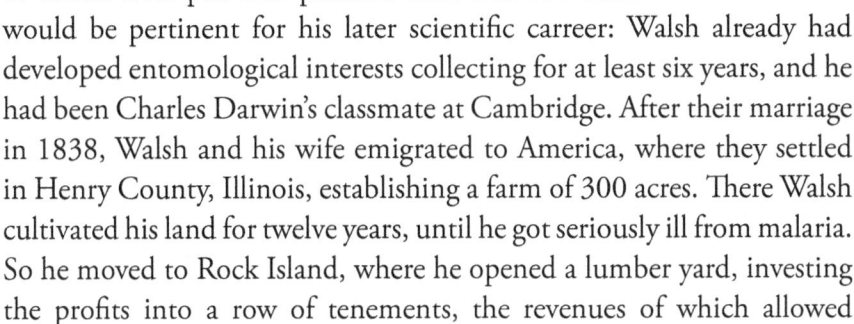

The thirty years Walsh lived in England are very different from those he spent in America. Walsh had graduated with a M.A. at Trinity College Cambridge in 1833, become a fellow in 1833 and had published a volume with a metric translation of several comedies of Aristophanes and, in 1837, a paper with suggestions for reforms of the University of Cambridge, nearly all of which were put into practice later. But two facts would be pertinent for his later scientific carreer: Walsh already had developed entomological interests collecting for at least six years, and he had been Charles Darwin's classmate at Cambridge. After their marriage in 1838, Walsh and his wife emigrated to America, where they settled in Henry County, Illinois, establishing a farm of 300 acres. There Walsh cultivated his land for twelve years, until he got seriously ill from malaria. So he moved to Rock Island, where he opened a lumber yard, investing the profits into a row of tenements, the revenues of which allowed him to retire from business in 1858, when he engaged himself with others in founding the Illinois Natural History Society, and to dedicate himself to entomology. By lectures and articles in newspapers he tried to disseminate knowledge on the effects of noxious insects on horticulture and their remedies by accurate scientific knowledge. The reputation won by these activities had the result that he was appointed the first Illinois State Entomologist in 1868, a position, the duties of which Walsh had exercised since 1867, but in the interim the formal employment had been thwarted politically. From 1860 Walsh had been in contact with many entomologists of renown (Osten Sacken 1860, Hagen, then still in Prussia, 1860, LeConte 1861, Uhler 1861, Scudder 1862) and he published in scientific journals. In 1865 he became associate editor of the *Practical Entomologist*, a journal dedicated to economic entomology, being left as sole editor in the journal's last year, 1867. In 1868 he became senior editor of the *American Entomologist*, O. Riley being junior editor. In these years Walsh ardently fought for Darwin's theory of evolution, providing arguments from his own observations, which Darwin included into later editions of his *Origin of Species*. In 1869 Walsh died as a result of an accident on a railway track. His collections, which had been bought by the State of Illinois, were destroyed in the great Chicago fire of 1871 except some Coleoptera and Lepidoptera. The scientific qualities of Walsh may be seen from a statement of Hagen, which is meant as praise for his abilities and erudition: "It is the scourge of science, and especially of Entomology, that we have always plenty of dilettantes and but very few with real knowledge, based upon regular and truly philosophical study."

Westfall, Minter Jackson Jr. (*January 28, 1916 Orlando, Orange County, Florida – †July 20, 2003 Gainesville, Hall County, Georgia) [164] [165] [166]

From his youth Westfall was interested in nature, mainly ornithology at first. Aged twenty he was busy banding birds around Orlando and in Alabama and employed as deputy game warden on Merritt Island, where the Kennedy Space Center now is. There he met E.M. Davis, Director of the Natural Science Museum of Rollins College in Orlando, who encouraged him

to study there, taking a job as research assistant as well. Later Davis introduced Westfall to J.G. Needham, who often stayed in Florida in winter. On his invitation, Westfall in 1941 after his B.Sc. at Collins transferred to Cornell University for graduate study and assisted with Needham's work on the 'Dragonflies of North America', which was finally published in 1955 and owes much to Westfall's accuracy. In 1943 service in the U.S. Army as a medical technician – the loss of his left eye at the age of seven did not allow combat duty – interrupted his study, which he resumed in 1944 completing his D.Sc. in 1947. After that he was hired for a teaching position in biology at the University of Florida by F.C. Byers, whose work on the Odonata of Florida he continued. Besides that and his teaching duties, in which he is said to have found time for any student who asked his help, he engaged in preparing a manual of the damselflies of North America with a focus on the taxonomy by taking the larvae into account many of which were unknown before. (This opus was published with the assistance of M.L. May in 1996). Another field of research was neotropic Odonata. For his odonatological research he visited the southwestern states of the U.S. (1956 - 1958), Cuba (1959), Jamaica and Haiti (1960), Costa Rica (1967), Guatemala (1977), Venezuela and Ecuador (1980). Westfall also was closely connected with the **S**ocietas **I**nternationalis **O**donatologica, which he served as North American representative, editor of the newsletter *Selysia* (1970-87), coeditor of *Odonatologica* and as president (1983-85). After his retirement from the University of Florida he became the first director of its newly created **I**nternational **O**donata **R**esearch **I**nstitute at Gainesville, Florida, which he had helped to establish. His collections he gave to IORI and FSCA. He became honorary member of SIO in 1979 and of DSA in 2002. Twelve Odonate taxa are named in his honor.

Westwood, John Obadiah (*December 22, 1805 Sheffield – †January 2, 1893) [167] [168] [169] was an English entomologist and antiquarian.

Westwood, son of a die engraver, may have learned his skills in drawing at home. He certainly was already interested in insects and their morphology as a schoolboy [170]. He was trained to be a lawyer and in 1821 for some time he was articled to a solicitor in London, but never really practised, because he preferred to follow his inclination for entomology and old books. He contributed to his living by illustrating works by other authors. He participated in founding the Entomological Society in 1833 and for some time was its secretary and acted as its president for more than one term. In 1861 he was the first Hope professor of invertebrate zoology at Oxford. When Darwin publicized his theories of selection and evolution, Westwood opposed them fiercely. Among his entomological publications, his comprehensive work *An Introduction to the Modern Classification of Insects* (1839-1840) may have been the most important, as it made available the ideas on systematics proposed by Latreille and others. For instance Brauer was stimulated to learn English by this work [171]. Besides entomology Westwood engaged with reproducing old manuscripts, illuminations, representations of old ivories and inscribed stones in his works. His contribution to odonatology is very small, naming one recent and four fossil species.

Williamson, Edward Bruce (*June 10, 1878 Marion, Indiana – †February 28, 1933 Ann Arbor, Michigan) [172] [173] [174] [175]

When Williamson was a boy his family moved to Bluffton, where he spent the greater part of his life. After graduating at the Ohio State University in 1898 and a short period as assistant curator of entomology in the Carnegie Museum at Pittsburgh and a fellowship at Vanderbilt University in 1900-01 for one year, he taught science in the high school at Salem, Ohio. In 1902 he returned to Bluffton, where he married and was employed in a bank, the director of which was his father. Later in 1918 Williamson himself became director of that bank, a post which he held until the institute closed in 1928 during the Depression. But in all his adult life he was a keen entomologist, specialising in Odonata. In 1916 the University of Michigan appointed him Associate Curator of Entomology in the Museum of Zoology. After his retirement, on being appointed research associate at Ann Arbor he decided to move there bringing his collections and his library to the museum. Besides extensive collecting trips to several regions of US he undertook expeditions to Middle America and the northern parts of South America including Barbados and Trinidad. He was in contact with many odonatologists, among them P.P. Calvert, C.H. Kennedy, but also with Selys and Förster. After the latter's death, when his family was impoverished, Williamson helped the sons to emigrate to the U.S. Williamson is acknowledged for his enthusiasm which enabled him to inspire others for the natural phenomena in which he engaged himself. Besides his professional and entomological interests he was a keen breeder of irises, for which task he established a farm near Bluffton, which after his death was taken over by an adopted daughter.

Endnotes

1. Courtesy of J.C. Abbott.

2. CARPENTER, F.M. & DARLINGTON, P.J. 1954. Nathan Banks. A Biographic Sketch and List of Publications. *Psyche* 61: 81-110.

3. MALLIS, A. 1971. *American Entomologists*. Rutgers University Press, New Brunswick, New Jersey: 180-183.

4. WASSCHER, M. 2014. On the Dutch Odonatologist Jean Belle. *Argia* 26(4): 30-31.

5. Manitoba Historical Society http://www.mhs.mb.ca/docs/people/bird_rd.shtml

6. HANDLIRSCH, A. 1905: Friedrich Moritz Brauer. *Verhandlungen der zoologisch-botanischen Gesellschaft Wien* 55: 129-166 (with portrait and list of publications).

7. REICHARDT, H.W.1876. Brittinger, Christian. in: *Allgemeine deutsche Biographie* 3. Leipzig, Duncker&Humblot: 335.

8. S(KOFITZ, A). 1860. Gallerie österreichischer Botaniker III: Christian Brittinger. *Österreichische botanische Zeitschrift* 10 (fasc. 7). 209-213.

9. WEISS, H.B. 1955 *Journal of the New York Entomological Society* 63: 1-7.

10. ALEXANDER, C.P. 1954 *Annals of the Entomological Society of America* 47(2): 375–376.

11. Courtesy of P.- M. Brunelle.

12. SCHNEIDER, K. 2006. Hermann Burmeister (1807-1892). Hallescher Gelehrter von Weltrang, *Entomologische Nachrichten und Berichte* 50 (4): 248–253.

13. FLIEDNER, H. 2006. Die wissenschaftlichen Namen in Burmeisters 'Handbuch der Entomologie'. *Virgo* 9: 5-23. Available in English translation at http://www.entomologie-mv.de/release/9-jahrgang-september-2006/

14. (As the two previous references are in German, the sources from ENDERSBY & FLIEDNER 2015, 89, 22sq might also be consulted).

15. WESTFALL, M. JR 1982. Obituary: Charles Francis Byers. *Odonatologica* 11: 245-249.

16. WHITE, HAROLD B. III. 1984 *Entomological News* 95(4): 155-162.

17. MALLIS, A. 1971. *American Entomologists*. Rutgers University Press, New Brunswick, New Jersey: 178-180.

18. REHN, J.A.G. 1962. Philip Powell Calvert (1871-1961). *Entomological News* 73:113-112.

19. Courtesy Rob Cannings

20. Rutgers (2010) http://www-rci.rutgers.edu/~carle/ [accessed 1 January 2014], augmented by Carle (pers. comm.).

21. ANONYMOUS 1995: Toussaint von Charpentier. p. 320 in: VIERHAUS, R. (ed.) (2005): *Deutsche Biographische Enzyklopädie*, vol. 2 Brann – Einslin. 2nd edition. K.G. Saur, München.

22. WEIDNER, H. 1960 Begegnungen mit Toussaint v. Charpentier. *Entomologische Zeitschrift* 70: 1-7, 27-30.

23. ANONYMOUS 2005. Nomination of Carl Cook as Honorary Member of the Dragonfly Society of the Americas. *Argia* 17 (2): 1 sq.

24. COOK, C. 1994. Over the Trails searching for Gomphids. Part I. Renewing Half-Century old Memories. *Argia* 5 (4): 8 sq.

25. WAGNER, D.L. 2011. The Society honors eight Charter Members. Carl Cook. *News of the Lepidopterist Society* 53 (1): 9.

26. Carl Cook, by letter.

27. KENNEDY, S.J. 1968. *Proceedings of the Royal Entomological Society of London* (C) 32: 59.

28. EDMUNDS, M.J. & MUESEBECK, C.F.W. 1961. Rolla Patterson Currie (1975-1960). *Proceedings of the Washington Entomological Society* 63: 137-139.

29. WARD, R.A. (ed.) 1976. *The United States Entomological Collections*. Smithsonian Institution Press: Washington, 49 pp. (for Bertha see p. 10).

30. WILLIAMSON, E. B. 1922. Notes on *Celithemis* with descriptions of two new species (Odonata). *Occ. Pap. Mus. Zool. Univ. Mich.* No. 108: 1–22. (for Bertha see p. 4).

31. Alers, E., Smithsonian Institution Archives: e-mail 2018-03-23.

32. https://www.findagrave.com/memorial/24507165/william-thomas-currie (accessed 2018-03-25)

33. EDMUNDS, M.J. & MUESEBECK, C.F.W. 1961. Rolla Patterson Currie (1975-1960). *Proceedings of the Washington Entomological Society* 63: 137-139.

34. FLINT, O.S. JR. 1991. The Odonata Collection of the National Museum of Natural History, Washington, U.S.A. *Advances in Odonatology* 5: 49-58.

35. https://www.pwrc.usgs.gov/resshow/perry/bios/CurrieRolla.htm

36. Courtesy of J.J. Daigle.

37. MALLIS, A. 1971. *American Entomologists*. Rutgers University Press, New Brunswick, New Jersey: 216-220.

38. PARSHLEY, H.M. 1951. On the Life of William T. Davis. *Entomological News* 62: 84-86.

39. TEALE, E.W. 1942. William T. Davis. An Appreciation. *Bulletin of the Brooklyn Entomological Society* 37: 118-126.

40. Davis, William Thompson. 2008. In: *Encyclopedia of Entomology*. Springer, Dordrecht (p. 1156) **DOI:** https://doi.org/10.1007/0-306-48380-7_1162//

41. https://books.google.de/books?id=i9ITMiiohVQC&pg=PA1156&lpg=PA1156&dq=Davis,+William+Thompson+entomologist&source=bl&ots=VYzmUvgMSQ&sig=4vnK_jFop-2GvDWvq1SISYFH3rcU&hl=de&sa=X&ved=0ahUKEwiyo_vsuZvYAhWE-qQKH-dRuATEQ6AEIPjAD#v=onepage&q=Davis%2C%20William%20Thompson%20entomologist&f=false

42. MICHALSKI, J. 2007. To Nick Donnelly on the Occasion of his 75th Birthday. *Argia* 19 (4): 6-9.

43. Nick and Ailsa Donnelly Fellowship. 2012. *Argia* 24 (4): 21.

44. WEISS, H. B. 1927. Dru Drury, Silversmith and Entomologist of the Eighteenth Century. *Entomological News* 27: 208-214.

45. Courtesy of Sid Dunkle and Dennis Paulson.

46. KLUG, J. F. C. 1850: Nekrolog [Erichson, W. F.]. *Entomologische Zeitung, Stettin* 11, 33-36.

47. HOFMANN, F. 1959: Fabricius, Johann Christian. p. 736 in: *Neue Deutsche Biographie* 4, Duncker & Humblot, Berlin.

48. NICKOL, M. 2010: http://www.uni-kiel.de/nickol/Garten/Johann-Christian-Fabricius.html (accessed 22.11. 2017).

49. WHITE, H.B. 2004. The Odonatological Legacy of George H. & Alice Beatty. *www1.udel.edu/chem/white/Odonata/BeattyLegacy.ppt*

50. *Obituary from Centre Daily Times*, State College, Pennsylvania, November 24, 1987 p. B-3.

51. MAYER, G. 1989. Friedrich Förster (1865-1918): badischer Schulmann, Forscher und Sammler. *Kraichgau. Beiträge zur Landschafts- und Heimatforschung* 11: 138-143.

52. ENDERSBY & FLIEDNER 2015, 59 sq.

53. BROWN, S.C.S. 1963. *Entomologist's Monthly Magazine* 99: 96.

54. HAINES, L.C. 1965. *Proceedings of the Royal Zoological Society of New South Wales* 1960-1964: 37-38.

55. KIMMINS, D.E. 1963. *Entomologist* 96: 94-95.

56. Cordulegastridae, Petaliidae, and Petaluridae.

57. Courtesy of R.W. Garrison.

58. VAN BRINK, J.M. & KIAUTA, B. 1977. To Mrs. Leonora K. Gloyd on her 75th birthday. *Odonatologica* 6: 143-149.

59. BEOLENS, B. 2018. *Eponym Dictionary of Odonata*. Whittles Publishing: Scotland. p. 154 with permission of the author.

60. VILARO, J. 1897. Sketch of John Gundlach. *Popular Science* 50 fasc.42: 691-697.

61. CALVERT, P.P. 1893. Dr. H. A. Hagen. *Entomological News* 4: 313-317.

62. HENSHAW, S. 1894. Hermann August Hagen. *Proceedings of the American Academy of Science* 29: 419-423.

63. MCLACHLAN, R. 1894. Obituary. Prof. Hermann August Hagen. *Entomologist's Monthly Magazine* 30: 18-20.

64. SCHEIDING, U. 1963. Über das Leben und Wirken von Hermann August Hagen. *Beiträge zur Entomologie* 13: 487-512.

65. OSTEN-SACKEN, C.R. 1903. *Record of my Life and Work in Entomology*. Cambridge/Mass.: 76.

66. CALVERT, P.P. 1900. Prof. F.L. Harvey. *Entomological News* 11: 451-452.

67. REYNOLDS, J.H. & THOMAS, D.Y. 1910. *History of the University of Arkansas* University of Arkansas: Fayetteville. pp. 469-470.

68. Courtesy of Troy Hibbits

69. KENNEDY, C.H. 1931. Obituaries. James Stewart Hine. *Ohio Journal of Science* 31: 510 sq.

70. KENNEDY, C.H. 1931. Obituary. (James Stewart Hine). *Entomological News* 42: 177-180.

71. University of Alabama, "University of Alabama Sixty-Eighth Annual Commencement Program, 1899," *Tuscaloosa Area Virtual Museum*, accessed May 17, 2018, http://tavm.omeka.net/items/show/2048

72. ROBB, F.O. 2016. Shot in Alabama. A History of Photography 1839-1941 and a List of Photographers. University Press, Tuscaloosa [about Hodges: p. VI, 160 and 181 sq.]

73. Nick Tew, by e-mail

74. BEOLENS, B. 2018. *Eponym Dictionary of Odonata*. Whittles Publishing: Scotland. p. 184 with permission of the author.

75. BRIDGES 1993 *hodgesi* q.v.

76. see ENDERSBY & FLIEDNER 2015 p.90 sq., endnotes 59-61.

77. BLEILE, A.M. 1898. David Simons Kellicott.*Transactions of the American Microscopical Society 20: 21-24.*

78. WEBSTER, F.M. & CALVERT, P.P. 1898. Obituary. Professor David Simons Kellicott. *Entomological News* 9: 160.

79. RILEY, N.D. 1953. The President's Address. *Proceedings of the Royal Entomological Society of London* (C) 17: 72.

80. MALLIS, A. 1971. *American Entomologists*. Rutgers University Press, New Brunswick, New Jersey: 470-472.

81. DONNELLY, N. 1999. History of American Odonata: Clarence Hamilton Kennedy (1879-1952). *Argia* 11 (4): 12-15.

82. MORICE, F. D. 1912. Obituaries. William Forsell Kirby. *Transactions of the Royal entomological Society London*: clxvi-clxviii.

83. ROWLAND-BROWN, H. 1912. Obituary. William Forsell Kirby, F.L.S., F.E.S. *The Entomologist* 45: 352-352.

84. W.E.K. [WILLIAM EGMONT KIRBY] 1912. Obituary. William Forsell Kirby (with portrait.). *The Entomologist's Record and Journal of Variation* 24: 314-317.

85. Courtesy of Kenneth Knopf.

86. Thesis details courtesy of Hal White.

87. Courtesy of E. Laudermilk.

88. ANONYMOUS [FRANCIS BOOTT] 1837. Obituary. William Elford Leach, MD, FRS. *Magazine of Natural History and Journal of Zoology, Botany, Mineralogy, Geology and Meteorology*. n.s. 1: 390.

89. SWAINSON, W. 1840. *Taxidermy: with biography of zoologists*. Printed for Longman, Orme, Brown, Green and Longmans: London (on Leach pp. 237-240).

90. SECCOMBE, T. 1892. Leach, William Elford. 311-312. in: Lee, Sidney. *Dictionary of National Biography*. **32**. London: Smith, Elder & Co.[accessed from internet 30. Nov. 2017].

91. ERIKSSON, G. 1980. *Svenskt biografiskt lexikon* 23: 700-715.

92. LINDROTH, S. 1949. *Svenska män och kvinnor* 5: 31-34.

93. TUXEN, S.L. 1973. Entomology systematizes and describes: 1700-1815: in: *History of Entomology*, ed. by Smith, R.F., Mittler, T.E. & Smith, C.N. Annual Reviews Inc. Palo Alto, Cal., 95-118 (on Linnaeus 105-109).

94. CALVERT, P.P. 1927. René Martin. *Entomological News* 38: 197-205.

95. BEOLENS, B. 2018. *Eponym Dictionary of Odonata*. Whittles Publishing: Scotland. pp. 279-280 with permission of the author.

96. WARE, J.L. & LA POLLA, J.S. 2012. A tribute to Michael L. May. *Organisms Diversity & Evolution* 12: 205-207.

97. https://entomology.rutgers.edu/personnel/michael-may.html (accessed November 5, 2018)

98. Michael May reminiscences (by e-mail).

99. ANONYMOUS 1904. (R. MCLACHLAN FRS) *Entomologist's Record and Journal of Variation* 16: 217.

100. CALVERT, P.P. 1904. Robert M'Lachlan. *Entomological News* 15: 226-228.

101. EATON, A.E. 1904. In Memoriam. Robert McLachlan. *Entomologist's Monthly Magazine* 40: 145-148.

102. MORTON, K.J. 1904. Robert M'Lachlan. Obituary. *Annals of Scottish Natural History* 13(52): 201-203.

103. LUCAS, W.J. 1904. Robert McLachlan. *Entomologist* 37: 195-196.

104. SAUNDERS, E. 1904. (Robert McLachlan, F.R.S., F.L.S., F.Z.S. &c) *Proceedings of the Linnean Society of London* 117: 42-43.

105. S[AUNDERS], E[DWARD] 1905. Robert McLachlan. 1837-1904. *Proceedings of the Royal Society of London* 75: 367-370.

106. JAMES, T. E. 1912. McLachlan, Robert. p. 530 sq. in: Lee, Sidney. *Dictionary of National Biography*, 1912 supplement. London: Smith, Elder & Co.

107. MCLACHLAN, R. 1894. [Obituary. Prof. Hermann August Hagen]. *Entomologist's Monthly Magazine* 30: 19.

108. MACKLIN, J.M. 1974. To Dr. B. Elwood Montgomery on his 75th birthday. *Odonatologica* 3 (4): 203-209.

109. ORTMAN, E.E. & WILSON, M. C. 1983. Basil Elwood Montgomery 1899–1983. *Bulletin of the Entomological Society of America* 29 (4): 63.

110. [EDITORS] 1983. In Memoriam Professor Basil Elwood Montgomery. *Odonatologica* 12 (1): 1-4.

111. DOW, R. 1937. The Scientific Work of Albert Pitts Morse. *Psyche* 44: 1-11.

112. CALVERT, P.P. 1943. *Entomological News* 54: 173-174.

113. ANONYMOUS 1944. *Annals of the Entomological Society of America* 37: 135.

114. EWAN, J. & EWAN, N.D. 1981. p. 160 in: *Biographical Dictionary of Rocky Mountain Naturalists*. Bohn, Scheltema & Holkema: Boston.

115. BASTERO MONSERRAT, J.-J. 1991. Longinos Navás, S.J. An Approach to his Life and entomological work. p. 581-584 in: ALBA-TERCEDOR, J. & SANCHEZ-ORTEGA, A. (EDS.) 1991: *Overview and strategies of Ephemeroptera and Plecoptera*. Sandhill Crane Press, Gainesville FLA (available: http://www.ephemeroptera-galactica.com/pubs/pub_b/pub-basteroj1991p581.pdf accessed 2 Dec 2017).

116. FLIEDNER, H. 1998. Die Namengeber der europäischen Libellen. Ergänzungsheft zu *Libellula Suppl.* 1. (Published by the author): 31-32.

117. MONSERRAT, V.J. 1986. Longinos Navás, His Neuropterological Work and Collection. pp. 173-176 in: J. Gepp, H. Aspöck, & H. Hölzel (eds.). *Recent Research* in *Neuropterology*. Proceedings of the 2nd International Symposium on *Neuropterology*, Hamburg 1984, *Graz, 1986* (in internet under https://www.zobodat.at/stable/pdf/MONO-ENT-NEURO_MEN2_0173-0176.pdf accessed 2 Dec 2017)

118. MALLIS, A. 1971. *American Entomologists*. Rutgers University Press, New Brunswick, New Jersey: 174-178.

119. DONNELLY, N. 1999. History of Odonata Study in North America — James G. Needham. *Argia* 11 (1): 24-26.

120. PALM, C.E., BERG, C.O. & BRADLEY, J.C. (without year). James George Needham. March 16, 1868 — July 24, 1957. (https://ecommons.cornell.edu/bitstream/handle/1813/19112/Needham_James_George_1957.pdf?sequence=2&isAllowed=y) (accessed 8 Feb. 2018).

121. ANONYMOUS 1876. Preface. *Zoologist* ser. II, 11: iii-xxii.

122. ANONYMOUS 1876. Obituary. *Entomologist's Monthly Magazine* 13: 45-46.

123. WESTWOOD, J.C. 1876. Obituary. Edward Newman , F.L.S., F.Z.S. &c. *Transactions of the Entomological Society of London* 1876: xlii-xliii.

124. COCKERELL, T.D.A. 1920. Biographical Memoir of Alpheus Spring Packard 1839-1905. *National Academy of Sciences Biographical Memoir* 9: 181-236.

125. MALLIS, A. 1971. *American Entomologists*. Rutgers University Press, New Brunswick, New Jersey: 296-302.

126. SMITH, J.B. 1905. The Entomological Work of Dr. A.S. Packard. *Psyche* 12: 33-35.

127. DEPPING 1843. Palisot de Beauvois (Ambroise-Marie-François-Joseph). in: Michaud, J.Fr. 1843. *Biographie universelle ancienne et moderne*. 2nd. ed. vol XXXII Pal-Pez. 14-17 (Reprint Graz, Akademische Druck- u. Verlagsanstalt)

128. Courtesy Dennis Paulson

129. DENNING, D.G. & ALLEN, W.W. 1965. Arthur Earl Pritchard (1915-1965). *Journal of Economic Entomology* 58: 807-808.

130. https://essig.berkeley.edu/holdings/pritchard/

131. MALLIS, A. 1971. *American Entomologists*. Rutgers University Press, New Brunswick, New Jersey: 106 sq.

132. PERRON, J.-M. 1990. Provancher, Léon. in *Dictionary of Canadian Biography*, vol. 12, University of Toronto/Université Laval, 2003–, accessed January 23, 2018, http://www.biographi.ca/en/bio/provancher_leon_12E.html

133. GRASLIN, A. DE 1872. Notice nécrologique sur le docteur Rambur, membre fondateur de la Société entomologique de France. *Annales de la Société Entomologique de France* (5) 2: 297-306.

134. HARPER, P. P. 2005. Adrien Robert c.s.v., un entomologiste d'envergure. *Le Naturaliste canadien* 129 (1): 5-8.

135. CALVERT, P.P. 1934. Obituary. Dr. Francis Metcalf Root. *Entomological News* 45: 285 sq.

136. MALLIS, A.1971. *American Entomologists*. Rutgers University Press. pp. 16–25.

137. Wikipedia: Thomas Say https://en.wikipedia.org/wiki/Thomas_Say (accessed 14 Dec 2017).

138. Thomas Say (1787-1834), father of American entomology https://faculty.evansville.edu/ck6/bstud/say.html

139. Noble Shor, E. (without year). "Say, Thomas." *Complete Dictionary of Scientific Biography*. Retrieved December 16, 2017 from Encyclopedia.com: http://www.encyclopedia.com/science/dictionaries-thesauruses-pictures-and-press-releases/say-thomas

140. Mayor, A.G. 1919. Samuel Hubbard Scudder 1837-1911. *National Academy of Science Biographical Memoirs*. 17 (3): 81-104. [pdf from internet: accessed Jan. 16, 2018].

141. Mallis, A. 1971. *American Entomologists*. Rutgers University Press, New Brunswick, New Jersey: 185-191.

142. Calvert, P.P. 1901 Baron Edmond de Selys-Longchamps. *Entomological News* 12: 33-37.

143. McLachlan, R. 1901. Obituary. Baron Michel Edmond de Selys-Longchamps *Entomologist's Monthly Magazine* 37: 78-80.

144. Wasscher, M.Th. & Dumont, H.J. (2013) Life and Work of Michel Edmond de Selys Longchamps (1813-1900), the Founder of Odonatology. *Odonatologica* 42: 369-402.

145. Beolens, B. 2018. *Eponym Dictionary of Odonata*. Whittles Publishing: Scotland. p. 392 with permission of the author.

146. Gantenbein, U.L. 2013: (7) Sulzer, Hans Heinrich: p. 126 in: *Historisches Lexikon der Schweiz* Bd. 12, Schwabe, Basel 2013.

147. Weidner, H. 1980: Entomologische Schriften der Zeitgenossen und Schüler von Carolus Linnaeus im Archiv der entomologischen Sammlungen des Zoologischen Instituts und Zoologischen Museums der Universität Hamburg. *Entomologische Mitteilungen aus dem Zoologischen Museum Hamburg* 6 (108/109): 309-379 [on Sulzer pp. 365-369.]

148. Courtesy of K.J. Tennessen.

149. Tough, J. 1892. A plea for the collector. *Entomological News* 3: 63-64.

150. Tough, J. 1900. A new species of *Gomphus*. *Occasional Memoirs of the Chicago Entomological Society* 1: 17–18.

151. Wyatt, A.K. 1941. The Chicago Entomological Society. *The Chicago Naturalist* 4 (2): 50-51.

152. Aurivillius, C. 1914. Filip Trybom †. Med porträtt. *Entomologisk tidskrift* 35: 81-86.

153. Flensburg, T. & Lindmann, S 1955. 1. Trybom, Arvid Filip. *Svenska män och kvinnor: biografisk uppslagsbok* 8: 52. Stockholm, Bonnier.

154. Howard, L.O. 1913. Philip Reese Uhler, LLD. *Entomological News* 24: 433-439.

155. Mallis, A. 1971. *American Entomologists*. Rutgers University Press, New Brunswick, New Jersey: 205-208.

156. Schwarz, E.A. (1914). "Philip Reese Uhler". *Proceedings of the Entomological Society of Washington*. 16 (1): 1–7.

157. Courtesy Timothy Vogt.

158. Corbet, P. 1969. Dr. Edmund Murton Walker (1878 [sic]-1969) in memoriam. *Tombo* 12: 2sq.

159. Nesbitt, H.H.J. 1970. E.M. Walker, 1877-1969. An Appreciation. *Canadian Entomologist* 102 (4): 385-388.

160. Wiggins, C.B. 1970. Obituary. Edmund Murton Walker 1877-1969. *Annals of the Entomological Society of America*. 63: 631 sq.

161. McNicholl, M.K. 2008. Walker, Edmund Murton. http://www.thecanadianencyclopedia.com/en/article/edmund-murton-walker/ (accessed 14. Dec. 2017).

162. Wikipedia: Edmund Murton Walker (https://fr.wikipedia.org/wiki/Edmund_Murton_Walker) (accessed 13. Dec. 2017).

163. Sheppard, C.A. 2004. Benjamin Dann Walsh. Pioneer Entomologist and Proponent of Darwinian Theory. *Annual Review of Entomology* . 49: 1-25 (p.1 for the place of birth).

164. Tennessen, K.J. 1986. Dr Minter Jackson Westfall, Jr: a Short Biographical Sketch and a Bibliography. *Odonatologica* 15 (1): 5-17.

165. Tennessen, K.J. 2004.Obituary. Dr Minter Jackson Westfall, Jr. *Odonatologica* 33 (1): 99-103.

166. Westfall, D.N. 2003. Profile: Minter Jackson Westfall, Jr. https://www.findagrave.com/memorial/109560528 (acessed Dec. 22, 2017).

167. McLachlan, R. 1893. Obituary. Professor John Obadia Westwood, M.A., F.L.S. &c. *Entomologist's Monthly Magazine* 29: 49-51.

168. Woodward, B.B. 1899. Westwood, John Obadiah. 381 sq. in: Lee, Sidney (ed.) *Dictionary of National Biography*, vol. 60.

169. (https://en.wikisource.org/wiki/Westwood,_John_Obadiah_(DNB00) (accessed 13 Dec 2017).

170. Westwood, J.O. 1842. Art. LXXVII. Observations on the Analysis of 'British Butterflies' (Entmol. 265). *Entomologist* 18: 285-287.

171. p. 136 in: Handlirsch, A. 1905: Friedrich Moritz Brauer. *Verhandlungen der zoologisch-botanischen Gesellschaft Wien* 55: 129-166.

172. Davis, J.J. 1934. Edward Bruce Williamson. *Proceedings of the Indiana Academy of Science* 43: 23-25.

173. Calvert, P.P. 1935. Edward Bruce Williamson. *Entomological News* 45, 1-13.

174. Gaige, F.M. 1933. Distiguished Michigan Scientist Dies. *The Michigan Alumnus* 39: 356.

175. https://www.google.de/search?q=Edward+Bruce+williamson&client=firefox-b&dcr=0&nirf=Edward+Bruce+williams&ei=PzQ6Wu7KJ8GlkwWp5IXAAQ&start=20&sa=N&biw=853&bih=512

The Etymologies

aaroni, Neoneura Calvert, 1903: 139
>"The material before me was probably collected by Mr. S. F. Aaron [1862-1947] in the vicinity of Corpus Christi in 1884."
>
>{noun in the genitive case}

abbreviatum, Amphiagrion (Selys, 1876a: 1299)
[Original designation: *Pyrrhosoma abbreviatum* Selys]
>L. *abbreviatus –a –um:* past participle of *abbrevio* = to shorten, from short abdomen.
>
>"Espèce bien extraordinaire par son abdomen à peine plus long que l'aile inférieure." [Very extraordinary species by its abdomen hardly longer than the hind wing].   {declinable past participle}

abbreviatus, Hylogomphus (Hagen in Selys, 1878: 464)
[Original designation: *Gomphus abbreviatus* Hagen in Selys]
>L. *abbreviatus –a –um*: past participle of *abbrevio* = to shorten, because of similarity to *G. brevis*. "♂ *Adulte*: Très-voisin du *G. brevis*." [Adult male very closely related to *Gomphus brevis* = *Hylogomphus adelphus* (Selys)].   {declinable past participle}

abdominalis, Tramea (Rambur, 1842: 37)
[Original designation: *Libellula abdominalis* Rambur]

> L. *abdominalis* –*is* –*e* = concerning the abdomen. The only feature of the abdomen which Rambur mentions in his short Latin description is: "abdomine postice maculis duabus vel tribus nigris" [the rear part of the abdomen with two or three black spots]. Therefore this may be at the base of the name. In his French description Rambur emphasizes the similarity of thorax and abdomen of this species to Linné's *Libellula carolina,* in the description of which he says it to have a red abdomen inflated at base with a large black spot on each of the last two segments. In his Latin description of that species he uses an almost identical wording with that for *abdominalis*.   {declinable adjective}

Acanthagrion Selys, 1876a: 304

> Gr. ἄκανθα = prickle, thorn, and *Agrion*, a name by which Fabricius (1775) included all damselflies. It is derived from Gr. ἄγριος – α –ον = wild, and probably meant 'living in the fields' as damselflies don't live in the domestic area like house flies. Later on controversies arose as to whether calopterygids or other taxa where the true agrionids. Therefore to settle arguments Kirby (1890) replaced the name by *Coenagrion* for non-calopterygid damselflies, which was later accepted by the ICZN. But –*agrion* is still part of many compound names for zygopteran genera, as in this case.

> The name *Acanthagrion* refers to an acute spine beneath s. 8 of the females, rather a feature common to the whole group of eight genera proposed in the paper where Selys names them 'sous-genres': (p. 250) "Une épine ou pointe aiguë au bout du 8ᵉ ségment de la femelle en dessous" [A spine or sharp point below the end of the 8th segment of the female] "Le nom d'*Acanthagrion* eût été parfaitement approprié pour désigner éventuellement ce grande genre." [The name *Acanthagrion* would have been perfectly appropriate to designate this great genus].
>
>   {Neuter, although Fabricius treated *Agrion* as feminine}

acuminatus, Ophiogomphus Carle, 1981: 272

"*O. acuminatus* [*–a –um*] ... (L. Part. "*furnished with a sharp point*", referring to the pointed adult male cerci)".

{declinable past participle}

adelphus, Hylogomphus (Selys, 1858: 673)
[Original designation: *Gomphus adelphus* Selys]

Gr. ἀδελφός – brother, kinsman. The name refers to its relationship with *Gomphus fraternus* (Say):"Il ressemble donc plutôt au *vulgatissimus* qu'au *fraternus* par le noir de la face et des lèvres, mais..." [It resembles rather *vulgatissimus* than *fraternus* by the black of the face and the 'lips', but ...] (Gr. adelphos – L. frater).
{noun in apposition}

adnexa, Coryphaeschna (Hagen, 1861: 127)
[Original designation: *Aeschna adnexa* Hagen]

L. *adnexus –a –um*: past participle of *adnecto* = to tie or bind to, attach [assimilated form: *annecto*, see *annexum*]. Hagen described the species from a mutilated ♀, so he was not sure about the taxonomic status of his specimen, and considered that it might pertain to a related species: "Is it *cyanifrons* Sel.?"

{declinable past participle}

aequabilis, Calopteryx Say, 1839: 33
[as *Calepteryx* Say, 1839. *C. aequabilis* was the only species name with the Leachean form of spelling of the genus name. See *Calopteryx*]

L. *aequabilis –is –e* = equal, similar, probably referring to the anal processes being almost of equal diameter for whole length. "anal processes curved inwards, and towards the tip a little downwards, of equal diameter, excepting that on the inner side they are a little dilated beyond the middle."

{declinable adjective}

aequalis, Micrathyria (Hagen, 1861: 167)
[Original designation: *Dythemis aequalis* Hagen]

> L. *aequalis –is –e* = equal, like. The name might allude to the same brassy-fuscous color of thorax and abdomen: "thorax brassy-fuscous, ... the sides brassy-fuscous, ..., abdomen ... brassy-fuscous." {declinable adjective}

Aeshna Fabricius, 1775: 424

> Derivation unknown. Some scientists thought Fabricius' name was derived from Greek αἰσχύνη = shame and explained the name from the observation that aeshnids were rarely seen in copula. Because of this derivation, the name was therefore emended to *Aeschna* [ILLIGER, 1802 p. 126]. As this emendation was widely accepted in the 19th century compound names established then are mostly written with c. But Fabricius himself kept to the orthography without c until his death. Because of this discrepancy the ICZN in opinion 34 decided, that *Aeshna* had to be maintained, as Fabricius had not explained his name in any way and an orthographical slip therefore could not be proven. In the 17th century in England *Aeschna* (with c) was in use for ephemerids (e.g. MOUFET, 1634, p. 69; CHARLETON 1677, p. 42) and from that Fabricius seems to have chosen his own orthography. {Feminine}

agrioides, Argia Calvert, 1895: 476

> Gr. suffix –ειδής = looking like, similar to *Agrion* (a word for damselfly) see *Acanthagrion*.

The source of the name is mentioned by Calvert: "Having sent a pair ♂♀ of this species to Baron de Selys, he wrote that it "est peut ètre une espèce inédite que j'ai nommé *A. agrioides* MS dans la collection de M. MacLachlan." [Is perhaps an unpublished species that I have named *A. agrioides* MS in the collection of Mr. MacLachlan]. (There is no further explanation of the similarity of the species to *Agrion* in the first description, but see *Argia*.) {adjective} *alabamensis, Neurocordulia* Hodges in Needham and Westfall, 1955: 356

From the type locality + *–ensis –is –e* = adjectival suffix indicating place of origin.

"We are greatly indebted to Dr. R. S. Hodges of Tuscaloosa, Alabama, for aid in treatment of this genus. With kind intent to make our volume more complete, he has given us for advance publication the description of a new species, *Neurocordulia alabamensis*." {declinable adjective}

alacer, Lestes Hagen, 1861: 67

L. *alacer –cris –e* = lively, brisk, quick, eager, excited. Allusion unknown. {declinable adjective}

alachuensis, Progomphus Byers, 1939: 50

From the type locality + *–ensis –is –e* = adjectival suffix indicating place of origin.

"Holotype male. Alachua Co.; Florida. Newman's Lake (4 miles east of Gainesville)." {declinable adjective}

alberta, Argia Kennedy, 1918a: 257

"I take pleasure in naming it after my father Albert Hamilton Kennedy". {declinable adjective}

albicincta, Somatochlora (Burmeister, 1839: 847)
[Original designation: *Epophthalmia albicincta* Burmeister]

L. *albus –a –um* = white + *cinctus –a –um* = girdled

"***albicincta*** has a white-ringed abdomen" (NEEDHAM & AL. 2000: 544 sq). {declinable adjective}

albistylus, *Stylogomphus* (Hagen in Selys, 1878: 460)
[Original designation: *Gomphus albistylus* Hagen in Selys]
> L. *albus –a –um* = white + *stilus* = a stake, a pointed instrument used by the Romans for writing upon wax tablets. The name applies to the anal appendages, that formerly were also called '*styli*'. "appendices aussi longs que le dernier segment, blancs" [appendages as long as the last segment, white].
> {declinable adjective}

albrighti, *Phyllogomphoides* (Needham, 1950: 1)
[Original designation: *Gomphoides albrighti* Needham]
> "This species is described from nine specimens, three males and six females, all taken by Paul [sic] N. Albright from the San Antonio river ..." Philip N. Albright (1901-1999).
> {noun in the genitive case}

alleghaniensis, *Macromia* Williamson, 1909: 376
> From the type locality + *–ensis –is –e* = adjectival suffix indicating place of origin.
>
> "Types. – Male and female in the author's collection, taken at Ohiopyle, Pennsylvania" (This locality is situated in the Alleghanies). {declinable adjective}

amanda, *Celithemis* (Hagen, 1861: 183)
[Original designation: *Diplax amanda* Hagen]
> L. *amandus –a –um* = lovable, one of the names reflecting the charming quality of dragonflies. {declinable adjective}

amata, *Calopteryx* Hagen, 1889: 244
> L. *amatus –a –um* = beloved, probably one of the names attributable to the charm or lovable characteristics of Odonata as shown by their French name demoiselles or names ending in –jungfer (= maid) in German, as found in the names *virgo* and *puella* given by Linnaeus. {declinable past participle}

amazili, Anax (Burmeister, 1839: 841)
[Original designation: *Aeschna amazili* Burmeister]
>In 1777 the French author J.F. Marmontel published a novel '*Les Incas, ou la destruction de l'Empire du Pérou*', in which an Inca heroine named Amazili plays a role. A genus of hummingbirds, *Amazilia*, is also called after her (cf. JOBLING 1991: 9) [H. Pieper, in litt.] {noun in apposition}

ambiguum, Sympetrum (Rambur, 1842: 106)
[Original designation: *Libellula ambigua* Rambur]
>L. *ambiguus –a –um* = doubtful, ambiguous. The only ambiguous thing mentioned in the first description is the provenance of Rambur's specimen: "D'après un seul individu femelle dont je ne connais pas la patrie, mais qui pourrait bien être exotique" [From one individual female whose homeland I do not know, but which could well be exotic]. {declinable adjective}

amelia, Neoneura Calvert, 1903: 138
>After Amelia Calvert, describer's wife (1876-1966). Although there is no direct acknowledgment in the original description there is in the introduction (p. xxx) "… to Mr. G. C. Champion, Dr. Henry Skinner, and my wife, for all the manifold assistance which they have so kindly rendered." {noun in apposition}

americana, Hetaerina (Fabricius, 1798: 287)
[Original designation: *Agrion americanum* Fabricius]
>Referring to type locality "Habitat in America. Dom. Hybner." {declinable adjective}

amnicola, Stylurus (Walsh, 1862: 396)
[Original designation: *Gomphus amnicola* Walsh]
>L. *amnis* = river + *–cola* (in compounds) = inhabitant
>
>"*G. fraternus, G. vastus* and *G. amnicola*, mihi, all likewise breed in the Missisippi River ... I suspect, that most, if not all, *Gomphi* breed in running, not in stagnant, water."
>{noun in apposition}

Amphiagrion Selys, 1876a: 284
>(for *Agrion* - damselfly see *Acanthagrion*)

>The name refers to the species *A. amphion*, brought forward in the same publication, which Selys thought to be typical for the new genus. In Greek myth Amphion was said to be a son of Antiope, the daughter of a river god, as a result of a tête à tête with Zeus, the supreme god. Amphion must have been something of a musical genius, who, when building the fortification of Thebes with his twin brother Zethus, charmed the stones into a wall by the force of his music. As Selys did not designate a type species for the genus himself (he might have thought that to be clear already by its name), KIRBY (1890) chose a different species in his revision. But it is to be noted that the species *amphion* no longer pertains to the genus *Amphiagrion*, but is synonymized with *Ischnura verticalis* (Say) [see GARRISON & VON ELLENRIEDER 2016, 19]. {Neuter}

Anax Leach, 1815: 137
>Gr. ἄναξ = lord of the house, perhaps referring to bulk of *A. imperator* or to its dominant behavior in its territory.
>{Masculine}

anceps, Argia Garrison 1996: 33
>L. *anceps* = two-headed; double, that extends on two opposite sides; doubtful, uncertain.

>The author explains: "Latin for double, in reference to its sibling relative *A. fissa*." But the meaning of the Latin word differs a little from the use in this name. {adjective}

angulatum, Coenagrion Walker, 1912: 256
>L. *angulatus –a –um* = angled, referring to shape of male cerci.

>"Superior appendages black, with a pale terminal tubercle."
>{declinable adjective}

angustifolia, Aphylla Garrison, 1986: 938

    L. *angustus –a –um* = narrow + *–folius –a –um* (in compounds) = leafed, referring to slight expansion of abdomen.

    The species is separated from *Aphylla protracta* by the width of the foliation of segment 8, which is lesser than in *A. protracta*: "The most useful character to separate *A. angustifolia* from *A. protracta* is the width of the abdominal foliation of segment 8. … the greatest width for males (0.56 mm) and females (0.32 mm) falls short of the minimum width observed for *A. protracta* (male 0.72 mm; female 0.52 mm)."   {declinable adjective}

angustipennis, Calopteryx (Selys, 1853: 9)
[Original designation: *Sylphis angustipennis* Selys]

    L. *angustus –a –um* = narrow + *–pennis –is –e* (in compounds) = winged.

    "ailes très-étroites" [wings very narrow].   {declinable adjective}

anna, Enallagma Williamson, 1900: 455

    "Named for Miss Anna Tribolet [1876-1950]," the later wife of the describer (HÄMÄLÄINEN 2016).   {noun in apposition}

annexum, Enallagma (Hagen, 1861: 87)
[Original designation: *Agrion annexum* Hagen]

    L. *annexus –a –um*: past participle of *annecto* = to tie or bind to, attach from similarity to Eurasian *E. cyathigerum*: "Allied to *A. cyathigerum* Charp., from Europe."   {declinable past participle}

annulata, Macromia Hagen, 1861: 133

    L. *an(n)ulus* = a small ring + suffix *–atus –a –um* = marked with, equipped with.

    The name refers to a pale ring on second abdominal segment: "Segment 2 with a transverse fascia".   {declinable adjective}

anomalus, Ophiogomphus Harvey, 1898: 60
> L. *anomalus –a –um* Latinized form of Gr. ἀνώμαλος = uneven, irregular.

> The anomaly at the base of the name is described thus "This male agrees with the characters given by Baron de Selys ... for *Ophiogomphus*, excepting the branches of the inferior appendage, which are strongly upcurved in their apical half, as in *Erpetogomphus*, instead of at the apex only, as in typical *Ophiogomphus*." {declinable adjective}

antennatum, Enallagma (Say, 1839: 39)
[Original designation: *Agrion antennata* Say]
> L. *antennatus –a –um* = having (remarkable) antennae.

> "antennae with the two basal joints much thicker than the others, equal in length, the first cylindric, the second attenuated at base". {declinable adjective}

antilope, Gomphaeschna (Hagen, 1874b: 354)
[Original designation: *Aeschna antilope* Hagen]
> medieval Gr. ἀντιλόπη = antelope, referring to male epiproct shaped like pair of horns: "the inferior appendage much narrower [than in *G. furcillata* (Say)], the two branches with an apical distance of a little more than 1 mm."
> {noun in apposition}

Apanisagrion Kennedy, 1920: 86
> Gr. prefix ἀπ(ο)- away from + ἄνισος – unlike; for *Agrion* see *Acanthagrion*.

> The name refers to a distinct difference from the genus *Anisagrion*, Selys 1876a "Characters as in *Anisagrion*, except that the wing is not petioled." The Selysian genus takes its name from differences from *Agrion* concerning the pterostigmata and the venation of fore and hind wings in the males. {Neuter}

apeora, Coryphaeschna Paulson, 1994: 380
>Latinized from Gr. ἀπήωρος –ος–ον = high in the air (with the accent on the o). In Greek there is no feminine form *apeora*, but only when the Greek word is Latinized. The name refers to the behavior of the species: "*apeora* is Greek, meaning 'on high', referring to the high foraging and patrol flight of this species." This species was first observed in the US by REID & RICKARD (2018). {declinable adjective}

Aphylla Selys 1854: 78
>Gr. ἄφυλλος – without leaves referring to reduced flanges on subterminal abdominal segments: "♂ 8ᵉ et 9ᵉ segments à peine dilatés, sans feuilles plissées;" [♂ 8th and 9th segments barely dilated, without folded leaves]. {Feminine}

apicalis, Argia (Say, 1839: 40)
[Original designation: *Agrion apicalis* Say]
>L. *apex* (stem *apic-*) = the extreme end + suffix *–alis –is –e* = concerning.

>The name refers to the abdomen's tip: "Two or three ultimate segments pearlaceous blue above ... A very common species, remarkable, when recent, by the color of the tip of the abdomen ..." {declinable adjective}

apomyius, Hylogomphus (Donnelly, 1966: 102)
[Original designation: *Gomphus apomyius* Donnelly]
>Gr. Ἀπόμυιος = averter of flies; in ancient times Zeus was invoked by this name at Olympia, when he was asked to drive away flies from the sanctuary: Why Donnelly named this species so, he explains "The specific name meaning 'one who drives away flies,' is very appropriate for this small but agressive dragonfly." {declinable adjective}

Archilestes Selys, 1862: 294
    Gr. (in compounds) ἀρχι- = first of / chief of + *Lestes* (q.v.)

There can be a double interpretation of this name: it might describe a primitive position of the genus among *Lestidae* or it may refer to the size of the only species Selys classifies in this genus, *Archilestes grandis*, which is the largest of all North American damselflies. Selys does not explain which possibility he had in mind.   {Masculine}

Argia Rambur, 1842: 254
    Gr. Ἀργεία = the woman from Argos:

In ancient mythology this was the name of the wife of Polyneikes, a son of Oedipus who, associated with six other heroes and their men, tried to regain rule over Thebes from where he had been expelled by his brother and rival Eteokles. However, it is probably not that figure from mythology at the base of the name, for all other genus names given by Rambur to Odonata describe a quality of the genus or compare it with a bird of prey. It rather seems that Rambur chose a name as near to *Agrion* as possible without causing confusion, to which genus the wing venation he says to be similar: "par le ptérostigma et les deux nervules du premier espace costal elles se rapprochent des *Agrion*" [by the pterostigma and the two small veins of the first costal space they are close to *Agrion*].   {Feminine}

argo, Tauriphila (Hagen, 1869: 263)
[Original designation: *Tramea argo* Hagen]

> Gr. Ἀργώ was the name of the mythical ship, in which Jason and his Argonauts fetched the Golden Fleece from Kolchis. The name of the ship was said to be due to her builder Ἄργος, who was one of the Argonauts, or it could be derived from the adjective ἀργός = shining or swift-footed. That Hagen had the ship in mind is to be seen by the capital letter with which the name is published. He does not give a full description, but only mentions characters by which *Tramea iphigenia* [a synonym of his *T. australis* which was described two years before] is distinguished from *argo*, which he erroneously thinks to have already been described in 1861. So there is no real clue why he chose that name. {noun in apposition}

Arigomphus Needham, 1897: 181

> Gr. ἀρι- (in compounds) = excellent + *Gomphus* (q.v.)

> Needham had first published this gomphid genus under the name *Orcus* (L. = the lower world, prison of the dead); but seeing that this name was preoccupied, he replaced it within the same publication. But as usual with Needham, he explains neither of the names. {Masculine}

arizonicus, Ophiogomphus Kennedy, 1917: 538

> After type locality + L. suffix *–icus –a –um* = belonging to, pertaining to.

> "Type. – ... A male. Huachuca Mountains, Arizona". {declinable adjective}

armata, Oplonaeschna (Hagen, 1861: 124)
[Original designation: *Aeschna armata* Hagen]

> L. *armatus –a –um* = armed, referring to the projection on tenth abdominal segment of the male.

> "the tenth segment, in the middle, above, with a long, compressed spine, bent backwards". {declinable adjective}

armatus, Dromogomphus Selys, 1854: 59
>L. *armatus –a –um* = armed, a reference to long spines of the metafemur.

>Very probably from "6-7 épines très-fortes aux derniers fémurs" [6-7 very strong spines on the posterior femurs] cf. SELYS, 1858, 383: "le présence des longues épines aux fémurs postérieurs, èloigne au premier abord ce *Gomphus* du *dilatatus* auquel il ressemble sous plusieurs rapports ..." [the presence of the long spines on the posterior femurs, at first sight removes this *Gomphus* from *dilatatus*, which it resembles in several respects].
>{declinable adjective}

aspersum, Enallagma (Hagen, 1861: 97)
[Original designation: *Agrion* (subgenus *Agrion*) *aspersum* Hagen]
>L. *aspersus –a –um* past participle of *aspergo* = to scatter or sprinkle, thus sprinkled, probably from black spots on the abdomen.

>"abdomen black, the sides blue ; segment 1 blue, with a quadrangular, basal, black spot ; 2 blue, with an apical, pyriform, black spot ; 3 blue, with a large, apical, reversed hastiform, black spot ; the apical half of 7, the whole of 8 and 9, and 10 with a large ovate spot each side blue".   {declinable past participle}

aspersus, Ophiogomphus Morse, 1895: 209
>L. *aspersus –a –um* past participle of *aspergo* = to scatter or sprinkle, thus sprinkled, probably referring to abdominal spots.

>"abdomen brown, marked with yellow as follows: ..."
>{declinable past participle}

attala, Erythemis (Selys in Sagra, 1857: 445)
[Original designation: *Libellula attala* Selys in Sagra]

    Selys does not explain why he chose the name, but it may well be that it was after *Atala*, a fictional native Indian heroine from a novel of François-Renè de Chateaubriand, published in 1801, which was so well known in the 19th century, that 1833 in the State of Mississippi Attala County was named after her. Otherwise the name of a male saint, who died at Bobbio in 627, or a female saint, died at Strasbourg in 741, could be at the base of the species name. {noun in apposition}

auripennis, Libellula Burmeister, 1839: 861

    L. *aureus –a –um* = adorned with gold, golden + *–pennis –is –e* (in compounds) = winged, referring to orange-yellow wings.

    "alis aureis rubro-venosis" [with golden wings, rich in red veins]. {declinable adjective}

australis, Lestes Walker, 1952: 65
[as *Lestes disjunctus australis* Walker]
L. *australis –is –e* = southern, referring to distribution south of *L. disjunctus*.

    "This subspecies belongs to the Austral region and is almost entirely confined to the United States" (different from the boreal *L. disjunctus*, which is confined to Canada and Alaska and to northern regions of the United States) from which Walker supposed it to be a southern subspecies. {declinable adjective}

australis, Ophiogomphus Carle, 1992: 142

    L. *australis –is –e* = southern

    "*O. australis* .., Latin 'southern', referring to the southern distribution of the species" [types from Louisiana and Mississipi]. {declinable adjective}

australis, *Phanogomphus* (Needham, 1897: 184)
[Original designation: *Arigomphus australis* Needham]
    L. *australis –is –e* = southern

    "One finely colored ♂ taken by Mr. A. Hempel at Orange Co, Fla."   {declinable adjective}

australis, *Tauriphila* (Hagen, 1867b: 229)
[Original designation: *Tramea australis* Hagen]
    L. *australis –is –e* = southern; referring to geographic range.

    The species is described from Cuba; a male Hagen supposes to be (and is) conspecific, is from Bogota.   {declinable adjective}

axilena, *Libellula* Westwood, 1837: 96
    Name seems to be intended as 'pertaining to axilla' (probably misspelled), referring to dark marking at wing base.

    "wings ... ; a very narrow black streak also is placed near these edges, close to the body, from whence it seems to issue, being about a quarter of an inch in length". As the formation of the name is not clear grammatically, it should be treated as a
    {noun in apposition}

azteca, *Tauriphila* Calvert, 1906: 297/298
    Although not mentioned in the original description the species is named after the Aztec Indians of the Mexican Plateau.

    "*Hab*. Mexico, Guadalajara [1 ♂], Atoyac [1 ♂] (Schumann) [1 ♀] in Vera Cruz, Teapa [1 ♂ (H H. Smith) in Tabasco."   {declinable adjective}

balteata, *Macrodiplax* (Hagen, 1861: 140)
[Original designation: *Tetragoneuria balteata* Hagen]
    L. *balteatus –a –um* = girdled, probably referring to ringed abdomen of female, which is not mentioned in the first description.   {declinable adjective}

barberi, Ischnura Currie, 1903: 302
>"Of this number one species, an *Ischnura,* is named in honor of Mr. Barber [H. S. Barber (1882-1950)], who devoted special attention to securing these insects." {noun in the genitive case}

barretti, Argia Calvert, 1902: 87
>"(*O. W. Barret* [1872-1950], *coll.* P.P.C.: 1 ♂)", collector of holotype. {noun in the genitive case}

Basiaeschna Selys, 1883: 735
>Gr. βάσις = base; *Aeshna* (q.v.)

>The name evokes the often free basal space in this genus: "espace basilaire souvent libre chez *Basiaeshna*" [basilar space often free in *Basiaeshna*]. {Feminine}

basidens, Enallagma Calvert, 1902: 114
>L. *basis* = base (borrowed from Greek) + *–dens* (in compounds) = with a tooth/ with teeth.

>The name refers to male cerci: "superior appendages ... apex almost truncated at right angles thereto, underside in its proximal half with a rather slender tooth directed downward almost at right angles, yet slightly distally, the tooth not quite half as long as the entire appendage". {adjective}

basifusca, Erythrodiplax (Calvert, 1895: 536)
[Original designation: *Trithemis basifusca* Calvert]
>L. *basis* = base (borrowed from Greek) + *fuscus –a –*um = dark, swarthy, dusky, tawny.

>This name describes the wings: "front wings slightly brownish at extreme base for not as much as the length of a cell, hind wings with a dark brown spot extending from just behind the costa to about the level of the apex of the membranule, and from the base of the wing outwards to a short distance beyond the first antecubital, this spot being usually cleft on its outer edge at the basilar space." {declinable adjective}

bella, Nannothemis (Uhler, 1857: 87)
[Original designation: *Nannophya bella* Uhler]
    L. *bellus –a –um* = pretty. "This beautiful little species ..."
                                                     {declinable adjective}

bellei, Progomphus Knopf & Tennessen, 1980: 247
    "This species is being named after Dr. Jean Belle [See p. 19], (The Netherlands) in honor of his extensive revision of *Progomphus*. The format and illustrations will follow that of BELLE, 1973."
    {noun in the genitive case}

berenice, Erythrodiplax (Drury, 1773: 48)
[Original designation: *Libellula Berenice* Drury]
    Drury never explains his names, which are almost always female names from Roman antiquity.

    Berenike [Gr. Βερενίκη, bearer of victory] was the name of several Ptolemaic princesses. One of them, queen of Cyrene, had dedicated a curl of her hair to the gods to secure a safe return of her husband, Ptolemy III., from war. This curl was transferred to the sky to form the constellation '*Coma Berenices*' by the court's poet Kallimachos, whose poem later was translated into Latin by Catullus (cf. BARTELS 1996: 212). There was also a Judean princess of that name (1st century BC), daughter of Salome I, a sister of Herod the Great and mother of Herod Agrippa I.
                                                     {noun in apposition}

bertha, Celithemis Williamson, 1922b: 8
    "Named for Miss Bertha P. Currie [See p. 30], of the Bureau of Entomology, U.S. Department of Agriculture, efficient and obliging custodian of dragonflies in the National Museum."
                                                     {noun in apposition}

bilineata, *Cordulegaster* (Carle, 1983: 61)
[Original designation: *Zoraena bilineata* Carle]
>L. *bi–* (in compounds) = two + *linea* = a straight line + suffix – *atus –ata –atum*, provided with.

The species differs from *C. diastatops* and *C. sayi* by only two (not more) yellow lateral thoracic stripes: "lateral mesepisternal pale stripes absent, mesepisternal stripes narrow".
{declinable adjective}

binotata, *Tramea* (Rambur, 1842: 36)
[Original designation: *Libellula binotata* Rambur]
>L. *bi–* (in compounds) = two, double + *notatus –a –um* = marked

The two marks probably refer to the brown proximal bands in the hindwings "Ailes postérieures bien moins larges à la base, ayant une petite band d'un brun roux au bord abdominal, encore plus étroite que dans l'*Abdominalis*, n'allant pas jusqu'à l'angle anal" [Hindwings much less broad at the base, with a small band of reddish brown on the proximal border, still narrower than in *abdominalis*, not going as far as the anal angle].

However, the reference might apply to "abdomine postice maculis duabus vel tribus nigris" [abdomen at the rear with two or three black spots]. {declinable adjective}

bipunctulata, *Argia* (Hagen, 1861: 90)
[Original designation: *Agrion bipunctulata* Hagen
>L. *bi–* (in compounds) = two + *punctulum* = little point, spot + suffix *–atus –a –um* = provided with = (marked with two small spots)

The species has apical points on each side of the second abdominal segment: "segment ... 2 has an apical point each side".
{declinable adjective}

bison, Ophiogomphus Selys, 1873b: 496

    Gr. βίσων = bison. The female occipital spines resemble bison horns.

    "Diffère de la femelle du *serpentinus*: par les cornes de l'occiput qui sont pointues" [Different from the female of *serpentinus*: by the horns of the occiput which are pointed].

    {noun in apposition}

boreale, Enallagma (Selys, 1875: 242)
[Original designation: *Aenallagma boreale* Selys]

    L. *borealis –is –e* – northern (from Gr. Βορέας = north wind/ god of the north wind), referring to northern distribution.

    "The materials from which this paper has been drawn up were collected in various parts of Newfoundland by my young friend Mr. John Milne, F.G.S."   {declinable adjective}

borealis, Leucorrhinia Hagen, 1890a: 231
[as *Leucorhinia* [sic] *borealis* Hagen]

    L. *borealis –is –e* – northern, referring to distribution.

    "Six males and four females from Saskatchewan River and Fort Resolution, Hudson's BayTerritory by Kennicott."

    {declinable adjective}

borealis, Phanogomphus descriptus (Needham in Needham and Betten, 1901: 453)
[Original designation: *Gomphus borealis* Needham]

    L. *borealis –is –e* – northern, referring to geographic range.

    "The variety was first received from Franconia N.H."

    {declinable adjective}

borealis, *Progomphus* McLachlan in Selys, 1873a: 764
   L. *borealis* –*is* –*e* – northern, distribution northerly for a *Progomphus*.

   "*Patrie:* L'Orégon, un mâle ..."   {declinable adjective}

Boyeria McLachlan, 1896: 424
   The name was given in honour of the Provençal entomologist E.L.J.H. Boyer de Fonscolombe (1772-1853) who described the first species to be included in this genus. McLachlan replaced the preoccupied denomination *Fonscolombia* Selys, 1883 with this name in 1896.   {Feminine}

Brachymesia Kirby, 1889: 280
   Probably Gr. βραχύς = short + μέσος = middle + suffix –ιος, -α, -ον = pertaining to.

   If so, it might refer to the lower appendage: "lower appendage very stout and short, not half the length of the upper ones" {= not reaching the middle of those}. Otherwise it may be a reference to short inflated basal section of abdomen as suggested by PAULSON & DUNKLE 2012, but it is not very likely that the base of the abdomen would be described as 'middle'.
   {Feminine}

Brechmorhoga Kirby, 1894: 264
   Gr. βρέχμα = front part of the head + ῥωγή = cleft.

   The name refers to "frontal tubercle bifid", a diagnostic feature, as in "*Macrothemis* the frontal tubercle is not bifid ..."
   {Feminine}

brevicincta, *Somatochlora* Robert, 1954: 419
   L. *brevis* –*is* –*e* = short + *cinctus* –*a* –*um* = girdled, referring to partial pale rings between some abdominal segments.

   "Similar to *S. albicincta*, but its abdomen lacks rings or they are reduced to small spots on the sides between segments 3 to 7."
   {declinable adjective}

breviphylla, Phyllocycla Belle, 1975: 65
> L. *brevis –is –e* = short + Gr. (in compounds) –φυλλος -η –ον = having leaves.
>
> The name refers to specially formed leaflike flanges on the sides of abdominal club: "The male [of *P. elongata*] is at once recognizable from that of this species by the lateral dilatations of the ninth abdominal segment, which are curved throughout and not acutely angulated at the basal half."
>
> {declinable adjective}

brevistylus, Hagenius Selys, 1854: 82
> L. *brevis –is –e* = short + *stilus* = a stake, a pointed instrument used by the Romans for writing upon wax tablets. From late antiquity until modern times y is often used instead of i thus converting *stilus* to *stylus*. The name applies to the anal appendages, that formerly also were called '*styli*'. "Appendices anals très-courts" [Very short anal appendages]. {declinable adjective}

byersi, Telebasis Westfall, 1957: 20
> "Named for C. Francis Byers [See p. 25], whose Contribution to the Knowledge of Florida Odonata published in 1930 is well known to students of these insects."
>
> {noun in the genitive case}

californica, Rhionaeschna (Calvert, 1895: 504)
[Original designation: *Aeschna californica* (Hagen MS) Calvert]
> From type locality + L. suffix *–icus –a –um* = belonging to, pertaining to.
>
> This was a manuscript name of Hagen whose type came from "1 ♂ California (Cal. Acad. coll.)" [Hagen. Proc. Bost. Soc. N.H. xviii, p. 73, 1875]. {declinable adjective}

californicus, Archilestes McLachlan, 1895: 20
[as *Archilestes californica* McLachlan]
>From type locality + L. suffix —*icus* –*a* –*um* = belonging to, pertaining to.

"I received this example from Mr. Edwards many years ago; it bears his printed locality label "California", without more precise indication. M. de Selys, to whom it was submitted, labelled it with the name I have adopted, but it has never been described." {declinable adjective}

Calopteryx Leach, 1815: 137
Gr. καλός –ή –όν = beautiful + πτέρυξ = wing.

For the genus name Leach chose the form *Calepteryx*, as if he had transcribed the two separate words into Latin, the first morpheme being an adjective adapted in gender to *pteryx* (feminine); but as compounds are formed differently it was later emended to *Calopteryx*. "This genus comprehends those *Agrionida* with colored wings." The wings of the males in the species of the genus known to Leach have a pretty metallic sheen. {Feminine}

calverti, Somatochlora Williamson & Gloyd, 1933: 1
"Before this paper was completed Mr. Williamson died quite unexpectedly. Throughout the period of his interest in Odonata, from his first paper in 1898 to his last in 1933, he carried on a friendly correspondence with Dr. Philip Calvert [See p. 26] of the University of Pennsylvania and greatly respected his scientific counsel and advice. It is in appreciation of this relationship that the new species is named for Dr. Calvert."

{noun in the genitive case}

calverti, Tramea Muttkowski, 1910: 179
"{Tramea}calverti n.n. *Syn. longicauda var.* CALVERT [See p. 26]; Proc. Cal. Acad., (2) 4, p. 514, 1895; descr."

{noun in the genitive case}

canadensis, Aeshna Walker, 1908: 384
> From the main area of distribution + *–ensis* –is –e = adjectival suffix indicating place of origin.

> "It is an abundant species in the Canadian division of the Boreal Zone, and it is also common in the Transition Zone from New England and the Maritime Provinces to Manitoba.
> {declinable adjective}

canis, Epitheca (McLachlan, 1886: 104)
[Original designation: *Tetragoneuria canis* McLachlan]
> L. *canis* = a dog. "*the apical portion* in this position *might be compared to a dog's (or a wolf's) head, with long profile and short, erect ears.*" ... "the shape of the apical portion of the superior appendages, seen laterally, is such as (in the absence of a figure) to have occasioned a familiar comparison, and it also suggested the specific name." {noun in apposition}

Cannaphila Kirby, 1889: 305
> Gr. κάννα = reed + -φιλός-ή –όν = loving.

> Kirby does not explain in the first description why he chose this name. {Feminine}

cara, Protoneura Calvert, 1903: 143
> L. *carus –a –um* = dear, precious, valued, esteemed, beloved.

> This seems to be one of the names, where especially damselflies are characterized as lovable creatures in a similar manner to names like *amabilis, amata, amanda.* {declinable adjective}

cardenium, Enallagma Hagen in Selys, 1876a: 530
> Name probably formed from *Cárdenas*, a city near Havana where early collections were made + L. adjectival suffix *–ius –a –um* = pertaining to.
>
> Whereas Cárdenas is mentioned in reference to other Odonata collected by Gundlach on Cuba, in the paper where the species was described it reads "Cuba, sur les fleuves, près de la Havane." [Cuba, on the rivers, near Havana]. {declinable adjective}

caribbea, Triacanthagyna Williamson, 1923b: 22
> L. *caribbeus –a –um* = Carribean.
>
> The species is distributed around the southern and eastern sides of the Caribbean. {declinable adjective}

carlcooki, Argia Daigle, 1995: 467
> "The species is named for Carl Cook [See p. 29], the founding editor of the North American journal *ARGIA*, in honor of his contributions to neotropical odonatology."
> {noun in the genitive case}

carolina, Tramea (Linnaeus, 1763: 411)
[Original designation: *Libellula carolina* Linnaeus]
> From "*Habitat in* Carolina. *Garden*". {declinable adjective}

carolus, Ophiogomphus Needham, 1897: 183
> L. name, engl Charles.
>
> There is no explanation of the name by Needham. In taxonomy the most prominent person of whom one might think with this first name is the founder of modern zoological nomenclature, Carolus Linnaeus. {noun in apposition}

carunculatum, Enallagma Morse, 1895: 208
> L. *carunculatus –a –um* = warty, referring to apical tubercle on male cerci.

"In profile the superior appendage, including the projecting tubercle, is half to two-thirds as long as 10."
{declinable adjective}

cavillaris, Phanogomphus (Needham, 1902: 276)
[Original designation: *Gomphus cavillaris* Needham]
> L. *cavillaris –is –e* = pertaining to jesting, allusion unknown.

Needham does not offer an explanation. {declinable adjective}

Celithemis Hagen, 1861: 147
> Gr. κηλίς = stain, spot, defilement + θέμις, -ιστος = law, as established by custom; personified as the goddess of order (now used in the sense of libellulid, corduliid or synthemistid dragonfly).

When describing the North American Odonata in 1861 Hagen saw that there were new Libellulid genera to be described. Inspired by generic names in *–etrum* (e.g. *Sympetrum*) suggested by NEWMAN 1833, which seemed not to have been adopted in odonatology, he wanted to avoid a change in gender from the feminine *Libellula*. Therefore he chose *–themis* as the second element of eight names, of which two [*Lepthemis, Mesothemis*] subsequently were synomisised with one of Hagen's new genera [*Erythemis*]. Hagen did not explain his choice except grammatically (HAGEN 1888), but it is probable, that the name was prompted by names of other gods in odonatology like *Nehalennia*. As an element of new libellulid names *–themis* was taken on by BRAUER 1868 and later also adopted for corduliid and synthemistid dragonflies.

Celithemis got its name from the colored patches on the wings of the two species on which Hagen based his genus. {Feminine}

cervula, *Ischnura* Selys, 1876a: 262
>L. *cervula* = little deer, alluding to the antler-like forked apex of tenth segment of male abdomen.

"L'éminence du 10ᵉ segment commençant dès la base comme chez *perparva*, mais fourchue dans plus de la moitié de son longueur, les branches s'écartant à angle aigu (droit chez *defixa*) un peu courbées et inclinées en dehors au bout." [The protruberance on the 10th segment starting from the base as in *perparva*, but forked for more than half of its length, the branches extending away at an acute angle (as in *defixa*) slightly curved and inclined outside at the end]. {noun in apposition}

Chromagrion Needham, 1903: 236
>Gr.χρῶμα = color + *Agrion* , a word for damselfly (see *Acanthagrion*)

The name probably indicates that coloration separates the species *C. conditum* from typically colored species of the genus *Erythromma*, where it was placed before Needham created this taxon: "In addition to the differences in coloration and appendages clearly stated by de Selys as distinguishing this species from the typical erythromma, there are differences of venation ..." (p. 246). {Neuter}

cingulata, *Somatochlora* (Selys, 1871a: 302)
[Original designation: *Epitheca cingulata* Selys]
>L. *cingulum* = girdle, sword-belt + suffix *–atus –a –um* = provided with, referring to pale abdominal rings.

"Abdomen brun noirâtre en dessus, 1ᵉʳ et 2ᵉ segments brun clair ainsi qu'une band latérale aux autres segments et l'articulation basale de 3-10ᵉ, formant un cercle jaune etroit." [Abdomen blackish brown on top, 1st and 2nd segments light brown as well as a side band on the other segments and the basal joint of 3-10th, forming a narrow yellow circle]. {declinable adjective}

citrina, *Tholymis* Hagen, 1867b: 218
> L. *citrinus –a –um* = lemon colored, citreous (in scientific names)

The only lemon colored feature of the species is the spots on the wings: "Auf den Unterflügeln ist aussen neben dem Nodus ein runder gelber Fleck, der bis zur Hälte der Flügelbreite reicht, am Vorderrande überragt er kaum den Nodus gegen die Basis hin. Ein ähnlicher, aber viel kleinerer gelber Fleck steht auf den Vorderflügeln unter den (!) Ursprung des Sect. nodalis." [On the hindwings there is distally beside the nodus a round yellow spot extending to half of the breadth of the wings; at the anterior margin it hardly exceeds the nodus in the direction of the wing base. A similar, but much smaller yellow spot occurs on the anterior wings beneath the origin of the nodal sector].
{declinable adjective}

civile, *Enallagma* (Hagen, 1861: 88)
[Original designation: *Agrion civile* Hagen]
> L. *civilis –is –e* = civil, of citizens.

Why he chose this name Hagen gives no information.
{declinable adjective}

clausum, *Enallagma* Morse, 1895: 209
> L. *clausus –a – um* = closed (past participle of *claudo* = to close)

In this species the male's cerci are contiguous at the base: "superior appendages short, blunt, very broad, contiguous at base for nearly half their length, the line of separation often only visible with difficulty". {declinable past participle} *clepsydra, Aeshna* Say, 1839: 12

Gr. κλεψύδρα = water clock, a device for measuring time by the amount of water discharged from vessel through a small orifice.

The name might be evoked by the feature: 'abdomen contracted at the base', which in Hagen 1861, 122 is described in more detail: "abdomen long, slender, equal, very much attenuated behind the inflated base". {noun in apposition}

Coenagrion Kirby, 1890: 148

Gr. κοινός = together, common +*Agrion* (a word for damselfly, see *Acanthagrion*)

Fabricius in 1775 created the genus *Agrion* to comprise all Zygoptera. Later on controversies arose as to whether calopterygids or other damselflies were the true agrionids. So Kirby 1890 partitioned the damselflies into *Agrion* for the calopterygids and *Coenagrion* for the remainder. But although Kirby (1890) admonished that "no generic name ought to be issued without a description" he did not stand by that principle when naming *Coenagrion*. Most probably the name means "common Agrion", but there might also have been intended the meaning "together Agrion", as most of the coenagrionids *sensu* Kirby oviposit in tandem. {Neuter}

collocata, Erythemis (Hagen, 1861: 171)
[Original designation: *Mesothemis collocata* Hagen]

L. *collocatus –a –um* : past participle of *colloco* = to place together.

Why he chose this name, Hagen does not say, but he placed the species as the second one of his genus *Mesothemis* directly after *Mesothemis simplicicollis* (Say) [now also in the genus *Erythemis*], so that placing them together might be the intention of the name. There is perhaps an alternative, as L. *colloco* may also mean to give into marriage, which semantically would correspond with names like *sponsa, nympha* or *nymphula*; but all these names denote damselflies. {declinable past participle}

colubrinus, Ophiogomphus Selys, 1854: 40
    L. *colubrinus –a –um* = snakelike.

    The species got its name because of its similarity to the European species *Ophiogomphus cecilia* (Fourcroy), then known as *Ophiogomphus serpentinus* (Charpentier) [L. *serpentinus* = of or like a snake].   {declinable adjective}

comanche, Libellula Calvert, 1907: 201
    After Comanche Indians of same area although its name is not explained by Calvert.

    "I have examined Rambur's presumed type of *flavida* at Oxford, England. It is identical with *plumbea* Uhler, and therefore different from *flavida* Hagen, which latter will require a new name." "For *flavida* Hagen (nec Rambur), I now propose *Libellula comanche*."   {noun in apposition}

composita, Libellula (Hagen, 1873b: 728)
[Original designation: *Mesothemis composita* Hagen]
    L. *compositus –a –um*: past participle of *compono* = to place together.

    Hagen described this species from Yellowstone after quoting three other species of his genus *Mesothemis* from there (all these four species pertain to different genera now). So the name probably just describes this fact. Or else it might refer to the similarity of the species mentioned immediately before: "The species is related to *M. corrupta*" (now *Sympetrum corruptum*).
    {declinable past participle}

compositus, *Erpetogomphus* Hagen in Selys, 1858: 660

L. *compositus –a –um*: past participle of *compono* = to place together, to compound.

Hagen does not explain his choice of the name, but his description of the species is peculiar in that he gives no description of it itself, but lists the differences from *E. designatus* described subsequently. "Elle ressemble beaucoup à celle du *designatus*. Voici les différences que j' observe:" [It is very similar to *designatus*. Here are the differences I observe:]. So the name might mean 'species placed together with *E. designatus*' but in the last part of the paragraph dedicated to this species it reads: "Il faut convenier que les femelles des deux espèces d'*Erpetogomphus* à ptérostigma noir (le *designatus* et le *compositus*) ressemblent par ce caractère et par le dessin à des *Onychogomphus*, au point qu'on ne pourrait pas les en séparer avec certitude, si l'on ne savait qu'elles appartiennent à des mâles qui forment un groupe naturel, distinct des *Onychogomphus* par les appendices anals moitié plus courts, des forme moins compliquée, caractères rendus plus importants par la notion géographique, ces espèces étant particulières à l'Amérique septentrionale, et les *Onychogomphus* étant restreints à l'ancien continent." [One must acknowledge that the females of the two species of *Erpetogomphus* with a black pterostigma (*designatus* and *compositus*) by this feature and by their pattern resemble those of *Onychogomphus* to the extent that they cannot be distinguished with certainty if one does not know that they belong to males which form a natural group distinct from *Onychogomphus*, by the half-shorter appendages, of less complicated form, rendered more important by the geographical concept, these species being peculiar to North America, and the *Onychogomphus* being restricted to the ancient continent]. {declinable past participle}

concisum, Enallagma Williamson, 1922c: 117
    L. *concisus –a –um* = short, concise: past participle of L. *concido* = cut up, cut to pieces.

The name refers to to the short mesostigmal lamina in the female: "Mesostigmal lamina largely pale, the upper half, anterior to the pale posterior inflated carina, and a very narrow border, posterior to this carina, black." {declinable adjective}

concolor, Anax Brauer, 1865: 508
    L. *concolor* = concolored i.e. of the same color.

In this species the frons, thorax and first two abdominal segments are of matching yellow-green color: "fronte viridi-flava immaculata, ... thorace flavo-viride (!) immaculato ... segmento primo et secundo flavo-viridibus [with an unstained yellowish green frons, ... an unstained yellowish green thorax, .. the first and second segment yellow-green]. {adjective}

conditum, Chromagrion (Hagen in Selys, 1876a: 1305)
[Original designation: *Erythromma?* conditum Hagen in Selys]
    L. *conditus –a –um*: past participle of L. *condo* = to put together, make by joining.

Hagen points out that the species is difficult to classify because it shows features of both *Erythromma* and *Pyrrhosoma*. "Elle est fort difficile à classér; tenant des *Erythromma* par le système de la coloration où le bleu domine, et des *Pyrrhosoma*, par la grande longueur des appendices inférieurs." [It is very difficult to classify; resembling *Erythromma* by the system of coloration in which blue dominates, and *Pyrrhosoma*, by the great length of the lower appendages]. {declinable past participle}

congener, Lestes Hagen, 1861: 67
    L. *congener –eris* = of same kind.

The name probably refers to *L. stultus* described directly above [as *L. stulta*]; the descriptions of the species correspond rather word for word, except in the overall coloration, which is described as black in *stultus* and brassy-black in *congener*. For *L. stultus* nothing is mentioned of the abdomen which seems to have been missing in the type. But also *L. vidua* is annotated: "It is similar to *L. congener* Hag.". Alternatively the name may also refer to that similarity.   {adjective}

consanguis, Stenogomphurus (Selys, 1879: lxvi)
[Original designation: *Gomphus consanguis Selys*]
    L. *consanguis –is –e* = of the same blood, related by blood, kindred, fraternal.

Selys mentions the near relationship to other *Gomphus* species: "Malgrè ma répugnance à voir une nouvelle espèce dans ce group si difficile et si nombreux des *Gomphus* américains, je ne puis rapporter ce mâle unique au *fraternus*." [Despite my reluctance to see a new species in this so difficult and numerous group of American *Gomphus*, I cannot relate this single male to *fraternus*]. In the following paragraph differences from other members of that *Gomphus* group are discussed, i.e. *G. adelphus* [Gr. brother Latinized], *sobrinus* [L. cousin on the mother's side] and *confraternus* [Medieval L. belonging to the same guild], the names of which all express a near relationship.
    {declinable adjective}

constricta, Aeshna Say, 1839: 11
    L. *constrictus –a –um* = past participle of *constringo* = to draw together, to compress.

The name refers to the abdomen: "The third abdominal segment is remarkably contracted."   {declinable past participle}

Cordulegaster Leach, 1815: 139
> Gr. κορδύλη = club, cudgel, bump, swelling + γαστήρ = paunch, belly, thus abdomen

> The genus is named from the clubbed abdominal shape of the males: "Abdomen of the male clavate".   {Feminine}

Cordulia Leach, 1815: 137
> L. *cordulia* feminine form of Latinized adjective derived from Gr. κορδύλη = club or cudgel) = clubbed.

> Leach introduced the name without explanation, but it certainly alludes to the shape of the abdomen in the males of this genus (as he states for his genus *Cordulegaster* in the same publication). Because of its origin, pronunciation should be accented on the 'i' (not the 'u' as is often done).   {Feminine}

cornutus, Arigomphus (Tough, 1900: 17)
[Original designation: *Gomphus cornutus* Tough]
> L. *cornutus –a –um* = horned, provided with antlers.

> In this species the superior appendages are similar to antlers, as to be seen in Tough 1900, 17 Fig. 1.   {declinable adjective}

corruptum, Sympetrum (Hagen, 1861: 171)
[Original designation: *Mesothemis corrupta* Hagen]
> L. *corruptus –a –um* = spoiled, corrupted (past participle of *corrumpo* = to destroy, spoil).

> Allusion unknown.   {declinable past participle}

Coryphaeschna Williamson, 1903: 2
> Gr. κορυφή = summit, extremity, tip + *–aeschna* see *Aeshna*.

> The name might refer to the location of the supplementary sector near wing tip: Williamson 1903, 2 note: "*Coryphe Gr. apex"; p. 3: "supplementary sector between the principal and nodal sectors originating far beyond pterostigma".   {Feminine}

costalis, Epitheca (Selys, 1871a: 273)
[Original designation: *Cordulia costalis* Selys]
> L. *costa* = rib; in entomology: anterior-most wing vein, forming front edge of the wing + suffix *–(a)lis –is –e* = concerning.

The female, from which Selys described the species, differs from *Epitheca cynosura* by a brown costal wing stripe.

"Stature et coloration du corps presque semblables a la *cynosura*. Elle en diffère parce que le bord costal des quatre ailes est brun opaque entre la nervure costale et la mediane jusqu'au nodus" [Stature and coloring of the body almost similar to *cynosura*, it differs because the costal edge of the four wings is opaque brown between the costal vein and the median as far as the nodus]. But that does not seem true for all females of the species (see PAULSON & DUNKLE 2012). {declinable adjective}

costiferum, Sympetrum (Hagen, 1861: 175)
[Original designation: *Diplax costifera* Hagen]
> L. *costa* = rib; in entomology the anteriormost wing vein, forming front edge of the wing + suffix *–fer –fera –ferum* = bearing.

The species has a costal wing stripe: "wings hyaline, the anterior margin and immediate base, flavescent". {declinable adjective}

crassus, Gomphurus (Hagen in Selys, 1878: 453)
[Original designation: *Gomphus crassus* Hagen in Selys]
> L. *crassus –a –um* = fat, stout.

"l'abdomen est remarquablement robuste et épais." [The abdomen is remarkably robust and thick].{declinable adjective}

croceipennis, Libellula Selys, 1868: 67
>L. *croceus* –*a* –*um* = of saffron, saffron-colored (from Gr. κρόκεος –ον = saffron-colored) + –*pennis* –*is* –*e* (in compounds) = winged.

In this species there are orange markings at the base of the wings of the male: "Elle en diffère principalement [from *L. saturata* Uhler] parce que l'éspace basilaire et les triangles des secondes ailes ne sont pas colorés en brun ochracé *plus foncée que le reste de la base des ailes*; et que cette couleur s'arréte au nodus au lieu de se prolonger le long de la côte jusqu'au pterostigma." [It differs principally [from *L. saturata* Uhler] because the basilar space and the triangles of the hind wings are not colored ochre brown *darker than the rest of the base of the wings*; and this color stops at the nodus instead of extending along the edge as far as the pterostigma]. {declinable adjective}

Crocothemis Brauer, 1868: 367
>Gr. κρόκος = saffron; for –*themis* see *Celithemis*.

This taxon got its name because in all species known at the time of the first description of the genus the wings are marked with saffron spots at the base. {Feminine}

crotalinus, Erpetogomphus (Hagen in Selys, 1854: 40)
[Original designation: *Ophiogomphus crotalinus* Hagen in Selys]
>L. *crotalinus* is derived from *crotalus* (a rattlesnake genus named by Linnaeus) [from Gr. κρόταλον = rattle, clapper] + suffix –*inus* –*a* –*um* = pertaining to.

The name is not explained in Selys 1854 and 1858, but certainly chosen because of the semantic closeness to names referring to snakes like *colubrinus* in the genera *Ophiogomphus* and later *Erpetogomphus* (q.v.). {declinable adjective}

cubensis, Idiataphe (Scudder, 1866: 190)
[Original designation: *Macromia cubensis* Scudder]
>From the type locality + *–ensis –is –e* = adjectival suffix indicating place of origin.

"The Isle of Pines, where the insects where obtained, which form the basis of the followings notes, is, zoologically speaking, a portion of Cuba ... The Odonata mentioned in the following pages were obtained at Santa Fé ... with the exception of one or two species which were taken in Cuba at an earlier date, but which became mingled in my collection, so that I was not able to distinguish them ..." {declinable adjective}

cultellatum, Neoerythromma (Hagen in Selys, 1876a: 524)
[Original designation: *Enallagma cultellatum*, Hagen in Selys]
L. *cultellus* = a little knife + suffix *–atus –a –um* = provided with.

The name refers to the male cerci: "Appendices anals supérieurs ... en lame de couteau presque droite" [Superior anal appendages ... as an almost straight knife blade]. {declinable adjective}

cuprea, Argia (Hagen, 1861: 96)
[Original designation: *Agrion cupreum* Hagen]
L. *cupreus –a –um* = coppery.

The first description emphasises the purple coppery appearance: "coppery-purple, head cupreous ... sides pale, above coppery". {declinable adjective}

cyanea, Libellula Fabricius, 1775: 424
L. *cyaneus –a –um* = dark blue, sea blue [from Gr. κύανος = lapis lazuli]

The name describes the blue body of mature male: "Corpus totum cyaneum" [The whole body blue]. {declinable adjective}

cynosura, Epitheca (Say, 1839: 30)
[Original designation: *Libellula cynosura* Say]
    Gr. κυνός οὐρά = a dog's tail.

    Say does not explain why he chose that name for the species, perhaps, because its body is rather hairy [cf. SELYS 1871a: 270]. Similarly a genus of grass with shaggy ears is called *Cynosurus*. Certainly *E. cynosura* is less pilose than other species of this genus (NEEDHAM & AL. 2000: 483); but it was the first one described. Another explanation is found in PAULSON & DUNKLE 2012. They think it might be an allusion to divergent male cerci looking like end points of the wag of a dog's tail in dorsal view.
                                                                    {noun in apposition}

daeckii, Enallagma (Calvert, 1903: 36)
[Original designation: *Telagrion? daeckii* Calvert]
    "named for the active and enthusiastic collector [E. Daecke (1863-1918), collector of one of types] who has added so much, for the last few years, to knowledge of the New Jersey insect fauna."   {noun in the genitive case}

damula, Ischnura Calvert, 1902: 126
    L. *damula* = little fallow deer.

    "very similar to *I. cervula*" [L. little deer], q.v.
                                                                       {noun in apposition}

danae, *Sympetrum* (Sulzer, 1776: 169)
[Original designation: *Libellula danae* Sulzer]

Danaë [Δανάη] is a figure from Greek mythology. She was said to be the beautiful daughter of Akrisios, king of Argos. A prophecy admonished the king, that he would be killed by his grandson. To prevent this happening he locked his daughter in an underground room. But Zeus entered the room in the form of golden rain, the result of which visit was the birth of the hero Perseus. When Akrisios noticed that, he ordered a chest to be prepared, in which Danaë with her child was thrown into the sea, hoping that they would perish. But they survived, and later the prophecy was fulfilled, because Perseus when grown up in an encounter with his grandfather was ignorant of the relationship. The name refers to yellow spots on the thorax of immature individuals. {noun in apposition}

davisi, *Enallagma* Westfall, 1943a: 103

"I wish to express my appreciation to ... and to Mr. E. M. Davis [Edward M. Davis (1888-1943), friend of describer] for material in this genus." {noun in the genitive case}

demorsa, *Ischnura* (Hagen, 1861: 81)
[Original designation: *Agrion* (subgenus *Ischnura*) *demorsum* Hagen]
L. *demorsus –a –um* : past participle of *de-mordeo* = to bite off.

Hagen's only specimen was damaged: "The abdomen of the female is partly destroyed". {declinable past participle}

denticollis, *Ischnura* (Burmeister, 1839: 819)
[Original designation: *Agrion denticolle* Burmeister]
L. *dens* (stem *dent–*) = tooth + *–collis –is –e* (in compounds) = –necked.

In this species the rear margin of the female's *pronotum* has a toothlike process in the middle and a triangular tubercle on each side (cf. SELYS 1876a: 1244). {declinable adjective}

deplanata, Ladona (Rambur, 1842: 75)
[Original designation: *Libellula deplanata* Rambur]
    L. *deplanatus –a –um*: past participle of *deplano* = to level off, flatten.

By this name the abdomen shape is described as having a superficial similarity to the European species *Libellula depressa* [L. *depressus –a –um* = depressed, referring to the flattened abdomen], but for size "Ressemblant un peu à la *Depressa*, mais n'ayant que cinq centim. d'envergure et trois et demi de long." [Somewhat resembling *depressa*, but wingspan only five cm, and three and a half long].   {declinable past participle}

descriptus, Phanogomphus (Banks, 1896: 194)
[Original designation: *Gomphus descriptus* Banks]
L. *descriptus –a –um* : past participle of *describo* = to describe.
    As Banks gives no explanation, the name might just say: the *Gomphus* described herein.   {declinable past participle}

designatus, Erpetogomphus Hagen in Selys, 1858: 661
    L. *designatus –a –um* : past participle of *designo* = to mark, designate.

The name probably refers to the black and yellow markings of the abdomen of the male, described elaborately in the first description.   {declinable past participle}

diadema, Cordulegaster Selys, 1868: 68
    Gr. διάδημα = band or fillet; especially band round the tiara worn by Persian kings.

Probably the following feature is at the base of this denomination: "Front noir en avant, jaune en dessus où cette couleur est entièrement entourée de noir" [Face black seen frontally, yellow on top where this color is entirely surrounded by black]. In the following part this is mentioned as a difference from *Cordulegaster bidentata*, a European species.
                                      {noun in apposition}

diastatops, *Cordulegaster* (Selys, 1854: 101)
[Original designation: *Thecaphora diastatops* Selys]
>Gr. διαστατός = standing apart, torn by faction + -οψ (in compounds) = with eyes, –eyed.

>In his description of the genus *Thecaphora* Charpentier, where he placed this species, Selys wrote in 1854: "Yeux non contigus, mais très- rapprochés." [Eyes not contiguous, but very close together]. {adjective}

didyma, *Micrathyria* (Selys in Sagra, 1857: 453
[Original designation: *Libellula didyma* Selys in Sagra]
>*didyma* = Latinized feminine form of Gr. δίδυμος –η –ον = double, twofold, twin.

>The reference is: "segmento septimo macula majore geminata" [on the seventh segment with a double major spot].
>{declinable adjective}

Didymops Rambur, 1842: 142
>Gr. δίδυμος –η –ον = double, twofold, twin + -οψ (in compounds) = with eyes, –eyed.

>In this genus the process at the rear of the eyes, typical for corduliids, has a shape which is grainlike and looks like an extra little eye, so that a pair of eyes seems to be present on each side of the head: "yeux contigus, ayant vers le milieu du bord postérieur un petit prolongement graniforme très-saillant" [eyes contiguous, having at the middle of the posterior margin a little prolongation like a grain, which is very prominent].
>{Femininine}

digiticollis, Telebasis Calvert, 1902: 118
  L. *digitus* = finger + *–collis –is –e* (in compounds] = –necked.

  The females of the species are said to differ from *T. vulnerata* (Hagen) in the coloring of the thorax "and in the shorter prothoracic processes, which latter have suggested the specific name". {declinable adjective}

dilatatus, Gomphurus (Rambur, 1842: 155)
[Original designation: *Gomphus dilatatus* Rambur]
  L. *dilatatus –a –um: past* participle of *dilato* = dilate, broaden, stretch, enlarge, extend.

  The widened abdominal club suggested this name: "Abdomen dilaté aux deux extrémités, surtout postérieurement, dont les trois pénultièmes segments, et surtout l'huitième, ont les bords latéraux fortement dilates." [Abdomen dilated at the two extremities, especially posteriorly, of which the three penultimate segments, and especially the eighth, have the lateral edges greatly dilated]. {declinable past participle}

dimidiata, Calopteryx Burmeister, 1839: 829
  L. *dimidiatus –a –um : past* participle of *dimidio* = to divide into two equal parts.

  The name might allude to the fact that in the females (Burmeister did not know the males) the wings seem to be divided as their distal parts are black whereas the proximal parts are only shadowed. {declinable past participle}

diminutus, Phanogomphus (Needham, 1950: 6)
[Original designation: *Gomphus diminutus* Needham]
  L. *diminutus –a –um* = past participle of *diminuo* = diminish

  The name is a reference to the small size: "This is a rather small green species" {declinable past participle}

discolor, *Orthemis* (Burmeister, 1839: 856)
[Original designation: *Libellula discolor* Burmeister]
    L. *discolor* = of another color, not of the same color.

    In this species the coloration of males and females is different: "rufescens (♂) vel testacea (♀)" [reddish (♂) or brick-colored (♀)].   {adjective}

disjunctus, *Lestes* Selys , 1862: 302
[as *Lestes disjuncta* Selys]
    L. *disjunctus –a –um* = separated, distant, disconnected, set apart [also past participle of *disjungo* = disunite, separate, part, estrange].

    In the first description the species is separated from the related Old World species *Lestes sponsa*: "Représente la *sponsa* en Amerique et n'en parait qu'une race locale…" [Represents *sponsa* in America and it seems only a local race …].
    {declinable adjective}

dissocians, *Micrathyria* Calvert, 1906: 222/226
    L. *dissocians* : present participle of *dissocio* = to put out of union, disjoin, disunite.

    "The specific name refers to the divergence of the tips of the superior appendages as seen in dorsal view." {present participle}

divagans, *Enallagma* Selys, 1876a: 521
    L. *divagans* : present participle of *divagor* = to wander about.

    Selys does not explain his choice of the name, but he emphasizes: "Très-voisin de l' *exsulans*" [very near to *exsulans* (L. = being in exile)]. So the similarity in meaning (= not being at home) might have produced the name.   {present participle}

domina, Palaemnema Calvert, 1903: 137
    L. *domina* = mistress, dame, she who rules.

Probably the name is given in the tradition of choosing denominations of females as names of dragonflies since Linnaeus 1758, e.g. his *Libellula virgo* (now *Calopteryx virgo*) or *L. puella* (now *Coenagrion puella*) or the calopterygid genus *Matrona* Selys. Calvert mentions the name to be from: "Hagen, in litt."
{noun in apposition}

domitia, Perithemis (Drury, 1773: 45)
[Original designation: *Libellula domitia* Drury]
    Drury never explains his names, which are almost always female names from Roman antiquity.

Domitia is the name of women from the *gens* of the *Domitii* of Ancient Rome. [*gens* signifies a family consisting of all those individuals who shared the same name and claimed descent from a common ancestor.] One candidate is Domitia Longina (c. AD 53-55–c. AD 126-130) who was an Empress of Rome and wife of the Roman Emperor Domitian. She was the youngest daughter of the general and consul Gnaeus Domitius Corbulo. {noun in apposition}

Dorocordulia Needham in Needham and Betten, 1901: 504
    Gr. δορός = leather bag or wallet + *Cordulia* (q.v.)

As Needham does not give a clue in the first description, the interpretation remains uncertain. The genus is distinguished from other corduliids by characteristics of the wing venation, which cannot be connected with a leather bag. Needham includes three species in this taxon, one of which is now placed in the genus *Williamsonia* (*C. lintneri* Hagen). A common feature of the males of all these three species is that the abdominal base is inflated (SELYS 1876a, 263 sq.; HAGEN 1890b, 372). So perhaps that feature might have made Needham think of a leather bag with a margin extended by a string drawn through. {Feminine}

dorsalis, Cordulegaster Hagen in Selys, 1858: 607
    L. *dorsalis –is –e* = dorsal.

The species has characteristic dorsal spots: "Abdomen ... à taches dorsales uniques sur chaque segment" [Abdomen ... with unique back splotches on each segment]. {declinable adjective}

doubledayi, Enallagma (Selys, 1850: 209)
[Original designation: *Agrion doubledayi* Selys]
"Je nommerai l'espèce américaine *Agrion Doubledayi* (De Selys) en l'honneur de M. Edw. Doubleday, qui l'à prise communément à St John Bluff, en Floride." [I will name this American species *Agrion Doubledayi* (De Selys) in honor of Mr. Edw. Doubleday [Edward Doubleday (1811-1849), English entomologist], who commonly captured it at St John Bluff, in Florida].
                                                            {noun in the genitive case}

Dromogomphus Selys, 1854: 58
    Gr. δρόμος = foot race + γόμφος = bolt, for shipbuilding or for other uses (see *Gomphus*).

The name seems to be inspired by the extraordinary long legs: SELYS 1854: "Fémurs postérieurs excessivement longs, portant 5-7 épines beaucoup plus fortes que l'autres." [Metafemurs excessively long, bearing 5-7 spines much stronger than the others.] and again emphasized by SELYS, 1858, 376: "J'avais établi pour ce type, qui, par ses longs pieds, se rapproche du Genre *Hagenius*, un sous-genre sous le nom de *Dromogomphus*, dans la Synopsis des Gomphines." [I had established for this type, which, from its long feet, approaches the Genus *Hagenius*, a subgenus with the name of *Dromogomphus*, in the Synopsis of the Gomphines]. {Masculine}

dryas, Lestes Kirby, 1890: 160
>Gr. Δρυάς = a Dryad, a nymph whose life was bound up with that of her tree.

>To replace the preoccupied name *Lestes nympha* Selys 1840 (Homonym of *Agrion nympha* Hansemann 1823, which was a synonym of *Agrion barbara* Fabricius 1798) Kirby chose a different type of nymph. As trees are without any importance for the European habitats of *Lestes dryas*, to interpret the name as a reference to habitat cannot be correct.{noun in apposition}

dubium, Enallagma Root, 1924: 321
>L. *dubius –a –um* = uncertain, doubtful, dubious.

>"... it seems best to describe this specimen as a new species. I propose for it the name of *E. dubium*, in recognition both of the doubtful advisability of basing a new species on a single specimen and of the possibility, that further study may indicate that *pictum, concisum* and *dubium* are all varieties of a single species." {declinable adjective}

dugesi, Rhionaeschna (Calvert, 1905: 184)
[Original designation: *Aeshna dugesi* Calvert]
>"Dr. A. Dugès: 1 ♂". Alfredo Dugès (birth name- Alfred Auguste Delsescautz Dugès; April 16, 1826 – January 7, 1910) was a French-born, Mexican physician and naturalist originating from Montpellier. He was the son of zoologist Antoine Louis Dugès (1797-1838). Alfredo Dugès is largely remembered for his extensive studies of Mexican herpetology. He collected the type specimen which bears his name.{noun in the genitive case}

durum, Enallagma (Hagen, 1861: 87)
[Original designation: *Agrion durum* Hagen]
>L. *durus –a –um* = hard, rough, troublesome.

>As Hagen gives no explanation, it remains uncertain how to interpret this name. {declinable adjective}

Dythemis Hagen, 1861: 162
    Gr. δύο = two + *–themis* see *Celithemis*.

    The name might refer to the bituberculated 10th abdominal segment in the females: "vulva disclosed, the lamina emarginated, the segment following it is carinated, bituberculated."
                                                             {Feminine}

ebrium, Enallagma (Hagen, 1861: 89)
[Original designation: *Agrion ebrium* Hagen]
    L. *ebrius –a –um* = drunken, allusion unknown.

    Why Hagen chose this name, he does not explain.
                                                          {declinable adjective}

edmundo, Ophiogomphus Needham, 1951: 41
    The species is named after the describer's grandson, Edmund Needham (not explained in the 1st description).
                                                   {noun in apposition}

eiseni, Enallagma Calvert, 1895: 486
    "This species is named after Dr. Gustav Eisen, the well known student of Oligochactous worms, to whose labors so much of the present paper is due." August Gustaf Eisen, (* 2. August 1847 in Stockholm, Schweden; † 29. October 1940 in Manhattan, New York, USA) was a Swedish–American zoologist and archaeologist. From 1892-1899 he was curator at the Natural History Museum in San Francisco. He published several works on earthworms and devoted himself to including chromosome research into entomology.   {noun in the genitive case}

elaps, Erpetogomphus Selys, 1858: 330
> *Elaps* is the former name of the coral snake genus *Micrurus* (inspired by Gr. ἔλαψ, which originally meant some seafish and was also interpreted as scaly or dumb). It is the type genus for the family Elapidae

> The name is not explained in SELYS 1858, but certainly chosen because of the semantic affinity to other names referring to snakes in the genera *Ophiogomphus* and *Erpetogomphus* (q.v.).
>
> {noun in apposition}

elisa, Celithemis (Hagen, 1861: 182)
[Original designation: *Diplax elisa* Hagen]
> The species is named after Johanna Maria Elise Gerhards (1832-1917), Hagen's wife (not mentioned in the 1st descr.).
>
> {noun in apposition}

elongata, Somatochlora (Scudder, 1866: 218)
[Original designation: *Cordulia elongata* Scudder]
> L. *elongatus –a –um* : past participle of *elongo* = to elongate.

> The name might be a reference to the pattern of the prothorax: "pleura with ... an elongated metathoracic spot brownish yellow (in life lemon yellow ...)"; but alternatively it might be a reference to the relatively long abdomen (the species exceeds the other ones described by Scudder in the genus *Cordulia* by far!)
>
> {declinable past participle}

emma, Argia Kennedy, 1915: 271
> "... which I have named for my mother [Emma Kennedy (*1850)], who has ever encouraged my interest in entomology."
>
> {noun in apposition}

Enallagma Charpentier, 1840: 21
>   Gr. ἐνάλλαγμα = change.

This name was meant by Charpentier as 'giving the possibility of confusion'. The taxon was intended to contain all Coenagrionids, the males of which had a blue abdomen with black markings and which were not distinguished easily. Within his delineation of *Agrion* he states "Omnes species permagnam, quod ad colorem et picturam attinet, inter se habent similitudinem (– qua de causa prius hoc subgenus "Enallagma" vocavi –) et utriusque sexus segmenta abdominis, imprimis priora, thoraci propiora, accurate sunt examinanda, quia eorum pictura diversa optime illae species distingui et secerni poterunt" [All species bear a very great resemblance to each other concerning color and pattern (– therefore previously I called this subgenus "*Enallagma*" –) and the abdominal segments, especially the first ones which are nearer to the thorax, of both sexes are to be examined accurately, because by their differing markings the species may be distinguished and separated best]. However his proposal had no effect until the valid description of the genus by Selys 1876a: 496 (Cowley 1934: 241). Charpentier's genus *Agrion*, used in this explanation, contains the rest of Zygoptera from the genus *Agrion* sensu Fabricius except *Epallage, Calopteryx, Lestes, Sympecma, Pyrrhosoma, Erythromma, Ischnura* and *Platycnemis*.
{Neuter}

ensigera, Somatochlora Martin, 1906: 29
>   L. *ensis* = sword + *–ger –gera –gerum* (in compounds) = bearing, referring to female ovipositor.

By this name Martin describes the female ovipositor: "écaille vulvaire très longue, en forme d'une épée pointue" [Vulvar scale very long, shaped like a pointed sword]   {declinable adjective}

Epiaeschna Hagen, 1875: 86

The Gr.prefix ἐπι-is plurivalent; among other meanings it may have a sense of addition (to) or superiority (over) + *–aeschna* see *Aeshna*.

As Hagen gives no explanation of the name, its interpretation is difficult. It probably denotes that a new Aeshnid genus is added to the other ones (in SELYS, 1883 *Epiaeshna* follows on p. 729 directly after *Aeshna* s.s.; there the first description of the characteristics of the genus are given). Alternatively, the name perhaps may allude to the size of the species *E. heros* being larger than other *Aeshna*.

There is a difficulty as to the naming of *Epiaeschna*. In HAGEN 1873a, *Proc.Boston Soc. nat. Hist.* 15, 271 the genus name is for the first time proferred, and it is done in combination with the species *A. heros* Fabr. This should constitute a valid description of the genus, the characteristics of which are given in SELYS 1883, 729. [in HAGEN 1875, 36 there is only: "*Aeshna heros* ♂♀ (subgenus *Epiaeschna* Selys)" without any other explanation].

{Feminine}

Epitheca Burmeister, 1839: 845

Gr. ἐπιθήκη = cover, referring to the spectacular vulvar plate in the females.

"Nomen ex vocabulis Graecis ἐπί et θήκη compositum, propter longissimas foeminae appendices ad valvam oviparam" [the name is composed of the Greek words ἐπί and θήκη because of the very long "appendages" of the oviparous valve] (CHARPENTIER 1840, 11). BURMEISTER (1839: 845) mentions that the genus *Epitheca* will be established by Charpentier. However, as he also reports on which species it would be based he already had given a valid description of the new genus and thus is recognised as its author now. The species, on which the genus was based, was not known to Burmeister but only from its description by Charpentier.

{Feminine}

eponina, *Celithemis* (Drury, 1773: 86)
[Original designation: *Libellula eponina* Drury]

    Drury never explains his names, which are almost always female names from Roman antiquity. One possibility could be: Eponina who was the faithful wife of Julius Sabinus, a Celtic prince, who led his people in a rebellion against the Roman emperor Vespasian. After the rebellion failed, she lived with her husband underground for almost nine years, until the couple were detected and executed at Rome. Plutarch, who has alone told this story of love unto death, concludes his tale by saying that there was nothing during Vespasian's reign to match the horror of this atrocious deed, and that, in retribution for it, the vengeance of the gods fell upon Vespasian, and in a short time after wrought the extirpation of his entire family. The story of the couple, with emphasis on the loyalty of Eponina (known as Éponine), became popular in France during the 18th and 19th centuries and was obviously known to Drury.

{noun in apposition}

eremita, *Aeshna* Scudder, 1866: 213

    L. *eremita* = hermit (from Gr. ἐρημίτης = of the desert {where the first hermits had taken refuge}).

Named after type locality New Hampshire, [Coos County], Hermit Lake. SCUDDER, 1866, 211: "some species of Odonata taken ... at the Glen, White Mountains. Most of them were taken at Hermit Lake." p. 213:"White Mts, August".

{noun in apposition}

Erpetogomphus Selys, 1858: 329
    Gr. ἑρπετόν = reptile, esp. snake + *Gomphus* (q.v.)

This genus was created for three American species, which Selys wanted to separate from the genus *Ophiogomphus* (serpent-gomphus, q.v.): "J'avais placé les trois espèces [*elaps – cophias – crotalinus*] que nous décrivons dans le sous-genre *Ophiogomphus*, qui a pour type le *serpentinus* d'Europe. Il a fallu les en séparer et créer un sous-genre distinct pour elles, parce que le pénis du mâle ne porte pas de dent au seconde article , et que nous avons considéré ce caractère, découvert par M. Hagen, comme assez important." [I had placed the three species [*elaps – cophias – crotalinus*] which we have described in the subgenus *Ophiogomphus*, which has for the type *serpentinus* from Europe. It was necessary to separate them and create a distinct sub-genus for them, because the penis of the male does not bear a tooth on the second segment, and we have considered this character, discovered by M. Hagen, as quite important]. {Masculine}

erratica, Ischnura Calvert, 1895: 491
    L. *erraticus –a –um* = erratic.

The species seems erratic in that that the females lack the ventral spine on the 8th segment differently from other *Ischnura*: "To write of the female that it possesses no ventral spine on the eighth segment is almost equivalent to excluding this species from *Ischnura*, but it is here so referred, with much hesitation, …" {declinable adjective}

erronea, Cordulegaster Hagen in Selys, 1878: 688
    L. *erroneus –a –um* = straying or erroneous.

Hagen does not explain the name. But, as according to the first description, it was observed in Kentucky in June and in North Carolina in July to September perhaps it is a reference to different times of observation in different States.

{declinable adjective}

Erythemis Hagen, 1861: 168
    Gr. ἐρυθρός = red + *–themis* see *Celithemis*.

Hagen based his taxon on three species, in which at least the abdomen of the males is red or ferruginous.   {Feminine}

Erythrodiplax Brauer, 1868: 368
    Gr. ἐρυθρός = red + *Diplax*.

Diplax is the name Charpentier (1840, 12) chose for a libellulid genus: "Nomen e Graecis vocabulis δίς et πλάξ derivatum ob prothoracis formam ... Prothorax in postica parte elevatus vel erectus in plagulam vel discum a duobus semicirculis formatum" [The name is derived from the Greek words δίς (= twice, doubly) and πλάξ (= anything flat and broad) because of the shape of the prothorax. ... The prothorax is elevated or erect in its hind part into a little area or disk formed by two semicircles]. That means this shape of the prothorax, which is at the base of the name, is similar to the upper case letter B. But Charpentier was unaware that this genus already had been described by Newman in 1833 under the name of *Sympetrum* (q.v.) [HAGEN 1888]. For a long time the priority of *Sympetrum* was overlooked. So many new genera split from Charpentier's libellulid genus have *–diplax* as the second element of their name, whereas *Diplax* itself is no longer in use.

The denomination 'red *Diplax*' suits the type species *E. corallina* [L. = coralline] but there is a difficulty; that species was classified as *Erythemis corallina* by BRAUER (1868: 722) on the very page on which he described the genus *Erythrodiplax*. For this he only listed species which are not red, except for one, *Libellula plebeia* Rambur, the name of which was preoccupied by the species *Libellula plebeja* Burmeister (now *Erythemis plebeja*). Its valid name is *Erythrodiplax corallina* (Brauer), the very species KIRBY (1889: 278) made type species of the genus.   {Feminine}

eurinus, Lestes Say, 1839: 36
   L. *eurinus –a –um* = eastern.

SAY (1839) describes three species from North America, which he deems to pertain to the genus *Lestes* Leach (one of them really being *Hetaerina americana* (Fabricius)). Of these, *eurinus* has the easternmost distribution. {declinable adjective}

eutainia, Erpetogomphus Calvert, 1905: 162
   Eutainia is the former name for a garter snake genus (from Gr. εὖ = well + ταινία = band, fillet).

The name is not explained in the first description but it is consistent semantically with other reptile names in the genus since its foundation. {noun in apposition}

exclamationis, Zoniagrion (Selys, 1876a: 1251)
   [Original designation: *Agrion exclamationis* Selys]

   L. *exclamationis*: genitive singular of *exclamatio* = exclamation.

In this species the antehumeral thoracic stripe forms an exclamation mark: "Devant du thorax noir jusqu'un peu au delà de la suture humérale, avec une large raie juxtahumérale commençant en bas et n'allant qu'à la moitié de la hauteur, et repairassant en haut contre les sinus en une point rond, ce qui forme le signe (!) d'exclamation." [In front of the black thorax up to a little beyond the humeral suture, with a broad antehumeral [?] line beginning at the bottom and going only half the height, and continuing upwards against the sinuses to a round point, which forms the exclamation mark(!)].
{noun in the genitive case}

exilis, *Phanogomphus* (Selys, 1854: 55)
[Original designation: *Gomphus exilis* Selys]
    L. *exilis –is –e* = slender.

The slenderness of the species is mentioned neither in particular in the first description nor in SELYS 1858, except that in the latter publication the French name on p. 416 is given as *Gomphus mince* [= slim, lean or slender *Gomphus*], which means that Selys thought the reason for the name to be self-evident when viewing a specimen. The first description says "abdomen un peu dilaté aux trois avant-derniers segments" [Abdomen slightly dilated on the penultimate segments] and in Selys 1858: 417, "L'abdomen est à peu près comme chez le *pallidus*" [The abdomen is about the same as in *pallidus*] [not like in *G. minutus*] and "♂ ressemble au *minutus* en petit" [♂ resembles a smallish *minutus*]. For *pallidus* from SELYS 1858: 406 "Abdomen un peu plus épais à la base et aux trois avant derniers segments" [Abdomen a little thicker at the base in the three last segments] which means that the differences in breadth are not so striking as in other *Gomphus* species.
                                         {declinable adjective}

exsulans, *Enallagma* (Hagen, 1861: 82)
[Original designation: *Agrion* (subgenus *Ischnura*) *exsulans* Hagen]
    L. *exsulans*: present participle of *exsulo* = to live in exile, to be a stranger.

Hagen does not explain why he chose this denomination, but the species name semantically is similar to *Argia extranea* described in the same publication (see below)   {present participle}

externus, Gomphurus (Hagen in Selys, 1858: 671)
[Original designation: *Gomphus externus* Hagen in Selys]
    L. *externus –a –um* = external.

The name refers to distinctive features on the outside of the legs: "Pieds assez longs, noirâtres, l'intérieur des fémurs antérieurs, une bande externe mal arrêtée aux autres, et une ligne étroite externe aux tibias, jaune pâle. Les fémurs ont des épines en tubercules; les postérieurs ont en outre une série externe d'épines, dont une douzaine sont successivement plus longues." [Feet fairly long, blackish, the interior of the anterior femurs [with], an external band discontinued on the others, and a narrow pale yellow external line to the tibiae. The femurs have spines on the tubercles; the posterior ones also have an external series of spines, of which a dozen are successively longer].
                                                {declinable adjective}

extranea, Argia (Hagen, 1861: 92)
[Original designation: *Agrion extraneum* Hagen]
    L. *extraneus –a –um* = extraneous, foreign, strange.

The name might refer to occurrence of the species just outside U.S: "*Hab*. Tampico, Mexico (Saussure)". {declinable adjective}

exusta, Ladona (Say, 1839: 29)
[Original designation: *Libellula exusta* Say]
    L. *exustus –a –um*: past participle of *exuro* = to burn up.

This name refers to the ashy abdominal pubescence of the males: "♂ Body yellowish brown, covered with a cinereous pubescence".   {declinable past participle}

fasciata, *Celithemis* Kirby, 1889: 326
>L. *fascia* = band, bandage + suffix *–atus –a –um* = marked with, equipped with.

By this name dark bands on the wings are referred to. Kirby describes the dark markings of the fore wings very extensively; on the hind wings he writes: "on the hind wing the apical patch and the middle band differ only in being more extended".
{declinable adjective}

ferruginea, *Orthemis* (Fabricius, 1775: 423)
[Original designation: *Libellula ferruginea* Fabricius]
>L. *ferrugineus –a –um* = rust-colored, ferrugineous.

Fabricius describes the species as: "corpore ferrugineo" [with a rust-colored abdomen], but that rather refers to females and immature males (or his dehydrated specimen), for mature males show a rosy purple color. {declinable adjective}

fervida, *Erythrodiplax* (Erichson, 1848: 584)
[Original designation: *Libellula fervida* Erichson]
>L. *fervidus –a –um* = boiling hot; fiery, torrid, roused, fervid; glowing; hot blooded.

Of the diverse meanings of Latin *fervidus* the only one sufficiently fitting seems to be the last but one, that is to say 'glowing', which evokes an impression of coloration. The author gives as overall impression: "Röthlich gelb. Die Stirn gleichfarbig" [Reddish yellow, the frons of the same color]. Subsequently extensive yellow markings of the "brown" abdomen are described, which contribute to an image of glowing matter with light sparks close to it. To refer the name to "the bright coloration in the wings" (PAULSON&DUNKLE 2018, 64) is rather not advisable, for these are described thus: "Flügel wasserklar, an der Wurzel beim Männchen breit, dunkelgelb. beim Weibchen ist nur der Wurzelrand der Hinterflügel gelblich" [Wings hyaline, at the base in the male broad, dark yellow. In the female only the margin of the base of the hind wings is yellowish].
{declinable adjective}

filosa, Somatochlora (Hagen, 1861: 136)
[Original designation: *Cordulia filosa* Hagen]
> L. *filum* = thread, string + *–osus –a –um* = full of, abounding with, spectacular by.

> The name might refer to the narrow thoracic stripes: "Thorax brassy-green, the sides, each, with two, obsolete, yellow lines".
{declinable adjective}

flavescens, Pantala (Fabricius, 1798: 285)
[Original designation: *Libellula flavescens* Fabricius]
> L. *flavescens*: present participle of *flavesco* = to become yellow. It is to be noted that compounds of color names ending with *–escens* often denote a lighter stage of coloration as if the process of dyeing had been prematurely halted (hence yellowish).

> The description evokes the coloration of tenerals and females: "L(ibellula) alis hyalinis: stigmate niveo, corpore flavescente" [Libellulid with hyaline wings: with a white pterostigma and a yellowish body]. {present participle}

flavida, Libellula Rambur, 1842: 58
> L. *flavidus –a –um* = yellowish.

> Rambur has "f{l}avo-rufa" [= reddish yellow] as the first words of the description; therefore the name pertains to the first impression of overall coloration of his female specimen.
{declinable adjective}

fletcheri, Williamsonia Williamson, 1923a: 96
> "At the suggestion of Mr. McDunnough I take pleasure in naming this Canadian dragonfly for Dr James Fletcher [1852-1908], 'first Dominion Entomologist, who was a keen collector in all orders' and whose work is comparable with that of Dr. Lintner, for whom the species from the United States is named." But it might be noted that there had been an interesting controversy between Williamson and Howe about naming the species (WHITE & O'BRIEN 2017). {noun in the genitive case}

floridensis, Didymops Davis, 1921: 110
> From the type locality + *–ensis –is –e* = adjectival suffix indicating place of origin.

"Type, male. Lakeland, Florida, March 28, 1912."
{declinable adjective}

forcipata, Somatochlora (Scudder, 1866: 216)
[Original designation: *Cordulia forcipata* Scudder]
> L. *forceps* (stem *forcip–*) = a pair of tongs, pincers + suffix *–atus –ata –atum* = provided with.

The males of the species have forceps-like cerci.

This is probably the explanation of the relevant morphology "inferior appendage triangular, bluntly pointed, the edge of the under surface raised to the basal half, curved upwards, the tip minutely uncinate above and fully reaching the tubercle of the superior pair." "Superior pair carinate inferiorly, and on the basal half exteriorly, sub-cylindrical; when viewed from above the basal half is straight, swollen, constricted just beyond the base, especially on the interior edge, the apical half bent slightly outwarts, then inwards, the inner edge rounded off to the pointed apex; when viewed laterally they are seen to be curved downwards considerably, the apex laminate, the lower edge with a small basal exterior tooth, beyond the middle a prominent tubercle, and between them the interior edge produced to a rather large rounded lamella, more prominent toward the base;" {declinable adjective}

forcipatus, Lestes Rambur, 1842: 246
> L. *forceps* (stem *forcip–*) = a pair of tongs, pincers + suffix *–atus –ata –atum* = provided with.

"appendices supérieurs tellement semblables à ceux de la *Forcipula* qu'il est difficile de voir des différences bien sensibles" [superior appendages so similar to those of *forcipula* [= diminutive of *forceps*] {= *L. sponsa* Hansemann} that it is difficult to see very subtle differences.] {declinable adjective}

forensis, *Libellula* Hagen, 1861: 154
> L. *forensis* –*is* –*e* = of the market, of the forum, public, forensic (in Hagen's time also used for external, foreign).
>
> Hagen does not explain his choice of name. So there is no certainty about its meaning. {declinable adjective}

forficula, *Lestes* Rambur, 1842: 247
> L. *forficula* = little scissors.
>
> The name probably refers to the male paraprocts, which are similar to those of the European species *Lestes sponsa* i.e. like scissors: "appendices inférieurs comme chez la *Sponsa*, laissant entre eux un éspace triangulaire" [Inferior appendages as in *sponsa*, leaving between them a triangular space].
>
> {noun in apposition}

franklini, *Somatochlora* (Selys, 1878: 195)
[Original designation: *Epitheca franklini* Selys]
> Named after the John Franklin (1768-1847), arctic explorer, during whose first expedition the described specimen was collected (see HÄMÄLÄINEN 2016a). {noun in the genitive case}

fraternus, *Gomphurus* (Say, 1839: 16)
[Original designation: *Aeshna fraterna* Say]
> L. *fraternus* –*a* –*um* = brotherly. Say explains the name thus: "It resembles *forcipata*, Fabr., very closely, but the feet are yellowish above; …". This statement sounds unambiguous, but it is not. For the reference species is not *Onychogomphus forcipatus* (Linnaeus, 1758), which by its spectacular appendages differs very much from the species in question, but *Gomphus vulgatissimus* (Linnaeus, 1758), which is now the type species of the genus *Gomphus* Leach. (For information on how this mistake came about see NEEDHAM 1901, 165 footnote).
>
> {declinable adjective}

frigida, Leucorrhinia Hagen, 1890a: 231
[as *Leucorhinia frigida* Hagen]
    L. *frigidus –a –um* = cold, chilling.

> The name probably refers to the range of the species in relatively cold (= northern) regions. A reference to "frost" on abdomen of mature males, as suggested by PAULSON & DUNKLE 2012 seems less probable, as Hagen describes a species *L. glacialis* [= icy, frozen], with a rather synonymic name in the same publication, where no pruinosity of the abdominal base occurs.
> {declinable adjective}

fugax, Dythemis Hagen, 1861: 163
    L. *fugax* = apt to flee, fleeing, timid, shy.

> This name seems to refer to behavior; but HAGEN 1861 based his description on the collection of C.R. von Osten-Sacken and other collections and a vast correspondence. At that time Hagen, living at Königsberg, Prussia [now Kaliningrad, Russia], had never seen any North American dragonfly alive. So it seems, that he first of all looked for short, easily memorable names, which would not have to be adapted, if the species might be transferred to a genus of different gender (When creating his genera with names ending in *–themis* he had done this to avoid change in gender for the species separated from the genus *Libellula* Linnaeus, see HAGEN 1888). In his newly created genus *Dythemis*, of the ten new species five have such names (*D. velox, fugax, mendax, praecox, pertinax*).   {adjective}

fumipennis, Argia (Burmeister, 1839: 819)
[Original designation: *Agrion fumipenne* Burmeister]
    L. *fumus* = smoke + *–pennis –is –e* (in compounds) = –winged.

> The species takes its name from the shadowed wings: "alis fumatis, venis omnibus pallidioribus" [with smoky wings, all the veins being paler], which feature however is not true for all populations of the species.   {declinable adjective}

funerea, Erythrodiplax (Hagen, 1861: 158)
[Original designation: *Libellula funerea* Hagen]
    L. *funereus –a –um* = funereal

    The name probably refers to the mostly black wings and coloration of mature males: "Black ... wings blackish fuscous".
{declinable adjective}

furcata, Brachymesia (Hagen, 1861: 169)
[Original designation: *Erythemis furcata* Hagen]
    L. *furca* = a two-pronged fork + suffix *–atus –ata –atum* = equipped with.

    The name may refer either to the male epiproct: "the inferior appendage short, quadrangular, the apex forked" or to the female genital lamina: "anterior genital lamina prominent, forked".
{declinable adjective}

furcifer, Arigomphus (Hagen in Selys, 1878: 458)
[Original designation: *Gomphus furcifer* Hagen in Selys]
    L. *furca* = a two-pronged fork + *–fer –fera –ferum* (in compounds) bearing, probably referring to branched male cerci.

    The name probably refers to branched male cerci: "la forme des appendices anals. Les supérieurs sont divariquées, plus courts que le 10e segment, fortement divariquès épais" [the form of the anal appendages. The superiors are divided, shorter than the 10th segment, strongly spread asunder, thick]. {declinable adjective}

furcillata, Gomphaeschna (Say, 1839: 14)
[Original designation: *Aeschna furcillata* Say]
    L. *furcilla* = little fork + suffix *–atus –ata –atum* = equipped with.

    The forked male epiproct is characteristic for this species: "This may readily be distinguished by the widely forked form of the inferior caudal process." {declinable adjective}

fusca, Erythrodiplax (Rambur, 1842: 78)
[Original designation: *Libellula fusca* Rambur]
    L. *fuscus –a –um* = dark, swarthy, dusky, tawny.

    Rambur describes his specimen as "fusco-rufa" [dusky red].
    {declinable adjective}

gaigei, Libellula Gloyd, 1938: 2
    "In recognition of his unfailing encouragement of studies on Odonata and of his personal association with zoological field work in Yucatán, I wish to name this species in honor of Professor Frederick M. Gaige of the University of Michigan [1890-1976]." {noun in the genitive case}

gemina, Ischnura (Kennedy, 1917: 497)
[Original designation: *Celaenura gemina* Kennedy]
    L. *geminus –a –um* = twin

    The name comes from the similarity to *Ischnura denticollis*: "This is a small species with coloration almost identical with that of *denticollis*." {declinable adjective}

geminatum, Enallagma Kellicott, 1895: 239
[as *Enallagma geminata* Kellicott]
    L. *geminatus –a –um*: past participle of *gemino* = to double, hence doubled, twinned, an allusion to the striking similarity to *E. divagans*, for which Kellicott had at first mistaken it: "the appendages of the male, except the inner tooth, which was first overlooked, are so nearly like those of *divagans*, that a mere description scarcely separates them". {declinable past participle}

geminatus, Hylogomphus (Carle, 1979: 423)
[Original designation: *Gomphus geminatus* Carle]
    L. *geminatus –a –um*: past participle of *gemino* = to double, hence doubled, twinned.

    "from *geminatus*, L. participle meaning "twinned", referring to the twin lateral brown stripes of the adult thorax."
    {declinable past participle}

georgiana, Somatochlora Walker, 1925: 98
> Type locality + L. suffix *–anus –ana –anum* = pertaining to.

> The name refers to the type locality: "*Holotype*. ♀ Leesburg, Georgia, July 6, 1923 (F.M. Root, U.S.N.M.)".
>
> {declinable adjective}

glacialis, Leucorrhinia Hagen, 1890a: 234
[as *Leucorhinia* [sic] *glacialis* Hagen]
> L. *glacialis –is –e* = icy, frozen, glacial.

> The name is probably due to the northern geographic range of the species: "I have sixteen males before me from Massachusetts; Cape Breton, Nova Scotia; London, Ontario; Michipicoten on Lake Superior; and Reno, Nevada (Mr. Morrison, 1878)".
>
> {declinable adjective}

Gomphaeschna Selys, 1871b: 413
> *Gomphus* (q.v.) + *–aeschna* (see *Aeshna*).

> The name refers to the forked male epiproct looking like that of a *Gomphus*: "Le sous-genre *Gomphaeshna* est crée pour recevoir la *Gynacantha quadrifida* de Rambur, dont les caractères sont mentionnés dans la description de l'espèce." [The subgenus *Gomphaeshna* is created to receive *Gynacantha quadrifida* of Rambur, the characteristics of which are mentioned in the description of the species.] [Selys 1883, 734: "Groupe très characterisé par ... l'appendice anal inferieur du mâle fourchu; cette dernière disposition ne se trouve chez aucune autre *Aeschnine*." [Group very much characterized by ... the inferior anal appendix of the male forked; this last arrangement is not to be found in any other *Aeschnine*]. {Feminine}

Gomphurus Needham, 1901: 446

γόμφος = bolt, for shipbuilding or for other uses + –ουρος –ος –ον (in compounds) –tailed [from οὐρά = tail; in entomology used for abdomen].

In the first description Needham does not give an explanation of this taxon, at first proposed as a subgenus. But in a later publication (Needham 1947, 327) it reads: "In form of body the species of *Gomphurus* are shorter and stockier [than those of *Stylurus*, (q.v.)] with a more heavily clubbed abdomen, as the generic name indicates." Therefore the clubbed abdomen in this genus is at the base of the name. {Masculine}

Gomphus Leach, 1815: 137

Gr. γόμφος = bolt, for shipbuilding or for other uses

Leach describes his genus *Gomphus*, which he based on the one species *Libellula vulgatissima* Linnaeus as follows: "Wings of the males angulated at their anal edge: Abdomen clavate in both sexes". This genus shares the first feature with Leach's genera *Cordulegaster* (q.v.) and *Aeshna*, from which he separated the forementioned two taxa and *Anax*. The genus therefore got its name in reference to the expanded posterior abdomen in both sexes; but for the females this is true only for a few species, while in many species this feature applies for the males. The genus *Gomphus* is no longer valid for North America, as WARE & AL., 2016 have established a new classification by which the 38 former *Gomphus* species are shifted to the taxa *Gomphurus*, *Hylogomphus*, *Phanogomphus* and *Stenogomphurus* (q. v.). These have been raised from subgeneric to generic rank. Therefore only old world taxa remain in the genus *Gomphus*. {Masculine}

gonzalezi, Gomphurus (Dunkle, 1992: 79)
[Original designation: *Gomphus gonzalezi* Dunkle]
> "Named for Enrique González Soriano [See p. 42], in recognition of his studies on Mexican Odonata."
>
> {noun in the genitive case}

gracilis, Nehalennia Morse, 1895: 274
L. *gracilis –is –e* = slender, slim, lean.

In the first description it reads: "similar to *N. irene*, but even slenderer". {declinable adjective}

grafiana, Boyeria Williamson, 1907a: 1
L. suffix *–anus –ana –anum* = pertaining to.

"This species is very properly named for J. L. Graf, a devoted and careful, though withal, silent student of nature, who first detected a difference in the Boyerias at Ohio Pyle."
{declinable adjective}

grandis, Archilestes (Rambur, 1842: 244)
[Original designation: *Lestes grandis* Rambur]
L. *grandis –is –e* = grand, large, great.

The name refers to its large size: "resemblant à la *Forcipula*, mais beaucoup plus grande" [similar to *forcipula*, but substantially larger].

Lestes forcipula is a junior synonym of the European species *L. sponsa* Hansemann. {declinable adjective}

graslinellus, *Phanogomphus* (Walsh, 1862: 394)
[Original designation: *Gomphus graslinellus* Walsh]
>L. suffix *–ellus –a –um* denotes a diminutive; *graslinellus* therefore = a little *graslini*.

>At the base of the name is the similarity to *Gomphus graslini* Rambur of Europe, named after Adolphe-Hercule de Graslin (1802-1882), French entomologist: "Its European representative, *G. graslini*, has ... two yellow vittae (anterior and posterior?) on the outside of all thighs, whereas *graslinellus*, like *fraternus*, has only a posterior yellow vitta on the anterior femora."
>{declinable adjective}

gravida, *Brachymesia* (Calvert, 1890: 35)
[Original designation: *Lepthemis gravida* (Hagen mss.) Calvert]
>L. *gravidus –a –um* = laden, filled, full, swollen, pregnant.

>The shape of the abdomen may have induced the name, for it is thickest on segment 6: "The abdomen is compressed at base, slightly narrower at 3, becoming a little wider at 6, thence decreasing slightly to the apex." {declinable adjective}

Gynacantha Rambur, 1842: 209
>Gr. γυνή = woman + ἄκανθα = thorn, prickle. This refers to the spines on the tenth abdominal segment of females. "… dernier segment chez les femelles, saillant et prolongé inférieurement, garni d'épines longues (2 à 3 seulement dans les espéces que je connais)" [last segment in females, prominent and extended below, furnished with long spines (only 2-3 in the species I know)]. {Feminine}

hageni, *Enallagma* (Walsh, 1863: 234)
[Original designation: *Agrion hageni* Walsh]
>"for which I now propose the name of *Agr. Hageni*". After Hermann A. Hagen (See p. 43), German-American odonatologist. {noun in the genitive case}

hageni, Tanypteryx (Selys, 1879: 68)
[Original designation: *Tachopteryx hageni* Selys]

"Je dédie à mon ancien ami et collaborateur, le Dr Hagen, cette espèce intéressante qui forme la seconde du genre connu jusqu'ici par la seul *T. Thoreyi* qui habite aux États-Unies les États orientaux" [I dedicate to my old friend and collaborator, Dr. Hagen [See p. 43], this interesting species which forms the second of the genus known hitherto only by *T. Thoreyi* which inhabits the Eastern States of the United States].

{noun in the genitive case}

hagenii, Micrathyria Kirby, 1890: 41

Although there is no explanation in the first description the species certainly is named after Hermann A. Hagen (See p. 43), German-American odonatologist.

{noun in the genitive case}

Hagenius Selys, 1854: 82

After Hermann A. Hagen (See p. 43), German-American odonatologist, with whom Selys closely collaborated in his epoch-making publications at least since 1850.   {Masculine}

harknessi, Argia Calvert, 1899: 378

"The specific name is in honor of Dr. H. W. Harkness, past President of the California Academy of Sciences, to whom much of the success attending the expeditions to Baja California and to Tepic is due." Harvey Willson "H.W." Harkness (1821–1901) was an American mycologist and natural historian best known for his early descriptions of California fungal species.

{noun in the genitive case}

hastata, Ischnura (Say, 1839: 38)
[Original designation: *Agrion hastata* Say]

L. *hastatus –a –um* = provided with a spear /spears.

The name is induced by the shape of the abdominal spots of the males: "tergum with green hastate spots and lines".

{declinable adjective}

Helocordulia Needham in Needham and Betten, 1901: 495
　gr.ἔλος = marsh meadow / backwater + *Cordulia* (q.v.).

The name seems to refer to a type of biotope, but Needham does not explain which one he had in mind when choosing the name. 　　　　　　　　　　　　　　　　　　　{Feminine}

herbida, *Brachymesia* (Gundlach, 1889: 261)
[Original designation: *Libellula herbida* Gundlach]
　L. *herbidus –a –um* = full of grass, grassy, but the word may also been taken for 'green' (like *pratum herbidum* – a green meadow).

The name *L. herbida*, which initially seems to refer to a biotope, was proferred by HAGEN 1868b (*Proc. Boston Soc. nat. Hist.* 11, 292) and GUNDLACH, 1889 supplied the description of a ♀ of the species, which does not contain any hint on habitat, but some to a greenish main color of the insect: "torax pardo olivado. Abdomen en los quatro primeros segmentos olivado-pardo, claro; los cinco siguientes son del mismo color, pero con una mancha triangular negra que con su base ocupa todo el bordo apical de los segmentos" [thorax brownish olivaceous. Abdomen in the first four segments clearly olivaceous brown; the five following segments are of the same color, but with a triangular black spot, the base of which occupies the whole apical margin]. So most probably the name was chosen due to coloration. 　　　　　　　　　　　　　　{declinable adjective}

heros, *Epiaeschna* (Fabricius, 1798: 285)
[Original designation: *Aeschna heros* Fabricius]
　Gr. ἥρως = a hero.

The name refers to large size. In his description Fabricius states the Eurasian species *Aeshna grandis* (Linnaeus) to be even larger "A. grandis adhuc maior"; but whereas that statement is not true, as DIJKSTRA & LEWINGTON 2006, 146 give for the total length of *Aeshna grandis* 70-77 mm and PAULSON 2009, 196 has 82-91 mm for this species, it shows that Fabricius had the large size in mind when naming the species. 　{noun in apposition}

Hesperagrion Calvert, 1902: 103
> Gr. ἕσπερος –ov = western; for *Agrion* (a word for damselfly) see *Acanthagrion*.
>
> The name reflects the geographic range of the genus: "*Hab.* UNITED STATES, Tombstone ..., in Arizona ...; MEXICO..."
> {Neuter}

Hetaerina Hagen in Selys, 1853: 30
> Gr. ἑταίρα = companion, courtesan + suffix –ινός –ή –όν = related to, like a...
>
> Whereas Hagen does not explain the name, it is clearly related to a female as often is concerning damselflies, as in Linné's species names *virgo* or *puella*. {Feminine}

heterodon, *Erpetogomphus* Garrison, 1994a: 230
> Originally *Heterodon* BAIRD & GIRARD, 1852 was a hognose snake genus [named from Gr. prefix ἕτερο- = of different ... + –οδων = –toothed, referring to the longer posterior palatine teeth].
>
> The anisopteran species name is not explained in the first description, but it is consistent with the semantic field of most *Erpetogomphus* names. {adjective}

heterodoxum, *Hesperagrion* (Selys, 1868: 69)
[Original designation: *Agrion heterodoxum* Selys]
> Gr. ἑτερόδοξος –ov = holding opinions other than the right (Latinized).
>
> It is clear that a damselfly species can hold no opinion; so the name most probably refers to an unusual characteristic, which in this case are the male cerci: "Appendices supérieurs très-extraordinaires" [Very extraordinary superior appendages].
> {declinable adjective}

hineana, Somatochlora Williamson, 1931: 2
>L. suffix *–anus –a –um* = pertaining to, combined with the name of the collector of the allotype specimen.

>"allotype female; same locality and date {near Indian lake, Logan County , Ohio, June 14, 1929}, James S. Hine collector".

>Professor James Stewart Hine (See p. 46), Curator of the Division of Natural History of the Ohio State Archaeological and Historical Museum, and a President of the Ohio Academy of Science. {declinable adjective}

hinei, Argia Kennedy, 1918a: 258
>"After I had taken *hinei* at Fillmore, Calif., I found, that Dr. Hine had taken it in Arizona, and his material was in Mr. Williamson's hand awaiting description." "I take pleasure naming it after Dr. Hine [See p. 46], a suggestion made by Mr. Williamson."
>{noun in the genitive case}

hodgesi, Phanogomphus (Needham, 1950: 8)
[Original designation: *Gomphus hodgesi* Needham]
>"On a visit to the University of Alabama, at Tuscaloosa, Dr. [Robert S.] Hodges [See p. 46] called my attention to a local specimen that is very similar to *G. brimleyi*, and then kindly sent it to me for study. Describing it herewith, I take pleasure in naming it in his honor." {noun in the genitive case}

howei, Ophiogomphus Bromley, 1924: 343
>"This species is named in honor of Dr.R. Heber Howe, Jr., whose writings on the Odonate fauna of New England have done much to encourage the study of this interesting order in this region." Reginald Heber Howe, Jr. (1875 – 1932) Naturalist (published on lichens, birds, and dragonflies). There is a detailed biography of him (WHITE 2016) and a meticulous description of the controversy about naming *Williamsonia fletcheri* (WHITE & O'BRIEN 2017), which also sheds evidence on the interrelations with other odonatologists of renown.
>{noun in the genitive case}

hudsonica, Leucorrhinia (Selys, 1850: 53)
[Original designation: *Libellula hudsonica* Selys]
    L. suffix *–icus –a –um* = belonging to (mostly in a geographical sense) [Latinized from Gr. –ικός –ή –όν]

Named after the type locality: "On trouve dans le nouveau Brunswick, près de la Baie d'Hudson, une Libellule excessivement voisine de celle-ci [i.e. *L. dubia*], qui m'a été communiquée par le Muséum Britannique, je la nomme: LIBELLULA HUDSONICA. De Sélys" [In New Brunswick, near Hudson Bay, there is a dragonfly which is exceedingly close to it [i.e. *L. dubia*], which was communicated to me by the British Museum, I call it: *Libellula hudsonica* Sélys].

        {declinable adjective}

hudsonica, Somatochlora (Hagen in Selys, 1871a: 301)
[Original designation: *Epitheca hudsonica* Hagen in Selys]
    L. suffix *–icus –a –um* = belonging to (mostly in a geographical sense) [Latinized from Gr. –ικός –ή –όν].

After the type locality "Fort Résolution, territoire de la baie d' Hudson" but note that Fort Resolution is on Great Slave Lake.
        {declinable adjective}

hybridus, Gomphurus (Williamson, 1902: 47)
[Original designation: *Gomphus hybridus* Williamson]
    L. *hybridus –a –um* = mongrel, hybrid.

The name is given because the male is similar to *Gomphus fraternus* and female to *G. externus*: "*Hybridus* differs most widely from *crassus*; the male is very closely related to *fraternus*, while the female has more resemblences to *externus* – a condition which justifies the specific name proposed."   {declinable adjective}

Hylogomphus Needham & Westfall 1955: 225 (*cf.* Needham, Westfall & May 2000: 333)

> Gr. ὕλη = woodland, forest + γόμφος = bolt for shipbuilding or for other uses.

> The taxon *Hylogomphus* was first announced by Needham, 1951, 23 endnote. The four species to be included were already mentioned in Needham 1947, 331 ff. as a nearly related group. Needham does not explain his choice of the name, but it is to be noted, that this genus is restricted to the eastern part of North America and the range of the species included is generally well-wooded.

> Needham, Westfall & May 2000: 333 explain the correction to nomenclature "Since Needham (1951) did not actually describe the subgenus or designate a type and Needham and Westfall (1955) also failed to specify a type, we take this opportunity to designate *Gomphus adelphus* Selys, 1858, as the type of *Hylogomphus*, thus making the latter name available under the rules of nomenclature." {Masculine}

hymenaea, Pantala (Say, 1839: 18)
[Original designation: *Libellula hymenaea* Say]

> L. *hymenaeus –a –um* = concerning a membrane, Latinized from Gr.ὑμήν = thin skin, membrane + suffix –αιος = concerning.

> Say does not explain this name, but at the end of his description he mentions a feature, by which this species might be identified: "Readily distinguishable by whitish nervures in the brown anal margin of the posterior wings and the snow-white anal membrane". So the snow-white anal membrane seems to have led to the name. {declinable adjective}

Idiataphe Cowley, 1934: 243

The name is an anagram of the original name *Ephidatia* Kirby 1889 [Gr.ἐφυδάτιος –η –ον = in / on the water] found to be preoccupied by *Ephidatia* Lecoq, 1862 a synonym of *Ephydatia* Lamouroux, 1816 (Animalia: Porifera).

So the name should not be referred to Gr. ἴδιος –α –ον= one's own and ταφή = burial. *Ephydatia* in antiquity was an epithet used for Nymphs, which seems to be suitable for an odonate genus. {Feminine}

illinoiensis, Macromia Walsh, 1862: 397

From the type locality + *–ensis –is –e* = adjectival suffix indicating place of origin.

"Except where otherwise stated the following species have been taken by myself within four miles of the city of Rock Island, [Rock Island County, Illinois]." {declinable adjective}

illotum, Sympetrum (Hagen, 1861: 172)
[Original designation: *Mesothemis illota* Hagen]
L.*illotus –a –um* = unwashed, dirty.

As Hagen does not explain the name, the allusion is unknown, but semantically it fits with species names like *immunda, pollutum, incesta* (cf. the remark on *fugax*).{declinable adjective}

imitans, Macrothemis Karsch, 1890: 367

L. *imitans*: present participle of *imito* = to imitate.

Karsch explains the name thus: "Diese *Macrothemis* Art zeigt in Grösse, Gestalt und Färbung eine so augenfällige Aehnlichkeit mit *Micrathyria didyma* Selys, dass sie namentlich im männlichen Geschlechte leicht mit dieser verwechselt werden kann" [this *Macrothemis* species has such a striking similarity to *Micrathyria didyma* Selys in size, shape and coloration that it easily might be mistaken for this species, especially the males]. But in fact the two species look and are quite different.

{present participle}

immunda, Argia (Hagen: 1861: 93)
[Original designation: *Agrion immundum* Hagen]
    L. *immundus –a –um* = unclean, impure, dirty, filthy, foul.

Perhaps the name is an allusion to the obscure luteous abdomen (as if it were dirty) ["abdomen obscure luteous"]. But certainly it fits semantically to names like *illotum* (q.v.) and others.
                                      {declinable adjective}

inacuta, Macrothemis Calvert, 1898: 318 (key), 328
    L. prefix *in–* = un–, not + *acutus –a –um* = sharp, pointed.

The name refers to the cerci of the males: "Tips of superior appendages of ♂ not acute but rounded." {declinable adjective}

inaequalis, Lestes Walsh, 1862: 385
    L. *inaequalis –is –e* = uneven, of different sizes.

In this species the male paraprocts are longer than the cerci: "Inferior appendages extending a third of a millimetre beyond the superiors". {declinable adjective}

incesta, Libellula Hagen, 1861: 155
    L. *incestus –a –um* = not religiously pure, unclean, impure, polluted, defiled, sinful, criminal.

Also in this case the first description offers no explanation for the name; but semantically it is consistent with names like *illotum, immunda, pollutum* (q.v.) {declinable adjective}

incurvata, Somatochlora Walker, 1918: 365
    L. *incurvatus –a –um*: past participle of *incurvo* = to bend, curve.

The incurved male cerci have caused the name: "In dorsal view the superior appendages ..., the apical inward curve nearly as in *semicircularis*". {declinable past participle}

incurvatus, *Ophiogomphus* Carle, 1982: 335
> L. *incurvatus* –*a* –*um*: past participle of *incurvo* = to bend, curve.

Carle 1982: 339: "Etymology. – *O. incurvatus* ... (L. mas. part. adj. 'bent inward,' referring to the incurvate male cerci)."
{declinable past participle}

inequiunguis, *Macrothemis* Calvert, 1895: 533
> L. prefix *in*– = un–, not ... + (*a*)*equus* = equal, like + –*unguis* –*is* –*e* (in compounds) = clawed.

The name refers to short tooth of the tarsal claw: "Tarsal nails toothed inferiorly before apex, tooth shorter than nail tip , hence departing from the normal form of *Macrothemis*".
{declinable adjective}

ingens, *Coryphaeschna* (Rambur, 1842: 192)
[Original designation: *Aeschna ingens* Rambur]
> L. *ingens* = huge, referring to large size.

Rambur describes the size: "Plus grande que l' *A. formosus* {=*Anax imperator*}" [Larger than *A. formosus*], the total length of which species is up to 84 mm. {adjective}

insularis, *Cannaphila* Kirby, 1889: 341
> L. *insularis* –*is* –*e* = of or belonging to an island (or, to islands), insular.

Kirby had specimens from Haiti and Jamaica: "*Hab*. Haiti (types in British Museum), Jamaica (Dublin)". {declinable adjective}

insularis, *Tramea* Hagen, 1861: 146
> L. *insularis* –*is* –*e* = of or belonging to an island (or, to islands), insular.

The name refers to the type locality: "*Hab*. Cuba".
{declinable adjective}

intacta, *Leucorrhinia* (Hagen, 1861: 179)
[Original designation: *Diplax intacta* Hagen]
    L. *intactus –a –um* = untouched, uninjured, intact.

    Hagen does not explain his choice of the name; so its meaning is not known.   {declinable adjective}

integricollis, *Nehalennia* Calvert, 1913a: 312
    L. *integer –gra –grum* = unimpaired, whole + *–collis –is –e* (in compounds) = –necked.

The name is due to the lack of emargination on the prothorax characteristic of some other *Nehalennia*: "Hind margin of prothorax convex, entire or nearly so."   {declinable adjective}

intensa, *Perithemis* Kirby, 1889: 326
    L. *intensus –a –um* = stretched, but also: intense, strenuous.

Kirby does not explain his choice of the name; it possibly refers to the elongate pterostigmata: "pterostigma red, rather long (slightly longer on the hind wings than on the fore wings)". But PAULSON & DUNKLE (2018) think that it might rather allude to the intense coloration of the wings, which is described thus: "Wings deep-brownish yellow.   {declinable adjective}

internum, *Sympetrum* Montgomery, 1943: 57
[named but not described by Hagen, 1875: 79]
    L. *internus –a –um* = internal, probably referring to the primarily interior geographic distribution.

Montgomery adopted the name, already published in HAGEN 1875 as *nomen nudum*, from labels in Hagen's collection for specimens of a species, which Ris (and other authors) erroneously had taken for *Diplax decisa* Hagen, 1874 (= *Sympetrum obtrusum*). There is no explanation of Hagen's name in the first description, but it is said: "A long series of specimens of this species from localities throughout the United States and Canada have been assembled for study and a detailed paper is in preparation."
    {declinable adjective}

interrogatum, Coenagrion (Hagen in Selys, 1876a: 1254)
[Original designation: *Agrion concinnum* race *interrogatum* Hagen in Selys]

>L. *interrogatus –a –um*: past participle of *interrogo* = to ask, question, inquire, interrogate.

>In Latin this participle does not exactly have the meaning of 'questioned' in the sense of being dubious, but it seems to have been used in that meaning by Hagen and Selys, because their specimen was a mutilated female, the last seven abdominal segments were missing so they were not sure about its taxonomic status, if it was a subspecies of the Eurasian species *Agrion concinnum* Johanson (now *Coenagrion johanssoni* Wallengren) or a species of its own.   {declinable past participle}

interrupta, Aeshna Walker, 1908: 381

>L. *interruptus –a –um*: past participle of *interrumpo* = to break apart, interrupted, referring to the thoracic stripes.

>"lateral thoracic band each divided into a superior and inferior spot; dorsal thoracic bands reduced to a pair of small elongate spots narrowed at both ends and not reaching the interalar sinus."   {declinable past participle}

intricatus, Stylurus (Hagen in Selys, 1858: 678)
[Original designation: *Gomphus intricatus* Hagen in Selys]

>L. *intricatus –a –um* = complex, tricky.

>The name probably reflects the similarity to two other *Gomphus* species: "C'est une espèce intermédiaire entre le *militaris* et le *minutus* ... On ne peut confondre cette espèce avec l'*exilis*..." [It is a species intermediate between *militaris* and *minutus* ... This species cannot be confused with *exilis* ...]. {declinable adjective}

The Etymologies

irene, Nehalennia (Hagen, 1861: 74)
[Original designation: *Agrion* (subgenus *Nehalennia*) *irene* Hagen]
    Latinized form of Εἰρήνη, the Greek goddess of peace, daughter of Themis and Zeus.

    The eponym of this species might be the Greek goddess of peace or, as Irene is also a common female first name, an unknown woman.   {noun in apposition}

Ischnura Charpentier, 1840: 20
    "Nomen e Graeco ἰσχνός et οὐρά compositum, ob abdominis eximiam tenuitatem. Signa distinctiva huius subgeneris sunt: abdomen, praecipue medium, valde attenuatum ..." [The name is combined from Greek ἰσχνός [= slender, lean] and οὐρά [= tail; in entomology used for abdomen] because of the extraordinary slenderness of the abdomen. A distinctive characteristic of this subgenus is that the abdomen, especially the middle part, is very thin ...].   {Feminine}

ivae, Stylurus Williamson, 1932: 12
    "In late September and early October, 1931, Mr. H. W. Ditzler, his wife Ivy [1882-1976], their daughter Laura, and myself, made a collecting trip which took us from Indiana as far as the southeast of Kentucky. ... Mrs. Ditzler and her daughter by their coöperation made this trip possible. It is appropriate, therefore, that these new species which, without their help would not have been discovered, should be named for them."   {noun in the genitive case}

janata, Basiaeschna (Say: 1839: 13)
[Original designation: *Aeshna janata* Say]
    The interpretation of this name is a problem, for it is not a word from Latin or Greek. Perhaps it might an attempt to Latinize the female first name Janet; but that would be unique among the odonate names given by Say; the only other proper name chosen by him for a dragonfly is *leda,* from the heroine visited by Zeus disguised as a swan. So the name seems to be a   {noun in apposition}

jesseana, Libellula Williamson, 1922a: 13
> "44 males, 2 females, collected by Jesse H. Williamson, for whom this handsome species is named" Jesse H. Williamson (1884-1964), cousin of the author (HÄMÄLÄINEN 2016).
>
> {noun in apposition}

julia, Ladona (Uhler, 1857: 88)
[Original designation: *Libellula julia* Uhler]
> *Julia* is the name of women from the *gens Julia* of Ancient Rome [*gens* signifies a family consisting of all those individuals who shared the same name and claimed descent from a common ancestor]. Uhler does not explain whom he had in mind, when he named this species. So the name might be a reference to an unknown female or a woman from Roman antiquity. If so, there are several candidates, the most prominent ones being the wife of Gaius Marius, the well known commander who was celebrated for his victory over Germanic tribes as 'third founder of Rome', and aunt of Julius Cesar, the dictator killed on the Ides of March 44 B.C., or the daughter of the latter, or the granddaughter of his grand nephew and adopted son, the emperor Augustus.
>
> {noun in apposition}

juncea, Aeshna (Linnaeus, 1758: 544)
[Original designation: *Libellula juncea* Linnaeus]
> L. *junceus –a –um* = of rushes (*Juncus*).
>
> This name points to a plant common in the habitat of the species. {declinable adjective}

junius, Anax (Drury, 1773: 47)
[Original designation: *Libellula junia* Drury]
> Drury never explains his names. Following his practice of mostly giving female names from antiquity to Odonata, Drury described this species as *Libellula junia*. The name was adapted in gender, when the species was transferred to *Anax*. Today that would not happen to a proper name. *Junius* means member of the clan of the *Iunii*. To that Roman family belonged Marcus Iunius Brutus, the famous founder of the Roman republic as well as one of the two assassins of Caesar, but none of them, being male, is involved in the origin of this name.
>
> {noun in apposition}

kellicotti, Ischnura Williamson, 1898: 209

"Named for Professor D. S. Kellicott, who first called attention to this species." David S. Kellicott (See p. 47), Professor of Zoology and Entomology at the Ohio State University, was President of the Buffalo Academy of Science and the Ohio State Academy of Science. {noun in the genitive case}

kennedyi, Somatochlora Walker, 1918: 371

"I take pleasure in naming this species after Mr. Clarence Hamilton Kennedy [See p. 48], in recognition of his valuable contributions to North American odonatology. Mr. Kennedy recognized this species as distinct independent of the writer and at about the same time, so that it is particularly fitting that it should bear his name." {noun in the genitive case}

kurilis, Phanogomphus (Hagen in Selys, 1858: 392)
[Original designation: *Gomphus kurilis* Hagen in Selys]

L. *kurilis –is -e* = of the Kurile Islands [between Kamchatka and Japan]

"Patrie. *Iles Kuriles*" was erroneously given as the type locality in the first description. {declinable adjective}

lacerata, Tramea Hagen, 1861: 145

L. *laceratus –a –um* = past participle of *lacero* = to mangle, rent, mutilate, lacerate.

The name describes the ragged edges of hindwing spots: "posterior wings with a broad, basal, fuscous band, which is ragged exteriorly". {declinable past participle}

lacrimans, Argia (Hagen: 1861: 95)
[Original designation: *Agrion lacrimans* Hagen]
>   L. *lacrimans*: present participle of *lacrimo* = to shed tears i.e. shedding tears, perhaps referring to teardrop-shaped abdominal spots.

>   Hagen in SELYS 1865, 386 describes the pattern of the male: "Abdomen lilas pâle, les segments 2ᵉ – 6ᵉ ayant de chaque côté une tache triangulaire noire" [Pale lilac abdomen, the 2nd – 6th having a black triangular spot on each side]. These spots seem to have reminded him of shed tears.   {present participle}

Ladona Needham, 1897: 146
>   Meaning unknown.

>   Gr. Λάδων = stream in Arcadia or a hound of Actaeon in Ovid's metamorphoses; but these would not explain the female form *Ladona*.   {Feminine}

lais, Apanisagrion (Selys, 1876b: 990)
[Original designation: *Nehalennia lais* Selys, 1876b]
>   Gr. Λαίς [the well-known one, from λαός = men, people] was a common name of courtesans.

>   At the base of the name is a superficial similarity of the male wingtip to the calopterygid genus *Lais* Selys 1853 (= *Mnesarete* Cowley, 1934): "Le bout extrême des ailes inférieures entre la costale et le secteur ultranodal contient environ douze cellules très-petites anastomosées, à nervules épassies, qui forment l'apparence d'une petite tache terminale arrondie noirâtre comme chez plusieurs Lais du groupe de l'*Aenea*." [The extreme end of the hindwings between the costal and the subnodal area contains about twelve very small anastomosed cells with veins, which form the appearance of a small black terminal spot, as in several of the *Lais* group of *Aenea*]. The name is credited by Selys to Brauer, who had applied it in the Imperial Collections at Vienna, where Selys had got to know the species. But as Brauer not had published any description of it, Selys is its author.
>   {noun in apposition}

lampropeltis, Erpetogomphus Kennedy, 1918b: 297

Lampropeltis = a king snake genus [Gr. λαμπρός –ά –όν = radiant + πέλτη = a light shield], named in reference to smooth dorsal scales.

As often in the genus *Erpetogomphus* the dragonfly species is named after a snake genus: "this is named after the handsome black-and-white banded king snake of California".

{noun in apposition}

Lanthus Needham, 1897: 166

This is one of the very few names for which Needham himself gives an explanation: "*Lanthus* (λανθανη contracted)". However there is no Greek word λανθανη which Needham cites either in ancient or in modern Greek, and its contraction would not be *Lanthus*, but it seems clear that Needham wanted to refer to the verb λανθάνω = to escape notice. {Masculine}

laterale, Enallagma Morse, 1895: 274

L. adjective *lateralis –is –e* from L. *latus* = the side, alluding to the lateral stripe on eighth abdominal segment. "a stripe each side on 8". {declinable adjective}

laurae, Stylurus Williamson, 1932: 3

"In late September and early October, 1931, Mr. H. W. Ditzler, his wife Ivy, their daughter Laura [Laura Buis (née Ditzler) (1911-2008)]; and myself, made a collecting trip which took us from Indiana as far as the southeast of Kentucky. ... Mrs. Ditzler and her daughter by their coöperation made this trip possible. It is appropriate, therefore, that these new species which, without their help would not have been discovered, should be named for them." {noun in the genitive case}

lentulus, Arigomphus (Needham, 1902: 275)
[Original designation: *Gomphus lentulus* Needham]
    L. *lentulus –a –um* = rather slow.

Needham does not give an explanation of the name in his first description. Two possible explanations come to mind: firstly, that the species is mostly found at lentic waters (see PAULSON 2009, 251); but in the first description Little Wabash River near Flora Ill. is given as the type locality. Alternatively it might represent a flight characteristic. But also of that there is no hint in the first description. So the basis of the name remains enigmatic.
        {declinable adjective}

leonorae, Argia Garrison, 1994b: 315
    "Named in honor of the late Leonora K. Gloyd [1902-1993; see p. 40], diligent odonate worker and researcher and specialist of the genus *Argia*."   {noun in the genitive case}

lepida, Dorocordulia (Hagen in Selys, 1871a: 264)
[Original designation: *Cordulia lepida* Hagen in Selys]
    L. *lepidus –a –um* = pleasant, agreeable, charming, fine, elegant, neat.

This is one of the many names in dragonflies evoking their charming character: "Cette jolie espèce ..." [This pretty species ...]. HAGEN *Proc. Bost. soc. nat. hist* 15, 1872-75, 271 "It is the smallest species of *Cordulia* known".   {declinable adjective}

Leptobasis Selys, 1877: 99
    Gr. λεπτός –ή –όν = thin, fine, lean + βάσις = (*inter alia*) base, pedestal.

The name refers to the petiolate wings in the genus: "Ailes pétiolées jusqu'à la nervule basale postcostale seulement; un peu avant l'origine du quadrilatère." [Wings petiolate only to the basal postcostal vein; a little before the origin of the quadrilateral.]   {Feminine}

Lestes Leach, 1815: 137

Gr. λῃστής = a robber; the Latinized form *Lestes* is accentuated on the first syllable.

Why Leach chose this name he did not say. It does not give any diagnostic clue either because all Odonata are predators.
{Masculine}

Leucorrhinia Brittinger, 1850: 333

Gr. λευκός –ή – όν = white + ῥίς (stem: ῥιν-) = nose + adjectival suffix –ιος –ία –ιον = pertaining to (Latinized). The name refers to the white frons as being the character which gives this genus its name.

Brittinger characterizes his new genus as follows: "Folgende Arten, welche durch ... einen dreieckigen, schwarzen Fleck an der Basis der Hinterflügel, und durch ihre weiße Stirn und Nase, eine sehr natürliche Gruppe bilden, habe ich schon 1845 als eigene Gattung geschieden, und unter dieser Benennung abgegeben" [The following species, which form a distinct natural group by ... a triangular black spot at the base of the hind wings, and by their white frons and rhinarium, I have separated already in 1845 as a genus of its own and under this denomination given it by other people.]
{Feminine}

Libellula Linnaeus, 1758: 543

L. *libellula*: diminutive of *libella* = mason's level [a diminutive of *liber* = book would be *libellus*, which is not at the base of the name].

It is a fascinating story how that instrument of carpenters and masons shaped like an inverted T, which was in use in ancient and medieval times, came to denote this odonate genus. The term *libella* in the 16th century was in use for the hammerhead shark because of the similarity in shape. It was transferred to zygopterous larvae by the French scientist G. Rondelet (1505-1566); from the 17th century on it was also used for adult dragonflies. Linné then chose the diminutive as the genus name for all dragonflies.
{Feminine}

libera, Dorocordulia (Selys, 1871a: 263)
[Original designation: *Cordulia libera* Selys]
    L. *liber –era –erum* = free.

    The name refers to a feature of wing venation: "triangles discoidaux libres" [discoidal triangles free].
                                                                  {declinable adjective}

linearis, Somatochlora (Hagen, 1861: 137)
[Original designation: *Cordulia linearis* Hagen]
    L. *linearis –is –e* = linear.

    In the first description it is said: "abdomen long, very slender", so that characteristic feature probably is at the base of the name.
                                                                   {declinable adjective}

lineatifrons, Gomphurus (Calvert, 1921: 222)
[Original designation: *Gomphus lineatifrons* Calvert]
    L. *linea* = thread, line + suffix *–atus –ata –atum* = provided with + *–frons* (in compounds) = –fronted.

    The name describes the black line bordering the anterior frons: "Black on the suture between frons and nasus (post clypeus) ... in *lineatifrons* a line or narrow stripe".   {adjective}

lineatipes, Paltothemis Karsch, 1890: 362
    L. *linea* = thread, line + suffix *–atus –ata –atum* = provided with + *–pes* (in compounds) = –footed, referring to striped legs.

    "Beine schwarz ... der Rücken der Schenkel und Schienen mit gelber Längslinie" [legs black ... the posterior side of femora and tibiae with a longitudinal yellow line].   {adjective}

lintneri, Williamsonia (Hagen in Selys, 1878: 187)
[Original designation: *Cordulia lintneri* Hagen in Selys]

Although there is no acknowledgment in the original description the species was named for Joseph Albert Lintner (*8 February 1822 in Schoharie, New York – †5 May 1898 in Rome) who was an American entomologist. He held the position of New York State Entomologist from 1881 following the creation of this post by the federal government. Selys (1878: 188) wrote "(Diagnose extradite d'une letter du Dr. Hagen)" [Diagnosis taken from a letter from Dr. Hagen] and that is where the acknowledgement lies (see also under *fletcheri*).   {noun in the genitive case}

lividus, Phanogomphus (Selys, 1854: 53)
[Original designation: *Gomphus lividus* Selys]

L. *lividus –a –um* = of a leaden color, bluish, a reference to dull coloration.

The original description refers to one female the color of which is described as mainly dark yellow or brown (jauneâtre or brunâtre) (also in SELYS 1858, 411). So it might be that Selys thought the word to have a somewhat different meaning. It seems probable that he wanted to point to the dull color of his specimen. {declinable adjective}

longipennis, Pachydiplax (Burmeister, 1839: 850)
[Original designation: *Libellula longipennis* Burmeister]

L. *longus –a –um* = long + *–pennis –is –e* (in compounds) = -winged.

In the first description the wings are described thus: "alis longis in basi umbra fulva, stigmatibus nigris" [with long wings, with a tawny shadow at the bases, with black pterostigmata]. "Ein Weibchen in Germar's Sammlung, ausgezeichnet durch sehr lange, aber breite Flügel und einen auffallend kurzen, dicken Hinterleib" [a female in Germar's collection, remarkable by very long, but broad wings and a conspicuously short thick abdomen]. {declinable adjective}

longipes, Anax Hagen, 1861: 118
>L. *longus –a –um* = long + *–pes* (in compounds) = –footed.

The name refers to the long legs of the species: "feet extremely long". {adjective}

lucifer, Leptobasis (Donnelly, 1967: 47)
[Original designation: *Chrysobasis lucifer* Donnelly]
>"*lucifer* [*–fera –ferum*] (Latin) : carrying a light, in allusion to the pale tip of the abdomen." {declinable adjective}

luctuosa, Libellula Burmeister, 1839: 861
>L. *luctuosus –a –um* = mournful.

It seems adequate to refer the name to the black cloak-like wing bases: "alis in basi late fuscis" [the wings broadly dark at base] as if they were a sign of mourning. But as Burmeister described the male from a specimen in the collection of M.C. Sommer, his father in law, as "♂ nigerrimus" [♂ deep black], this might be at the base of the name, whereas living adult males are whitish pruinose. {declinable adjective}

lugens, Argia (Hagen, 1861: 95)
[Original designation: *Agrion lugens* Hagen]
>L. *lugens*: present participle of *lugeo* = to be in mourning, to wear mourning apparel.

The species is described from a single female specimen chronologically between *A. moesta* [= sad, unhappy, q.v.] and *A. lacrimans* [= shedding tears, q.v.] the three names being semantically close. The specimen is described as luteous (of an orange-yellow or greenish yellow color), which would not be the color of mourning apparel, but Hagen mentions some dark markings: "head above with an arcuated, angulose line, and a postoccipital fascia, blackish brown; posterior margin of the prothorax subrotund, with an arcuated black spot ... thorax luteous a dorsal middle streak and two narrow stripes each side, fuscous ... abdomen thick, luteous, a broad stripe each side, confluent at the apices of the segments, blackish-brown". So the semantic affinity to the neighboring species and the dark markings may be at the base of the name. {present participle}

luteipennis, Remartinia (Burmeister, 1839: 837)
[Original designation: *Aeschna luteipennis* Burmeister]
>L. *luteus –a –um* = yellow + *–pennis –is –e* (in compounds) = –winged, referring to colored wings of old individuals.

>In the first description it reads: "alis luteis, venis stigmatibusque nigris" [with yellow wings with black veins and pterostigmata].
>{declinable adjective}

lydia, Plathemis (Drury, 1773: 47)
[Original designation: *Libellula lydia* Drury]
>Drury never explains his names, which are almost always female names from Roman antiquity. While Lydia was a name for female slaves who came from Lydia in Asia Minor, it is possible that Drury chose Lydia of Thyatira (Λυδία) a woman mentioned in the New Testament who is regarded as the first documented convert to Christianity in Europe. Several Christian denominations have designated her a saint. Lydia's name is an ethnicon, deriving from her place of origin.
>{noun in apposition}

lynnae, Gomphurus (Paulson, 1983: 60)
[Original designation: *Gomphus lynnae* Paulson]
>"This species is named after Lynn Erckmann (formerly Mary Lynn Paulson [* 1942]), who discovered it, knew it was something interesting, and shared my excitement when I realized it was undescribed. She also produced the fine illustration reproduced herein and furnished the moral support necessary to embark on my first description of a new species of dragonfly."
>{noun in the genitive case}

Macrodiplax Brauer, 1868: 366
>Gr. μακρός –ά –όν = long, tall, large, great; for *Diplax* (a junior synonym of *Sympetrum* Newman) see *Erythrodiplax*.

>Whereas it is not explained in the first description, the name refers to the large size in relationship to dragonflies in the old libellulid genus *Diplax*. {Feminine}

Macromia Rambur, 1842: 137

    Gr. μακρός –ά –όν = long, extensive, + ὦμος = shoulder + feminine form of the suffix –ιος –ια –ιον = concerning.

Williamson (1899: 231, 307), with advice from Calvert, gives the etymology as "(macros Gr., great, long; omos Gr., equally) ... the name probably referring to the equally long tarsal nails." This is based on Rambur's "onglets fortement bifides" [strongly bifid tarsal claws]. Rambur also states "elles se distinguent bien des *Cordulia* par la forme des onglets" [they are well distinguished from *Cordulia* by the form of their tarsal claws]. In commenting on *Cordulia* [= *Macromia*] *splendens*, SELYS (1843) says "Les principaux caractères qui distinguent les Macromies des Cordulies sont d'avoir les onglets des tarses entièrement bifides" [The main characteristics that distinguish the macromines from cordulines are having the tarsal claws fully bifid].

However, the Calvert/Williamson interpretation is not correct on philological grounds. ὁμῶς translates to equally, likewise or alike and is an adverb, from which a derivation *–omia* would be hazardous and not likely to have been made by Rambur, whose names in the main are philologically correct. At the base of the name is the Gr. noun ὦμος– shoulder as explained above. The passage in RAMBUR 1842:137 to which it seems to refer is: "Ailes ayant la partie humérale du bord costal au moins deux fois aussi longue que la partie cubitale jusqu'au pterostigma" [Wings with the humeral part of the costal edge at least twice as long as the cubital as far as the pterostigma].

    [see ENDERSBY & FLIEDNER 2015 p. 174 sq]   {Feminine}

Macrothemis Hagen, 1868a: 281

Gr. μακρός –ά –όν = long, tall, large, great; for *–themis* see *Celithemis*.

On the first look one might think that the name is to be understood as 'large libellulid'; but that can't be true, for more than half of the species Hagen 1861 included in the genus *Dythemis*, from which *Macrothemis* is separated, are larger than any of the four species comprising the new genus. So a different interpretation is needed. Hagen 1868a, 283 states that his genus *Dythemis* as founded in 1861 was inhomogeneous and a group of four South American species were to form a new genus differing from the others "durch die eigenthümliche Bildung der Tarsen. Selbe sind nämlich genau wie bei Macromia und [sic! erroneously for 'an'] der Spitze verdoppelt, d. h. der untere Zahn an die Spitze gerückt, so lang wie der obere, und an den vier Hinterfüssen sogar stärker, so dass der untere Zahn eigentlich das Ende der Tarsenkralle zu bilden scheint, und der obere gleichsam einen dünneren Anhang bildet."[by the peculiar form of the tarsi. For these are exactly like those of *Macromia* doubled at the tip, i.e., the inferior tooth reaches to the tip, being as long as the superior one, and at the four posterior feet even stronger, so that the inferior tooth seems to be the actual end of the tarsal claw and the superior one virtually constitutes a thinner appendix]. In the following paragraph he mentions that, differently from *Macromia*, in the females the inferior tooth in all feet is somewhat shorter than the superior one. So the name means 'libellulid similar to *Macromia*'. {Feminine}

maculata, *Calopteryx* (Palisot de Beauvois, 1805: 85)
[Original designation: *Agrion maculatum* Palisot de Beauvois]

L. *macula* = spot, stain + suffix *–atus –a –um* = provided with, referring to white pterostigma of female.

"alis fuscis, subnigris, albomaculatis" [with brown, blackish wings spotted white].

{declinable adjective}

maculata, Cordulegaster Selys, 1854: 105
[as *Cordulegaster maculatus* Selys]
    L. *macula* = spot, stain + suffix *–atus –a –um* = provided with.

The name refers to the abdominal spots: "Abdomen à demi-anneaux médianes jaunes, suivis d'un demi-anneau terminal jusqu'au 6ᵉ segment; ces demi-anneaux réduits les uns et les autres á deux taches arrondiés, separées par l'arrête dorsale." [Abdomen with half medial rings, followed by a terminal half-ring up to the 6th segment; these half-rings reduced to one and the others to two rounded spots separated by the dorsal ridge].
                                                                 {declinable adjective}

madidum, Sympetrum (Hagen, 1861: 174)
[Original designation: *Diplax madida* Hagen]
    L. *madidus –a –um* = moist, wet, soaked.

What Hagen had in mind when choosing this name he does not say, so it remains enigmatic.
                                                                   {declinable adjective}

magnifica, Macromia MacLachlan in Selys, 1874: 22
    L. *magnificus –a –um* = splendid, magnificent, stately.

In the first description the name is not explained. Even though other *Macromia* species are even larger, this is a very impressive dragonfly. So the name probably refers to size.
                                                      {declinable adjective}

mainensis, Ophiogomphus Packard in Walsh, 1863: 255
    From the type locality + *ensis –is –e* = adjectival suffix indicating place of origin.

This name is a reference to the type locality Maine [implied]: "After the above was in the hands of the printer, I received from Mr. A.S. Packard, jun., [see p. 62] of the state of Maine, the following brief description of the ♀ of what is evidently an undescribed species of *Ophiogomphus*."   {declinable adjective}

marcella, Miathyria (Selys in Sagra, 1857: 452)
[Original designation: *Libellula marcella* Selys in Sagra]
>The species is named after an unknown woman or a saint from the 4th century. Marcella (325–410) is a saint in the Roman Catholic Church and Eastern Orthodox Church. She is known primarily for her role in the founding of monasticism. After the death of her husband, she commenced a life of abstinence and many other women in Rome at the time followed suit.
>{noun in apposition}

margarita, Macromia Westfall, 1947: 32
>"Named in honor of my good wife, Margaret S. Westfall [1922-2000], whose help and encouragement are a great aid in my dragonfly work." {noun in apposition}

margarita, Somatochlora Donnelly, 1962: 235
>"The new species is named for Miss Margaret Stevenson, a delightful companion of my wife and myself on all of our collecting trips during the spring of 1961, and a very great help to us during the bizarre maneuvres which were required to net this most elusive and beautiful insect." {noun in apposition}

martha, Celithemis Williamson, 1922b: 4
>"Named for Miss Mattie Wadsworth [1862-1943], for nearly thirty years a careful and unselfish collector and student of Maine dragonflies, who collected many specimens of the species here named in her honor." For informations on the eponym's life and her contributions to Odonatology see WHITE & CALHOUN 2009. {noun in apposition}

maxwelli, Arigomphus (Ferguson, 1950: 93)
[Original designation: *Gomphus maxwelli* Ferguson]
>"Four males of the species herein described as new, were collected by Dr. Richard E. Maxwell in Hardin County; Texas, May 11, 1940."
>{noun in genitive case}

maya, *Dythemis* Calvert, 1906: 272, 275
>"The specific name proposed alludes to the [Mayan, Indian] human tribe whose area of distribution partly coincided with that of this species." {noun in apposition}

melinogaster, *Leptobasis* González Soriano, 2002: 181
>L. *melinus* –*a* –*um* = of or belonging to honey, honey + Gr. γαστήρ = paunch, belly i.e. abdomen.
>
>p. 182: "From the latin "melinus" or yellow-honey colored, refering [sic] to the coloration of dorsum of last three abdominal segments." {noun in apposition}

mendax, *Brechmorhoga* (Hagen, 1861: 164)
[Original designation: *Dythemis mendax* Hagen]
>L. *mendax* = lying, false, deceptive, elusive.
>
>The name might refer to a female from Tampico the assignment of which was dubious to Hagen: "I saw a female from Tampico (Saussure) which had the head chalybeous [bluish black with a steely luster] above: is it different?" {adjective}

mexicana, *Gynacantha* Selys, 1868: 69
>L. *mexicanus* –*a* –*um* = of Mexico.
>
>"Reçue du Mexico, par M. de Bonvouloir, qui me l'a communiquée" [Received from Mexico, by M. de Bonvouloir, who communicated it to me]. {declinable adjective}

Miathyria Kirby, 1889: 269
>Gr. μία = one (feminine) + θύρα = door, entrance, occasionally shutter of a window + adjectival suffix –ιος –ια –ιον = concerning.
>
>The following feature might be at the base of the name: "subtriangular space consisting of one very large pentagonal cell". {Feminine}

michaeli, *Neurocordulia* Brunelle, 2000: 39
> "*Neurocordulia michaeli* in celebration of Michael Erin Brunelle, born 14 March 1991 [son of describer]." In Latin the genitive of the name Michael normally is Michaelis, but the author has treated Michael as a modern name according to ICZN 31.1.2
> {noun in the genitive case}

Micrathyria Kirby, 1889: 303
> Gr. μικρος –ά –όν = small + ἄθυρος –ον = without door.

> The name might refer to small size of the type species, which has "no supratriangular nervures" in fore and hind wings. If referring to small cells, the name correctly would be: *Microthyria*.
> {Feminine}

militaris, *Phanogomphus* (Hagen in Selys, 1858: 676)
[Original designation: *Gomphus militaris* Hagen in Selys]
> L. *militaris* –*is* –*e* = military.

> According to PAULSON & DUNKLE 2012 the species was collected on an expedition supported by the military, whereas in the first description the specimens are said to be provided by the Smithonian Institution. {declinable adjective}

minor, *Somatochlora* Calvert in Harvey, 1898: 86
[as *Somatochlora elongata* var. *minor* Calvert in Harvey]
> L. *minor* –*or* –*us* = smaller.

> It is evident that the name refers to the minor size of this taxon compared to 'normal' *S. elongata*. {declinable adjective}

minuscula, *Erythrodiplax* (Rambur, 1842: 115)
[Original designation: *Libellula minuscula* Rambur]
> L. *minusculus* –*a* –*um* = rather small.

> The first description emphasizes the smallness of the species: "Près de moitié plus petite que la *Vulgata* {= the Eurasian species *Sympetrum vulgatum*}, à laquelle elle ressemble" [Almost half as small as *vulgata* which it resembles]. {declinable adjective}

minusculum, Enallagma Morse, 1895: 207
  L. *minusculus –a –um* = rather small.

The measures given in the first description show that the name is justified: "Abd. 20 mm., hind wing, 14-15 mm."
{declinable adjective}

minuta, Nehalennia (Selys in Sagra, 1857: 464)
[Original designation: *Trichocnemis minuta* Selys in Sagra]
  L. *minutus –a –um* = little, small, minute.

The name refers to its smaller size in comparision to most coenagrionids: "Long circa, 27; alae inf., 16; lat. alae inf., 3 millim." which is also to be seen by the French name *Trichocnemis petite* given by Selys and his remark: "La *Minuta* diffère, en tous cas, de la *Tibialis* des États-Unis par sa taille moitié moindre ..." [In any case *Minuta* differs from *Tibialis* from the United States being only half its size]. {declinable adjective}

minutus, Phanogomphus (Rambur, 1842: 161)
[Original designation: *Gomphus minutus* Rambur]

L. *minutus –a –um* = little, small, minute, referring to small size.

"Plus pétit que l' *Unguiculatus*" [Smaller than (the Eurasian taxon *Onychogomphus forcipatus) unguiculatus*].
{declinable adjective}

mithroides, Erythemis (Brauer, 1900: 266)
[Original designation: *Mesothemis mithroides* Brauer]
  Gr. suffix (-o-)ειδής = looking like ..., similar, referring to [*Erythemis*] *mithra,* synonym of *Erythemis attala.*

In the first description the only remark conducive to the interpretation is: "Flügel wie bei *attala* Selys, nur das Pterostigma kleiner" [wings as in *attala* Selys, but pterostigma smaller], as on p. 262, 11 the synonymy of *E. mithra* Selys and *E. attala* Selys is declared immediately before (under number 12) the species *E. mithroides* is mentioned for the first time. {adjective}

modestus, *Gomphurus* (Needham, 1942: 72)
[Original designation: *Gomphus modestus* Needham]
>L. *modestus –a –um* = modest, possibly alluding to the modesty of the collector, Alice L. Dietrich, in not describing species herself.

>"Among the dragonflies of a fine collection made by Mrs. Dietrich in Mississippi and recently presented to Cornell University, there are two new species of *Gomphus* that she has modestly asked me to describe." {declinable adjective}

moesta, *Argia* (Hagen, 1861: 94)
[Original designation: *Agrion moestum* Hagen]
>L. *moestus –a –um* [classical orthography *maestus*] = connected with mourning; containing, causing, or showing sadness.

>As usual in his publication, Hagen does not explain why he chose this name. It might refer to the dark coloration of the male as if it were wearing a vestment of mourning: "Fuscous … dorsum of the thorax fuscous … sides brassy fuscous … abdomen brassy fuscous". It is to be noticed that the names of the following two species in HAGEN 1861 are semantically near to this one: they are *A. lugens* (= mourning) and *A. lacrimans* (= shedding tears). {declinable adjective}

molesta, *Neurocordulia* (Walsh, 1863: 254)
[Original designation: *C.? molesta* Walsh (as *Cordulia* on p. 257)]
>L. *molestus –a –um* = troublesome, annoying, unmanageable.

>The name is due to the doubt of the author concerning the correct genus of the new species: "It is with misgiving that, in absence of the ♂, I refer the above unique ♀ to *Cordulia*". {declinable adjective}

morrisoni, Ophiogomphus Selys, 1879: 45
"Patrie: Le territoire de Nevada (États-Unies); par M. Morrison"

Herbert Knowles Morrison (1854-1885), American entomologist, was one of the original members of the Cambridge Entomological Club, and was also a member of the Boston Society of Natural History. He was a member of the first excursion party of the Cambridge Entomological Club to Mount Washington, in 1874. {noun in the genitive case}

multicolor, Rhionaeschna (Hagen, 1861: 121)
[Original designation: *Aeschna multicolor* Hagen]
L. *multicolor* = many-colored.

As this species does not show significantly more colors than other aeshnids described by Hagen in the same publication, the name probably refers to the feet which are described thus: "feet black, femora rufous above, the apex black, anterior femora beneath, luteous". {adjective}

munda, Argia Calvert, 1902: 96
[as *Argia vivida* var. *munda* (Hagen, MS) Calvert]
L. *mundus –a –um* = clean, nice, neat, elegant perhaps in opposition to *immunda*.

A female described by Selys as 'un peu douteuse' [a little doubtful] as that of *A. vivida* shows characteristics which Calvert identifies as typical for *Argia immunda* (the real ♀♀ of *A. vivida* Calvert 1895, 478 had identified from specimens found in copula with males of the species). As to the name var. *munda* (Hagen, MS) Calvert explains "This name was attached by Hagen to the specimens in the M. C. Z. from Arizona, which do not differ from *A. vivida* in the form of appendages of the male, nor in that of the mesostigmal laminae of the female". But the specimens of the new variety are said to be different in colors. So the opposing name might be intended by Hagen to emphasize this difference. {declinable adjective}

mutata, Rhionaeschna (Hagen, 1861: 124)
[Original designation: *Aeschna mutata* Hagen]
 L. *mutatus –a –um*, past participle of *mutare* = to alter, change.

Neither the first description nor Hagen 1875, 35 gives a clue why this name might have been chosen. The species is described from a single female specimen, which is described by Williamson 1908a, 301, who gives the first description of the male, as "an imperfect female". So this imperfectness might be at the base of the name. But perhaps another explanation is true: Paulson & Dunkle, 2012 suppose the name might be alluding to the species being like a mutant of *A. multicolor*, and that might be justified, as Calvert, 1901, 183 deems the species of Hagen to be a synonym of *R. multicolor*.   {declinable past participle}

nahuana, Argia Calvert, 1902: 99
 L. *nahuanus –a –um* = concerning the Nahua people.

"The varietal name is modified from the Nahua, or Nahuatlan, family of tribes, the members of which inhabited much the same region as does this variety."   {declinable adjective}

Nannothemis Brauer, 1868: 369
 From the Gr. νᾶνος or νάννος = dwarf + Gr. θέμις = law as established by custom (see *Celithemis*).

Brauer gives no indication of relative sizes in his key to genera where this taxon is first named, but the first (and now only) species of the genus he mentions is *N. bella* (Uhler), the smallest anisopteran of North America.   {Feminine}

Nasiaeschna Selys in Förster, 1900: 93
 L. *nasus* = nose + *Aeshna* (q.v.).

The name refers to a significantly hollow projection of the frons (nasus): "Le genre *Nasiaeshna* differre du genre *Epiaeshna, Brachytron* et *Acanthaeshna* par le nasus *notablement excavé*." [The genus *Nasiaeshna* differs from the genera *Epiaeshna, Brachytron* and *Acanthaeshna* by the considerably hollow nasus].
   {Feminine}

nayaritensis, Phyllogomphoides Belle, 1987: 11
>From the type locality + *–ensis –is –e* = adjectival suffix indicating place of origin.

"Holotypus: ♂, Mexico, Staat Nayarit, Acaponeta., 2.XI.1923. J.H. Williamson leg.". E.B. Williamson had sent the specimen, which had been caught by his cousin Jesse, to the Swiss odonatologist F. Ris as *P. pacificus*. After Ris' death it was included in his collection that had been sent to the Museum Senckenberg at Frankfurt/Germany, where Jean Belle, who had been asked to check the identification, found out that it was a new species, which he named after the type locality. Nayarit is a word of the Cora people from that region meaning "Child of God, who is in heaven and the sun".*

{declinable adjective}

needhami, Libellula Westfall, 1943b: 22
[as *Libellula* (*Holotania*) *needhami* Westfall]

"Named for Dr. James G. Needham, from whom I have received much inspiration and assistance in my study of Odonata."

James George Needham (1868 –1957) was an American entomologist. After studying with John Henry Comstock at Cornell University (1896–1898) he taught biology at Lake Forest University (1898–1907). In 1908 he returned to Cornell as assistant professor of limnology. When Comstock retired in 1914, Needham became head of the Department of Entomology at Cornell until his retirement in 1935. Needham published numerous scientific articles, educational papers, and textbooks but is best known for the Comstock-Needham system for describing insect wing venation. (See also p. 60).

{noun in the genitive case}

---

* see https://es.wikipedia.org/wiki/Nayarit (accessed 4. Nov.2018)

Nehalennia Selys, 1850: 172
   Named for a river goddess of the Rhine.

   "(*) Nom d'une déesse de la Gaul Belgique dont on a trouvé un temple dans l'ile de Walcheren en Zeelande." [Name of a goddess of Belgian Gaul whose temple was found on the island of Walcheren in Zeeland {The Netherlands}.]   {Feminine}

Neoerythromma Kennedy, 1920: 86
   Gr. νέος = new + *Erythromma*, a coenagrionid Old World genus, named from Gr. ἐρυθρός = red + ὄμμα = eye.

   Although it is not mentioned in the first description, this genus is restricted to the New World. Most probably that is the explanation for the first part of the compound name. The reference to the Old World genus is due to: "Penis characters as in *Erythromma*", whereas *Neoerythromma* does not share the males red eyes in most species.   {Neuter}

Neoneura Selys, 1860: 459
[as *Neonevra* Selys (subgenus of *Protonevra*)]
   Gr. νέος = new + adj. suffix –νευρος –ος –ον (Latinized) [from νεῦρον = any linear feature in an organism, so sinew, tendon, vein, nerve, fibre in plants; in entomology used for wing veins].

   As Selys describes the taxon as a subgenus of *Protoneura* (q.v.) in reference to wing venation, he seems to have seen something more modern in this taxon than in the nominal genus. Which feature it was he does not explain.   {Feminine}

nervosa, Gynacantha Rambur, 1842: 213
   L. *nervus* = nerve, string; in entomology also used for wing veins + adj. suffix *–osus –a –um* = rich in, remarkable by.

   The name evokes the dense wing venation of the species: "alis nervis rufescentibus, nervulis numerosis marginatis" [the wings with reddish veins and bordered by numerous small veins] and : "trente-deux nervules au premier espace costal" [thirty two little veins in the first costal space].   {declinable adjective}

Neurocordulia Selys, 1871a: 278
[as *Nevrocordulia* Selys]

    Gr. νεῦρον = any linear feature in an organism, so sinew, tendon, vein, nerve, fibre in plants; in entomology used for wing veins + *Cordulia* (q.v.).

    SELYS, 1871a, 277-279 divides his "sous-genre" *Epitheca* into three "sections", which now all have generic rank, viz. this genus, *Epitheca* s.s. and *Somatochlora*. The genus *Neurocordulia* is set apart from the other two by a feature of wing venation: "une nervule dans l'espace basilaire" [a little vein in the basal space].   {Feminine}

nigrescens, Dythemis Calvert, 1899: 390
[as *Dythemis velox* Hagen, var.(?) *nigrescens* Calvert]

    L. *nigrescens*: present participle of *nigresco* = to become black.

    "*Male* very similar to *sterilis*, but ... a crescentic black spot on the nasus, labrum black, but green along the base in the younger individuals, lateral labial lobes barely edged with black on their inner edge, or this black as wide as one-fifth of the width of the lobe."   {present participle}

nodisticta, Libellula Hagen, 1861: 151

    L. *nodus* = a knot + Gr. στικτός -ή -όν = tattooed, spotted, dappled (Latinized).

    The name refers to small brown nodal wing spots: "wings hyaline, a basal fascia and a nodal point, black".   {declinable adjective}

notatus, Stylurus (Rambur, 1842: 162)
[Syn. *Gomphus notatus* Rambur]
    L. *notatus –a –um*: past participle of *noto* = to mark.

    The species has a distinct yellow marking on the front of thorax (mentioned by Rambur): "thorace antice lineolis duabus flavis, subabbreviatis" [frontally at the thorax two little yellow lines]. "Thorax jaunâtre en dessous, ayant antérieurement, où il est plus obscur, deux lignes un peu obliques, s'écartant un peu l'une de l'autre de haut en bas, un peu plus larges inférieurement, jaunes:" [Thorax yellowish below, having anteriorly, where it is more obscure, two rather oblique lines, a little wider from each other from top to bottom, inferiorly somewhat broader, yellow].   {declinable past participle}

novaehispaniae, Enallagma Calvert, 1907: 381
[as *Enallagma coecum* subspecies *novae-hispaniae* Calvert]
    L. *novae hispaniae* = of New Spain (= Latin America) [genitive case]
    As localities around the Carribean are cited in the first description, the species is named from its Latin American distribution.
    {noun in the genitive case}

obliqua, Cordulegaster (Say, 1839: 15)
[Original designation: *Aeshna obliqua* Say]
    L. *obliquus –a –um* = oblique.

    The name describes the two oblique stripes at the front of the thorax: "Thorax brown, with two oblique yellow vittae before".
    {declinable adjective}

obscurus, Progomphus (Rambur, 1842: 170)
[Original designation: *Diastatomma obscurum* Rambur]
    L. *obscurus –a –um* = obscure, dark.

    In the first description the overall impression is described as "Fuscum" [= dark, swarthy, dusky, tawny].{declinable adjective}

obsoleta, Neurocordulia (Say, 1839: 28)
[Original designation: *Libellula obsoleta* Say]
    L. *obsoletus –a –um*: past participle of *obsolesco* = to wear out, grow obsolete, fade; (of color) dirty looking, dingy.

    The name probably was chosen by Say because: "The brown spots of the anal base and the submarginal spots of the wings, are sometimes obsolete, or altogether wanting". In addition, the coloration of the species as described by NEEDHAM & AL. (2000, 527) "Ground color olivaceous, heavily suffused with brown" might have looked to the author as if these anisopterans were soiled with brown. {declinable past participle}

obtrusum, Sympetrum (Hagen, 1867a: 95)
[Original designation: *Diplax obtrusa* Hagen]
    L. *obtrusus –a –um* : past participle of *obtrudo* = to thrust upon, obtrude; allusion unknown, but perhaps Hagen wanted to say *obtusum* (blunt, edgeless), referring to the external branch of the hamule, which he describes as 'broad, truncated' (HAGEN, 1861, 177 in connection with *Sympetrum rubicundulum* (Say)). {declinable past participle}

occidentis, Ophiogomphus Hagen, 1885: 259
    L. *occidentis* = of the west (genitive case).

    The species was described from nymphs collected in Oregon and Washington territory. {noun in the genitive case}

Octogomphus Selys, 1873a: 759
    Gr. ὀκτώ = eight + *Gomphus* (q.v.)

    The name refers to the eight-branched male adominal appendages: "appendices ... l'uns et les autres complétement fourchus, de sorte que le abdomen se termine en huit pointes" [Appendages ... both completely forked, so that the abdomen ends in eight points]. {Masculine}

oenea, *Argia* Hagen in Selys, 1865: 407
> Gr. οἶνος = wine + L. adj. suffix *–eus –ea –eum* = consisting of, having the color of.

> Although not mentioned in the first description it was probably named from the coppery red (= wine colored) front of the thorax in the males. {declinable adjective}

oklahomensis, *Phanogomphus* (Pritchard, 1935: 1)
[Original designation: *Gomphus oklahomensis* Pritchard]
> From the type locality + *–ensis –is –e* = adjectival suffix indicating place of origin.

> "Holotype male and allotype female taken in copulation; Fourche Maline Creek, 8 miles north of Wilburton [Latimer County] Oklahoma, April 28, 1934, A. E. Pritchard collector." {declinable adjective}

olivaceus, *Stylurus* (Selys, 1873a: 749)
[Original designation: *Gomphus olivaceus* Selys]
> L. *oliva* = an olive + adj. suffix *–(c)eus –a –um* = consisting of, having the color of.

> Olive-green elements of coloration probably have led to the name: "occiput ...et le derrière des yeux d'un jaune olivâtre clair ... Prothorax brun mélangé d'olivâtre ... Abdomen assez épais ... les articulations, les côtés et le dessous jaune verdâtre ainsi qu'il suit ..." [occiput and the hind part of the eyes of a clear dark olivaceous yellow ... Prothorax brown mixed with dark olivaceous ... Abdomen very stout ... its articulations, its sides and underneath dark green yellow as follows ...]. {declinable adjective}

onusta, *Tramea* Hagen, 1861: 144
> L. *onustus –a –um* = burdened, loaded.

> Probably the large hindwing spots which remind one of lateral loads on a pack animal are at the base of the name as also suggested by the vernacular name Red Saddlebags.
> {declinable adjective}

Ophiogomphus Selys, 1854: 39
> Gr. ὄφις = snake, serpent + *Gomphus* (q.v.).

By this name Selys wanted to show that he saw the taxon *Gomphus serpentinus* (Charpentier) [= *O. cecilia* (Fourcroy)] as typical for the new genus choosing a Greek term to reflect the Latin species name *serpentinus* [= of or belonging to a serpent].
{Masculine}

Oplonaeschna Selys, 1883: 735
> Gr. ὅπλων = of the armour (genitive of ὅπλα) + *Aeshna* (q.v.).

The species which in Selys' opinion showed the characteristics of the new genus best was *Aeshna armata* (= armed *Aeshna*). For the genus name, a Greek term was chosen.
{Masculine}

ornata, *Celithemis* (Rambur, 1842: 96)
[Original designation: *Libellula ornata* Rambur]
> L. *ornatus –a –um* : past participle of *orno* = to ornament, adorn.

The name refers to complicated markings of wings and body: "Ailes transparentes, à résau clair, les postérieurs ayant une tache basilaire, d'un brun roux, réticulée de jaune, divisée en trois parties, avec un peu de jaune antérieurement et une bande de la même couleur entre les deux dernières parties" [Transparent wings with a clear network, the posteriors having a basilar spot of a reddish brown, reticulated with yellow, divided into three parts, with some yellow anteriorly and a band of the same color between the last two parts]. {declinable past participle}

Orthemis Hagen, 1861: 160
> Gr. ὀρθός = straight + *–themis* (see *Celithemis*).

A distinctive feature of these libellulids is given in the first description: "The first sector of the triangle straight".
{Feminine}

ozarkensis, Gomphurus (Westfall, 1975: 91)
[Original designation: *Gomphus ozarkensis* Westfall]
From the type locality + *–ensis –is –e* = adjectival suffix indicating place of origin.

"the new species, known only as yet from Arkansas, is named for the famous Ozark Mountains in which the holotype was collected." {declinable adjective}

ozarkensis, Somatochlora Bird, 1933: 1
From the geographic range + *–ensis –is –e* = adjectival suffix indicating place of origin.

"I am calling the species *ozarkensis* after the area which is known in physiography as the Ozark plateau." {declinable adjective}

Pachydiplax Brauer, 1868: 368
Gr. παχύς –εῖα –ύ = thick, stout + *–diplax* (see *Erythrodiplax*).

The name refers to the stout female abdomen in comparison with other members of the old libellulid genus *Diplax*: "Hinterleib dick und kurz" [abdomen thick and short] (BRAUER, 1868, 722). {Feminine}

pacifica, Macromia Hagen, 1861: 134
L. *pacificus –a –um* = peacemaking, peacable.

The holotype was collected on a Pacific Railroad survey: "*Hab.* North America, Pacific R. R. Survey, Lat. 38°".
{declinable adjective}

Palaemnema Selys, 1860: 434
Gr. παλαιός –ά –όν = old, ancient + μνῆμα = memory.

The correct interpretation of the name is found in CALVERT, 1931, 2 note 1: "Dr. Ris has told me ... that from hints which Baron de Selys dropped he had received the impression that the Baron intended the generic name *Philogenia* to allude to his love for his living family, *Palaemnema* to his pious memory of his forebears." {Neuter}

pallens, Argia Calvert, 1902: 98
[Original designation: *Argia violacea* var. *pallens* Calvert]
    L. *pallens* : present participle of *palleo* = to be pale.

    The name refers to the overall coloration: "As the varietal name indicates, the chief difference from *A. violacea*, Hagen, is in the smaller amount of black on the thorax and on the seventh abdominal segment." {present participle}

pallidula, Nehalennia Calvert, 1913b: 373
    L. *pallidulus –a –um* = somewhat pale, rather colorless.

    Calvert chose the name "in allusion to the narrower metallic green area of the thoracic dorsum" compared to other *Nehalennia*. {declinable adjective}

pallidum, Enallagma Root, 1923: 202
    L. *pallidus –a –um* = pale, pallid,

    The species is named from overall coloration in both sexes: "♂ pale blue ... ♀ pale green". {declinable adjective}

pallidus, Arigomphus (Rambur: 1842: 163)
[Original designation: *Gomphus pallidus* Rambur]
    L. *pallidus –a –um* = pale, pallid.

    The overall pale brick-colored appearance is at the base of the name: "pallide testaceus ... thorax velu, d'un jaune testacé pâle, avec apparence de trois lignes un peu obscures, ... Abdomen de la même couleur" [Pallid testaceous ... thorax hairy, of a pale brick yellow, with the appearance of three slightly obscure lines, ... Abdomen of the same color]. {declinable adjective}

pallipes, *Sympetrum* (Hagen, 1874a: 589)
[Original designation: *Diplax pallipes* Hagen]
    L. *pallidus –a –um* = pale, pallid + *–pes* (in compounds) = –footed.

    Hagen justifies that name with the explanation that the legs of the new species are paler that those of *Diplax decisa* (= *Sympetrum obtrusum*). But that is only true for some of its populations. So PAULSON (2009, 467) calls the name a misnomer.   {adjective}

palmata. *Aeshna* Hagen, 1856: 369
    L. *palmatus –a –um* = palmate.

    Although not explained in the first description, the name refers to the shape of the male cerci.   {declinable adjective}

Paltothemis Karsch, 1890: 362
    Gr. παλτόν = missile, dart, light spear; for *–themis* see *Celithemis*.

    There is no explanation in the first description and, as Karsch only knew one specimen from the Berlin Museum collection, it is not likely that he would be able to describe the flight style of the living animals by the name. He rather wanted to refer to the distinctive unbranched form of the hamulus characteristically different from that of *Macrothemis*: "durch ... und einem des äußern Astes entbehrenden Hamulus gegenüber *Macrothemis* äußerst charakteristischen Gattung" [a genus being extremely characteristic compared with *Macrothemis* by ... and a hamulus lacking the exteriour branch].   {Feminine}

Pantala Hagen, 1861: 141
    Gr. παντ– (in compounds) = all + ἄλη = wandering or roaming without home or hope of rest.

    The name describes the cosmopolitan distribution and vagrant behaviour of the species *P. flavescens*: "It encircles the whole world; no other species occupies so many countries." (HAGEN, 1861, 142).   {Feminine}

parvidens, Hylogomphus (Currie, 1917: 223)
[Original designation: *Gomphus parvidens* Currie]
    L. *parvus –a –um* = small + *–dens* (in compounds) = with a tooth, with teeth.

    The shorter length of the spine on the cercus, which is at the base of the name, is not specifically mentioned in the first description, but clearly to be seen on pl. 28 fig. 3 in comparision with *G. abbreviatus*, *G. viridifrons* and *G. brevis* (fig. 4-6).
                      {adjective}

parvulus, Lanthus (Selys, 1854: 56)
[Original designation: *Gomphus parvulus* Selys]
    L. *parvulus –a –um.* = very small.

    For a gomphid it is a small species: "Abdomen environ 25. Aile inférieure environ 23. [mm]".   {declinable adjective}

patricia, Leucorrhinia Walker, 1940: 12
    The species is described in a paper "Odonata from the Patricia portion of the Kenora District of Ontario with description of a new species of *Leucorrhinia*".   {noun in apposition}

pentacantha, Nasiaeschna (Rambur, 1842: 208)
[Original designation: *Aeschna pentacantha* Rambur
    Gr. πέντε = five + ἄκανθα = prickle, thorn.

    Spines at the underside of the female's abdomen have led to the name:"... le dernier segment; celui-ci ayant le dessous saillant, portant cinq épines courtes." [the last segment; the latter having the underside protruding, bearing five short spines].
                      {noun in apposition}

Perithemis Hagen, 1861: 185
   Gr. περί = around, round about; for *–themis* see *Celithemis*.

   The name probably refers to the narrower abdomen at the base (= around the body) as a distinguishing feature: "abdomen much shorter than the wings, broad, depressed, narrower at base."
   {Feminine}

perparva, Ischnura McLachlan in Selys, 1876a: 263
   L. *perparvus –a –um* = very little, thoroughly small.

   This is a very small *Ischnura* species: "Par sa petite taille, elle diffère des toutes les autres *Ischnura* du groupe de l'*elegans*" [By its small size, it differs from all the other *Ischnura* of the *elegans* group].   {declinable adjective}

persephone, Aeshna Donnelly, 1961: 193
   Περσεφόνη = Greek goddess, queen of Hades, who was obliged to spend a third of each year (the winter months) in the underworld, and the remaining part of the year with the gods above. The myth of her abduction represents her function as the personification of vegetation, which shoots forth in spring and withdraws into the earth after harvest; hence, she is also associated with spring as well as the fertility of vegetation.

   "The name is suggested by the habitat of this large and colorful dragonfly. In contrast to the sunny streams and ponds favored by most of its North American congeners, it inhabits mountain streams, which are lit by the sun's rays for only a few hours each day, though it ascends periodically through the forest gloom to the sunlit mountains slopes."   {noun in apposition}

pertinax, Brechmorhoga (Hagen, 1861: 166)
[Original designation: *Dythemis pertinax* Hagen]
   L. *pertinax* = persevering, unyielding, obstinate, pertinacious, stubborn.

   Allusion unknown, but see *fugax*.   {adjective}

peruviana, *Erythemis* (Rambur, 1842: 81)
[Original designation: *Libellula peruviana* Rambur]
    L. *peruvianus* –*a* –*um* (adjective) = of Peru

> "Décrite d'après un individu mâle en mauvais état de la collection du général Dejean, ètiqueté du Perou par Latreille" [Described from a male individual in poor condition in the collection of General Dejean, labeled as Peruvian by Latreille].
>
> {declinable adjective}

petechialis, *Epitheca* (Muttkowski, 1911: 10)
[Original designation: *Tetragoneuria petechialis* Muttkowski]
    medical L. *petechialis* –*is* –*e* = spotted, referring to dark spots on wing [(med.) *petechia* – a small red or purple spot caused by bleeding into the skin]

> MUTTKOWSKI 1910, 95: "Wings with brown spots at internodal sections, sometimes with spaces filled"; ibid. 104: "The species is at once distinct from the others by the narrow abdomen, the form of the appendages and the conspicuous spots at each antenodal of the hind wings."   {declinable adjective}

Phanogomphus Carle, 1986: 296
    Gr. φανός = torch, lamp, lantern + γόμφος = bolt for shipbuilding or for other uses.

> This taxon, proposed by Carle as a subgenus of *Gomphus* s.s., was elevated to generic rank by WARE & AL 2016. The author wants the name to be an allusion "that imparts the notion of an obscured lantern, referring to the subdued male abdominal club of this gomphid group as opposed to the wide and brightly colored abdominal clubs of related groups" (PAULSON, by e-mail). But as in modern Greek φανός may also mean floodlight the allusion at the base of the name may not easily be discerned.
>
> {Masculine}

Phyllocycla Calvert, 1948: 62
    Gr. φύλλον = leaf + κύκλος = anything circular.

The name is an anagram of the older name *Cyclophylla* referring to rounded leaflike flanges on sides of abdominal club: "***Phyllocycla*** new generic name for *Cyclophylla* Selys preoccupied." (SELYS 1854, 78: "♂8ᵉ segment dilaté en feuilles plissées, souvent un vestige analogue en 9ᵉ," [♂ 8th segment expanded into folded leaves, often an analogous rudiment in the 9th]).
                                                                                         {Feminine}

Phyllogomphoides Belle, 1970: 112
    Gr. φύλλον = leaf + *Gomphus* (q.v.) + Gr. suffix –ειδής = looking like, similar to.

The name refers to the abdominal flanges by which the taxon differs from the genus *Gomphoides* Selys, in which the type species of the new genus (*P. fuliginosus*) was classified initially: "Foliaceous expansion of abdominal segments 8 and 9 well developed and leaf-like."   {Masculine}

pictum, Enallagma Morse, 1895: 207
    L. *pictus –a –um* = painted, colored, variegated, of various colors.

The species is named for the contrasting yellow and black coloration: "Coloration black and yellow".
                                                                          {declinable adjective}

pima, Argia Garrison, 1994b: 323
    "Named for the Pima Indians of Southern Arizona."
                                                                           {noun in apposition}

plagiatus, Stylurus (Selys, 1854: 57)
[Original designation *Gomphus plagiatus* Selys]
>Gr.πλάγιος –α –ov = athwart, transverse, oblique + L. suffix *–atus –a –um* = marked with, equipped with.

>Perched, in life (PAULSON 2009, 279), or in the specimen that Selys would have examined, the thoracic stripes appear oblique. This is probably the source of the name. "Devant du thorax noirâtre avec une collier mésothoracique étroit, interrompu au milieu, deux bandes droites assez larges, presque confluentes avec lui et un gros point huméral supérieur jaunes. Les côtes jaunes avec deux lignes noirâtres fines, la première interrompue." [In front of the blackish thorax with a narrow mesothoracic collar, interrupted in the middle, two straight bands broad enough, almost confluent with it and a big yellow upper humeral spot. The yellow sides with two fine blackish lines, the first interrupted]. This description is re-iterated in Selys 1858, 419 "Sur les côtés du thorax, aux sutures, sont deux lignes fines noirâtres, la première interrompue" [On the sides of the thorax, to the sutures, are two fine black lines, the first interrupted].
>{declinable adjective}

plana, Argia Calvert, 1902: 96
[Original designation: *Argia vivida* var. *plana* (Hagen, MS)]
>L. *planus –a –um* = flat, level, plain; (but also) clear, distinct.

>The name probably was chosen because Hagen thought this taxon to be a distinct variety. {declinable adjective}

Planiplax Muttkowski, 1910: 169
>L. *planus –a –um* = flat, level, plain + Gr. πλάξ = anything flat and broad.

>This is a replacement name for the preoccupied name *Platyplax* Karsch (Gr. πλατύς –εῖα –ύ = flat, level), referring to the flattened frons, especially in males : "Stirn oben beim ♀ schwächer, beim ♂ stärker abgeflacht und stark mit querkantigem Vorderrand versehen" [frons above with the ♀ lesser, with the ♂ more flattened, furnished with a prominent traversely bordered anterior margin]. {Feminine}

Plathemis Hagen, 1861: 149
    Gr. πλατύς –εῖα –ύ = flat, level; for *–themis* see *Celithemis*.

This is one of the eight names in *–themis* Hagen created for libellulid dragonflies. It refers to the flattened abdomen in this genus: "the abdomen short, broad, flat".   {Feminine}

plebeja, Erythemis (Burmeister, 1839: 856)
[Original designation: *Libellula plebeja* Burmeister]
    L. *plebeius –a –um* = belonging to the common people, plebeian, common, perhaps refers to its being common or ordinary.

Burmeister does not explain his choice of the name, but in the first description it reads: "griseo-fusca ... alis griseis" [gray brown ... with gray wings]. The mentioning of gray wings is unique among the 81 species Burmeister classified into the genus *Libellula*, and so this feature of his specimen combined with the dark overall impression may have reminded him of the lower classes, the clothes of which were dull colored and many of whom had livid faces. According to Paulson (in litt.) Burmeister's specimen must have been unusual, as the wings of this species are not any grayer than in other libellulids. But perhaps Burmeister only wanted to state that the species was very common. Rambur (1842: 107) chose the name *plebeia* for a different species to evoke the similarity to the Eurasian species *Sympetrum vulgatum*; both species names can be translated as 'common'.
                                                            {declinable adjective}

pollutum, Enallagma (Hagen, 1861: 83)
[Original designation: *Agrion* (subgenus *Ischnura*) *pollutum* Hagen]
    L. *pollutus –a –um*: past participle of *polluo* = to soil, defile, stain, foul, pollute, make unclean.

The name perhaps refers to the dark coloration, which is described as "Brassy-fuscous". There are other similar names (cf. *immunda*).   {declinable past participle}

posita, Ischnura (Hagen, 1861: 77)
[Original designation: *Agrion* (subgenus *Ischnura*) *positum* Hagen]
    L. *positus –a –um* = placed, situated, set, planted, standing, lying [past participle of *pono*].

    As Hagen does not explain his choice of the name, the allusion is unknown.   {declinable past participle}

potulentus, Stylurus Needham, 1942: 71
[as *Gomphus* (*Stylurus*) *potulentus* Needham]
    L. *potulentus –a –um* = tipsy, rather drunk.

    The name seems to be chosen as an allusion to the type locality: "A single male specimen from Whisky Creek; near Leaf, Mississippi".   {declinable adjective}

praecox, Brechmorhoga (Hagen, 1861: 164)
[Original designation: *Dythemis praecox* Hagen]
    L. *praecox* = ripe before its time, early ripe, premature, precocious.

    There is no explanation in the first description, so the allusion is unknown; but cf. *fugax*.   {adjective}

praevarum, Enallagma (Hagen, 1861: 88)
[Original designation: *Agrion praevarum* Hagen]
    L. *praevarus –a –um* = very irregular, very unsteady.

    There is no hint in the first description how the name is to be understood, but it is the only *Agrion* species in that publication for which Hagen states: "having the posterior margin of the prothorax each side excised". So that feature might be at the base of the name.   {declinable adjective}

princeps, Epitheca Hagen, 1861: 134
    L. *princeps* = first, chief, foremost.

    The name refers to large size relative to other *Epitheca*: "A large specimen (♂) from Georgia, has 72 millims. length; alar expanse 102 millim."   {noun in apposition}

prognata, Ischnura (Hagen, 1861: 83)
[Original designation: *Agrion* (subgenus *Ischnura*) *prognatum* Hagen]
 L. *prognatus –a –um* = born, descended, sprung from.

 As there is no reference by Hagen, the allusion remains unknown.   {declinable adjective}

Progomphus Selys, 1854: 69
 Gr. prefix προ– = prior in rank or order + *Gomphus* (q.v.).

 The name is probably meant as 'preceding *Gomphus* phylogenetically', referring to the primitive position of the genus. This explanation is probable because, before this genus, a genus *Hemigomphus* = half a *Gomphus* is described. {Masculine}

Protoneura Selys, 1857: 470
[as *Protonevra* Selys]
 Gr. πρῶτος –η –ον = foremost, first, earliest + adj. suffix –νευρος –ον –ον (Latinized) [from νεῦρον = any linear feature in an organism, so sinew, tendon, vein, nerve, fibre in plants; in entomology used for wing veins].

 Probably Selys thought the genus to be primordial according to features of the wing venation. (see SELYS 1860, 431 "J'appelle *incomplètes* les Agrionines de cette sous-division, parce que, chez elles le secteur inférieur du triangle est nul ou rudimentaire" [I call the Agrionines of this subdivision incomplete, because in them the lower sector of the triangle is missing or rudimentary]).
   {Feminine}

protracta, Aphylla (Selys, 1859: 546)
[Original designation: *Cyclophylla protracta* Selys]
 L. *protractus –a –um*: past participle of *protraho* = to lengthen, to extend.

 There are posterolateral extensions in the abdominal segment 10 of the males: "remarquable par sa grande taille et par un prolongement latéral inférieur terminal du 10e segment du mâle, rappellant les *Aphylla*." [remarkable for its large size and a lower lateral extension of the 10th segment of the male, reminiscent of *Aphylla*]. {declinable past participle}

provocans, Somatochlora Calvert, 1903: 39
    L. *provocans* : present participle of *provoco* = to challenge, provoke, exasperate.

    The name refers to the difficulty of capture: "The insect usually keeps at a considerable distance above one's head, both when in flight and at rest. We have seen other individuals which we believe to be of this species, but in spite of special trips to secure them and patient waiting in the hope that they might come in one's reach, only these two males are known to have been taken in ten years." {present participle}

proxima, Leucorrhinia Calvert, 1890: 38
[as *Leucorhinia proxima* (Hagen mss.) Calvert]
    L. *proximus –a –um* = nearest, next.

    The name might be alluding to the similarity to other *Leucorrhinia* (in HAGEN 1875, 79 without a description it is placed between *L. glacialis* and *L. frigida*) or, being Hagen's manuscript name, it might just say 'next *Leucorrhinia* in my collection'.
    {declinable adjective}

pseudimitans, Macrothemis Calvert, 1898: 319
    Gr./L. prefix *pseud(o)–* = false (from Gr. ψεῦδος = falsehood, lie, fallacy) + *imitans* (q.v.).

    Calvert had in 1895 erroneously given a description of this species under the name of *M. imitans* Karsch, which error he rectifies by the new name: "*Macrothemis pseudimitans* nom. nov." {adjective}

Pseudoleon Kirby, 1889: 274
    Gr./L. prefix *pseud(o)–* = false (from Gr. ψεῦδος = falsehood, lie, fallacy) + λέων = lion.

    The wing pattern in this genus is like that of some antlions: "wings rather short and broad, of an extremely iridescent hyaline, mottled with brown or purplish brown as in many *Myrmeleonidae*". {Masculine}

psilus, *Rhionaeschna* (Calvert, 1947: 4)
[Original designation: *Aeshna psilus* Calvert]
    Gr. ψιλός = soldier without heavy armor (Latinized).

The name refers to a difference from *A. cornigera*, from which the species is separated: "♂. Anterior lamina with very short spine on each side".   {noun in apposition}

pulchella, *Libellula* Drury, 1770: 115
    L. *pulchellus –a –um* = beautiful little one.

There is no explanation of the name in the first description; so it might be a reference to the mature male's pretty color pattern or it could be the first scientific name referring to the loveliness of dragonflies.   {declinable adjective}

quadratum, *Acanthagrion* Selys, 1876a: 309
[as *Acanthagrion gracile* var. *quadratum* Selys]
    L. *quadratus –a –um* = square.

The name evokes the distinctive spot on the first abdominal segment of the male: "le 1er segment offre une tache carrée basale noir" [the first segment has a square black basal spot].   {declinable adjective}

quadricolor, *Phanogomphus* (Walsh, 1863: 246)
[Original designation: *Gomphus quadricolor* Walsh]
    L. *quadri–* (in compounds) = four + *–color* (in compounds) = colored.

The adults of this species are four-colored: "There are four distinct colors in this insect, viz.: black, lilac, green and yellow, whence the specific name".   {adjective}

quadrimaculata, Libellula Linnaeus, 1758: 543
[as *Libellula 4-maculata* Linnaeus]
> L. *quadri–* (in compounds) = four + *macula* = spot, stain + suffix *–atus –a –um* = provided with.

> The species has black marks at the nodus of each wing which together with the pterostigmata make eight spots: "L(ibellula) alis posticis basi omnibusque medio antico macula nigricante" [A dragonfly with a blackish spot at the base of the hind wings and moreover in every wing in front of its middle part].
>
> {declinable adjective}

ramburii, Ischnura (Selys, 1850: 186)
[Original designation: *Agrion ramburii* Selys]
> "Ce que M. Rambur a donné une variété du senegalense, envoyé de Yucatan, et qu'il a très-bien signalée, page 277 de son ouvrage, forme une espèce distincte que nous nommerons *Agrion Ramburii*." [That which M. Rambur has given is a variety of the *senegalense*, sent from Yucatan, and which he has very well pointed out, page 277 of his work, forms a distinct species which we shall call *Agrion Ramburii*]. Jules Pierre Rambur (See p. 66), was an early French entomologist who, after Burmeister (1839), was the second entomologist in the 19th century who tried to describe the dragonflies from around the world.
>
> {noun in the genitive case}

rectangularis, Lestes Say, 1839: 34
> L. *rectangularis –is –e* = rectangular.

> The name probably refers to the shape of the male cerci in lateral view: "forceps shorter than the two ultimate segments taken together, with two oblique, very acute teeth beneath; beyond the middle curved downward and inward, so as to become nearly perpendicular to the basal half".   {declinable adjective}

recurvatum, Enallagma Davis, 1913a: 15
> L. *recurvatus –a –um*= recurved: past participle of *recurvo* = to bend or curve backwards.

> "The species has been named *recurvatum* on account of the male's superior appendages."   {declinable past participle}

Remartinia Navás, 1911: 479
> "*Etimologia*. He formado este nombre genérico en obsequio del ilustre odonatólogo D. Renato Martin, à quien debo innumerales obsequios en el estudio de los Odonatos." [*Etymology*. I have formed this generic name in favor of the illustrious odonatologist Dr. René Martin, to whom I owe innumerable favors in the study of Odonates]. René Martin (See p. 53), a French entomologist was an early monographer of Aeshnidae.
>   {Feminine}

resolutum, Coenagrion (Hagen in Selys, 1876a: 1263)
[Original designation: *Agrion resolutum* Hagen in Selys]
> L. *resolutus –a –um*: past participle of *resolvo* = to loosen, to relax.

> This word is not directly at the base of the name, but it is a reference to the type locality Fort Resolution [Northwest Territories]. "Patrie . Territoire de la baie d'Hudson (Saskatchvan, Red River et Fort Résolution; près de grand lac de l'Esclave)" [Home country. Territory of the Hudson Bay (Saskatchewan, Red River and Fort Resolution, near to the Great Slave Lake)].
>   {declinable past participle}

Rhionaeschna Förster, 1909: 220
>Gr. ῥίον = any jutting part of a mountain, whether upwards or forwards + *Aeshna* (q.v.).

>The name refers the prominent vertex in the type species: "Sehr merkwürdig ist die Bildung der Ocellenblase. Sie ist von vornher eingestülpt, sodaß sie eine Art Haube bildet, unter welcher die mittelste Ocelle sitzt. Vor der Ocelle ist die Stirn mit einer kreisförmigen Mulde versehen. Gesicht etwas kugelig vorgewölbt; die Stirn sanft nach oben und hinten gerundet, ohne Vorderkante, da die Kantenlinie fast in die Mitte der Oberseite zu liegen kommt" [The formation of the vesicule near the ocelli is very remarkable. It is concave anteriorly, so that it forms some kind of hood, under which the middle ocellus is positioned. In front of the ocellus the frons has a circular depression. The face bulges somewhat forward globularly; the frons is rounded softly upwards and backwards, without an anterior edge, as the line of the edge is positioned nearly in the middle of the upper side].
>
>{Feminine}

rhoadsi, *Argia* Calvert, 1902: 92
>"(Rhoads: 1 ♂)". Collector of the holotype, Samuel Nicholson Rhoads (1862 – 1952) was a founder of the Delaware Valley Ornithological Club. From 1902, for about 20 years, he maintained the Franklin Book Store in Philadelphia.
>
>{noun in the genitive case}

rogersi, Stenogomphurus (Gloyd, 1936: 1)
[Original designation: *Gomphus rogersi* Gloyd]
"The species is named in honor of Dr. J. Speed Rogers of the University of Florida, in appreciation of the many specimens of Odonata which he has presented to the Museum."

Dr James Speed Rogers (1891-1955) was an American biologist and entomologist who was the Director of the Museum of Zoology at the University of Michigan. He had spent three years, from 1919 to 1921, as Assistant Professor of Zoology at Grinnell College before joining the staff at the University of Florida as Professor and Head of the Department of Biology. Professor Rogers remained at Florida for twenty four years. (He was also the collector of the type specimen).

{noun in the genitive case}

rubicundulum, Sympetrum (Say, 1839: 26)
[Original designation: *Libellula rubicundula* Say]
L. *rubicundulus –a –um* = somewhat red (diminutive of *rubicundus –a –um* = suffused with red, ruddy).

In the first description Say says: "tergum bright sanguineous". This is not only true for adult males, but also for some of the females when mature (cf. PAULSON 2009, 465).

{declinable adjective}

rupinsulensis, Ophiogomphus (Walsh, 1862: 388)
[Original designation: *Erpetogomphus?* [sic] *rupinsulensis* Walsh]
L. *rupes* = a rock, cliff + *insula* = island + *–ensis –is –e* = adjectival suffix indicating place of origin.

The name refers to the type locality; TL: Illinois, [Rock Island County], Rock Island: "Except where otherwise stated the following species have been taken by myself within four miles of the city of Rock Island". {declinable adjective}

sabino, Argia Garrison, 1994b: 329
    "Named for Sabino Canyon, Arizona. ... I collected *A. sabino* on large boulders near the stream's edge in Upper Sabino Canyon in September 1988."   {noun in apposition}

sahlbergi, Somatochlora Trybom, 1889: 7
    After Johan R. Sahlberg (1845-1920), Finnish entomologist.

    Sahlberg was a member of the expedition during which Trybom detected the species. In Trybom's paper Sahlberg is said to have captured a female of the species, which is described next to his eponym species under a different name [*S. théeli*] which indeed is the female of *S. sahlbergi*. "Prof. J. SAHLBERG fångade en hona vid Chantaika $^{19}/_7$, hvilken, då hon kom mig tillhanda för bestämning, visserligen var mycket skadad, men som dock af qvarlefvorna visar sig så nära öfverensstammände med den nyss beskrifna, att jåg icke tvekar att anse dem såsom tillhörande samma art." [Prof J Sahlberg caught a female at Chantaika 19/7, which, when it arrived to me for determination, certainly was much damaged but, as is evident from the remains, it is so closely consistent with that newly described that I do not hesitate to consider them as belonging to the same species].
    {noun in the genitive case}

salva, Telebasis (Hagen, 1861: 85)
[Original designation: *Agrion* (subgenus *Pyrrhosoma*) *salvum* Hagen]
    L. *salvus –a –um* = unharmed, saved, unhurt.

    Named in opposition to the Carribean species *Agrion vulneratum* [= damaged *Agrion*, now *Telebasis vulnerata*] described as the next one in HAGEN 1861 from a truncated specimen "the posterior lobe of the prothorax larger, margined with yellow, the sides obliquely truncated". This is different in *Telebasis salva*.
    {declinable adjective}

sandrius, Phanogomphus (Tennessen, 1983: 743)
[Original designation: *Gomphus sandrius* Tenessen]
    "Etymology- *G. sandrius* [*–a –um*] ... "Sandra's Gomphus," for my wife [* 1947]."   {declinable adjective}

sanguiniventris, Planiplax Calvert, 1907: 327
>   L. *sanguineus –a –um* = bloody, blood-colored, blood-red + *venter* (stem *ventr–*) = belly + adjectival ending *–is –is –e*.
>
>   The name refers to the color of the abdomen of the species: "abdominal segments 3-10 and the appendages bright red".
>   {declinable adjective}

sarracenia, Cordulegaster Abbott & Hibbitts, 2011: 61
>   Named after *Sarracenia*, a genus of pitcher plants: "The Latin word sarracenia ... is the genus of eastern North American insectivorous pitcher plants found in bogs and seepages at the type locality: The pitcher plant genus was named after D. Sarrazin, a 17th-century botanist from Quebec, Canada."
>   {noun in apposition}

saturata, Libellula Uhler, 1857: 88
>   L. *saturatus –a –um* : past participle of *saturo* = to drench, saturate.
>
>   The name refers to the coloration of the wing bases: "wings humeral portion saturate reddish-yellow".
>   {declinable past participle}

saucium, Amphiagrion (Burmeister, 1839: 819)
[Original designation: *Agrion saucium* Burmeister]
>   L. *saucius –a –um* = wounded, hurt.
>
>   A special feature of the coloration of the male is described by the name: "segmentis 7-9 supra nigris, linea media sanguina" [segments 7-9 black above, with a blood-red middle line] which feature makes them look wounded. BURMEISTER (1839: 856) took a female of this species and one of a different species to be conspecific varieties and described them as *Agrion discolor* [differently colored *Agrion*]. From that synonym KIRBY (1890: 143) made the type species of the genus *Amphiagrion* (CALVERT 1898: 38).
>   {declinable adjective}

sayi, Cordulegaster Selys, 1854: 104
>The species is named after Thomas Say (See p. 69), the first American entomologist, who contributed to the knowledge of Odonata by describing 27 new species.
>
>{noun in the genitive case}

scudderi, Stylurus (Selys, 1873a: 752)
[Original designation: *Gomphus scudderi* Selys]
>"*Patrie* : États-Unis. Communiquée par M. Scudder (Coll. Selys)."
>
>Samuel Hubbard Scudder (See p. 70) was an American entomologist and palaeontologist.
>
>{noun in the genitive case}

secreta, Remartinia (Calvert, 1952: 262)
[Original designation: *Coryphaeschna secreta* Calvert]
>L. *secretus –a –um*: hidden; private, secret; remote; apart, separate (from).
>
>"The proposed name refers to the long concealment of this large insect in spite of much biological exploration of Cuba."
>
>{declinable adjective}

sedula, Argia (Hagen, 1861: 94)
[Original designation: *Agrion sedulum* Hagen]
>L. *sedulus –a –um* = attentive, persistent, busy, sedulous.
>
>Whereas the Latin adjective can have numerous meanings, none seems very suitable for a dragonfly. As Hagen does not explain his choice, the allusion remains unknown.
>
>{declinable adjective}

selysii, Helocordulia (Hagen in Selys, 1878: 189)
[Original designation: *C[ordulia] selysii* Hagen in Selys]
>The species is named after Michel Edmond De Selys-Longchamps (See p. 71), the eminent Belgian odonatologist.
>
>{noun in the genitive case}

semiaquea, *Epitheca* (Burmeister, 1839: 858)
[Original designation: *Libellula semiaquea* Burmeister]
>L. *semi–* (in compounds) = half + *aqueus –a –um* = consisting of water, being like water.

>From Burmeister's description is not to be seen with certainty which feature is meant: "alis hyalinis, posticis late fuscis, macula elongata diaphana" [wings hyaline, the hind ones broadly dark, with an elongate diaphanous spot]. So the name possibly alludes to half of hindwing as clear as water or rather to that quality of both forewings in contrast to the colored hindwings.
>{declinable adjective}

semicinctum, *Sympetrum* (Say, 1839: 27)
[Original designation: *Libellula semicincta* Say]
>L. *semi–* (in compounds) = half + *cinctus –a –um* = girt, girdled (past participle of *cingo* = to go around, surround, gird, wreathe).

>The name refers to wing bands: "wings tinted on the basal half with pale ferrugineous". {declinable adjective}

semicirculare, *Enallagma* Selys, 1876a: 517
>L. *semicircularis –is –e* = semicircular.

>The shape of male cerci is at the base of the name: "vus en dessus, ils s'écartent d'abord un peu l'une de l'autre, pour se rapprocher en demi-cercle à la pointe" [Seen from above, they move away at first a little from each other, to approach in a semicircle at the point]. {declinable adjective}

semicircularis, *Somatochlora* (Selys, 1871a: 295)
[Original designation: *Epitheca semicircularis* Selys]
>L. *semicircularis –is –e* = semicircular.

>Also for this species the name refers to the outline of male cerci in dorsal view: "le bout des appendices courbé semi-circulairement" [the tips of appendages curved semicircularly].
>{declinable adjective}

semifasciata, Libellula Burmeister, 1839: 862
> L. *semi–* (in compounds) = half + *fascia* = band, bandage + suffix *–atus –a –um* = marked with, equipped with.

> In this species there are dark bands on the wings starting from the end of the nodus in the middle of the wings: "alis in basi fulvis, linea fusca flavo-venosa, tum fascia dimidia ad finem subcostae et macula in apice inde ab initio stigmatis dimidie fusca, dimidia fulva" [the wings reddish-yellow at base, with a dark yellow veined band, then half a band at the end of the subcosta and, at the apex from the origin of the pterostigma, a mark half dark brown, half reddish-yellow].
>   {declinable adjective}

sepia, Epitheca (Gloyd, 1933: 2)
[Original designation: *Tetragoneuria sepia* Gloyd]
> L. *sepia* = the cuttlefish; the ink of the cuttlefish (borrowed from Gr. σηπία).

> The name refers to the mainly brown coloration: "Synthorax, dorsally a rich medium brown (Roman sepia), laterally olivaceous brown." "The greatly reduced basal wing spots and the rich brown color of the whole insect in general immediately set it apart from other members of the group (p. 4)."
>   {noun in apposition}

septentrionalis, Aeshna Burmeister, 1839: 839
> L. *septentrionalis –is –e* = northern [the word is interesting, because it is an adjective derived from the constellation the Romans called *septem triones* (= seven oxen used for threshing) – now known as the Great Bear – which metaphorically also signifies the North].

> The type locality is at the base of the name: "Aus Labrador" [From Labrador].   {declinable adjective}

septentrionalis, *Somatochlora* (Hagen, 1861: 139)
[Original designation: *Cordulia septentrionalis* Hagen]
    L. *septentrionalis* –*is* –*e* = northern.

    This species also has a northern geographic range: "*Hab.* Labrador".   {declinable adjective}

septima, *Gomphurus* (Westfall, 1956: 253)
[Original designation: *Gomphus septima* Westfall]
    Named after Septima Cecilia Smith (1891-1984), American odonatologist: "This species is named for Dr. Septima Smith in recognition of the contribution she has made to our knowledge of the Odonata of Alabama."   {noun in apposition}

septima, *Triacanthagyna* (Selys in Sagra, 1857: 460)
[Original designation: *Gynacantha septima* Selys in Sagra]
    L. *septimus* –*a* –*um* = the seventh; but Septima is also a modern female name.

    As Selys gives the French name as Gynacanthe septime, not septième, it is not the numeral at the base of the denomination, but the female name. However, as Selys does not explain whom he wants to honor, her identity remains uncertain.
    {noun in apposition}

servilia, *Crocothemis* (Drury, 1773: 112)
[Original designation: *Libellula servilia* Drury]
    Drury never explains his names, which are almost always female names from Roman antiquity. It is most likely that this species was named after Servilia (**ca.* 104 BC, †. after 42 BC) who was the mistress of Julius Caesar, mother of one of Caesar's assassins, Brutus, mother-in-law of another assassin, Cassius, and half-sister of Cato the Younger.   {noun in apposition}

severus, *Ophiogomphus* Hagen, 1874a: 591
    L. *severus* –*a* –*um* = serious, sober, grave, strict, austere, stern, severe.

    As Hagen gives no explanation, the allusion of this name remains unknown.   {declinable adjective}

shurtleffii, Cordulia Scudder, 1866: 217

"The following notes have references mostly to the colors during life of some species of Odonata taken in the summer of 1862 by my valued friend; the late Mr. C. A. Shurtleff [1840-1864], and myself during a visit of a few weeks at the Glen, White Mountains." {noun in the genitive case}

sigma, Lestes Calvert, 1901: 49

The Greek letter name σίγμα is here applied for the shape of the letter "S".

"The **S**-shape of the inferior appendages recalls that of *L. unguiculatus* Hagen, and has suggested the specific name." {noun in apposition}

sigmastylus, Stylogomphus Cook & Laudermilk, 2004: 5

The Greek letter name σίγμα is here applied for the shape of the letter "S" + L. *stylus* (medieval orthography for stilus) = a pointed instrument. (Note: in ancient times the Greek letter sigma was formed like a C, so that with the Romans it was in use for a semicircular couch for reclining at meals or a bathing tub of the same shape).

p. 14 "Etymology From "sigma" Gr. = letter "S" in Greek alphabet, and "stylus" L. = "sharp pointed", alluding to the sharp-pointed "S" shaped cerci. The specific epithet is an adjective." {declinable adjective}

signatum, Enallagma (Hagen, 1861: 84)
[Original designation: *Agrion* (subgenus *Ischnura*) *signatum* Hagen]

L. *signatus –a –um*: past participle of *signo* = to mark.

Hagen describes the species as "fuscous", with yellow and black spots and lines on diverse parts of the body. So that color pattern is at the base of the name. {declinable past participle}

signiferum, *Sympetrum* Cannings & Garrison, 1991: 474
>L. *signifer –fera –ferum* = sign-bearing.

>"Etymology. *S. signiferum* is named for its most characteristic feature, the dark brown triangular spot at the base of the hindwing. Combined with the orange basal wash anteriorly, these wing markings are unique in the genus – thus: *signiferum* (Latin): bearing marks, signs, or flags."   {declinable adjective}

simplicicollis, *Erythemis* (Say, 1839: 28)
[Original designation: *Libellula simplicicollis* Say]
>L. *simplex* (stem *simplic-*) = simple, plain + *–collis –is –e* (in compounds) = –necked.

>Say does not explain his choice of the name and his description does not give a clue. HAGEN, 1861, 170 in his description of the genus *Mesothemis*, to which he transfers the species, says "posterior lobe of the prothorax large, broad, bilobed" which seems not to be a feature to be described as 'plain', adding to the enigma.   {declinable adjective}

sitchensis, *Aeschna* Hagen, 1861: 119
>From the type locality + *–ensis –is –e* = adjectival suffix indicating placc of origin.

>"*Hab.* Russian America [now Alaska], Sitka."
>   {declinable adjective}

smithi, *Ophiogomphus* Tennessen & Vogt, 2004: 540
>"Named for our colleague and co-discoverer of the species, William A. Smith [See p. 72], biologist, Department of Natural Resources, State of Wisconsin."
>   {noun in the genitive case}

Somatochlora Selys, 1871a: 279
    Gr. σῶμα (stem σωματ-) = body + χλωρός –ά –όν = pale green.

The name evokes the green metallic sheen of the species which CHARPENTIER (1840) knew when naming his (sub)genus *Chlorosoma*. As that name was preoccupied, it was changed into *Somatochlora* by SELYS (1871a: 279).   {Feminine}

specularis, *Octogomphus* (Hagen in Selys, 1859: 544)
[Original designation: *Neogomphus? specularis* Hagen in Selys]
    L. *specularis –is –e* = like a mirror.

There is no clue in the first description for the choice of the name, perhaps – although philologically incorrect – it could mean the assignment to the genus *Neogomphus* is speculative.
    {declinable adjective}

spicatus, *Phanogomphus* (Hagen in Selys, 1854: 54)
[Original designation: *Gomphus spicatus* Hagen in Selys]
    L. *spicatus –a –um*: past participle of *spico* = to furnish with spikes, probably a reference to spines on male cerci.

"Appendices anals bruns; les superieurs pointus, avec une forte dent latérale externe submédiane, très-visible en dessus; l'autre, aussi submediane, mais au bord interne, très penchée vers le bas, non visible en dessus. Appendice inférieur à branches plus écartées que les superieurs." [Anal appendages brown; the superior pointed, with a strong lateral submedian external tooth, very visible from above; the other, also submedian, but at the inner edge, very inclined downwards, not visible from above. Inferior appendage with branches shorter than superiors] SELYS 1858, 415: "Ses appendices anals singuliers rappellent ceux du *G. Graslini* d'Europe; si ce n'est qu'ils possèdent une dent interne qui manque chez le *Graslini*." [Its singular anal appendages recall those of *G. graslini* of Europe; except that they have an internal tooth missing from *graslini*].   {declinable past participle}

spiniceps, *Stylurus* (Walsh, 1862: 389)
[Original designation: *Macrogomphus? spiniceps* Walsh]
    L. *spina* = thorn, prickle, spine + *–ceps* (in compounds) = headed.

There are spines on the female vertex, to which the name refers: "between each of these extremities and the eye is a slender acute black thorn".   {adjective}

spinigera, *Epitheca* (Selys, 1871a: 269)
[Original designation: *Cordulia spinigera* Selys]
    L. *spiniger –era –erum* = thorn-bearing, referring to male cerci.

"Les appendices anales supérieurs portent en dessous intérieurement une longue épine penchée en bas" [The superior anal appendages carry internally a long spine bent downwards].   {declinable adjective}

spinosa, *Epitheca* (Hagen in Selys, 1878: 188)
[Original designation: *Cordulia spinosa* Hagen in Selys]
    L. *spinosus –a –um* = full of thorns, spiny.

The males of the species have spines on the cerci: "... les appendices anals supérieurs qui portent *en dessus* à leur dernier quarte une dent courte mais épaisse mais aiguë; très distincte lorsqu'on regarde l'appendice en profil." [...the upper anal appendages which carry in their last quarter a short but thick, sharp tooth; very distinct when looking at the appendix in profile].   {declinable adjective}

spinosus, *Dromogomphus* SELYS, 1854: 59
L. *spinosus –a –um* = full of thorns, spiny.
    The name is a reference to the long spines of the metafemur: "5 épines très-fortes aux derniers fémurs" [5 very strong spines on the hind femora] these are the only spines mentioned there; cf. SELYS, 1858, 381: "les femurs postérieurs très-longs, dépassant un peu le 2e segment avec 5 épines très-fortes en dehors" [the hind femora very long, a little longer than the second segment with five very strong spines on the outer side].   {declinable adjective}

spoliatus, Dromogomphus (Hagen in Selys, 1858: 669)
[Original designation: *Gomphus spoliatus* Hagen in Selys]
    L. *spoliatus –a –um* = despoiled, impoverished, bare (past participle of *spolio* = to plunder, strip).

Probably the name reflects the absence of a black band between frons and nasus: "On voit que le caractère principal réside dans l'absence de bande noire entre le front et le nasus" [One sees that the main characteristic lies in the absence of a black band between the frons and the nasus].   {declinable past participle}

spumarius, Lestes Hagen in Selys, 1862: 309
[as *Lestes spumaria* Hagen in Selys]
    L. *spuma* = foam, froth, spume + suffix *–(a)rius –a –um* = relating to, pertaining to.

The pruinosity of the interalar space is probably at the base of the name: "Espace interalaire saupoudré" [Interalar space sprinkled with powder].   {declinable adjective}

stella, Epitheca (Williamson in Muttkowski, 1911: 96)
[Original designation: *Tetragoneuria stella* Williamson in Muttkowski]
    "This species is named for Stella Mullin Deam [1870-1957], who has collected much botanical and zoological material in Florida ... I am indebted to her for the specimens of this new species as well as for many other dragon flies from Florida."
  {noun in apposition}

Stenogomphurus Carle, 1986: 296
    Gr. στενός = narrow / close, confined + *Gomphurus* (q.v.).

Carle does not say why he chose this name, but it appears that he thinks the new subgenus to be closely related to *Gomphurus*. An explanation is found in WARE & AL. 2016, 7: "abdomen ... relatively slender and with lateral margins of S8-S9 only slightly expanded in *Stenogomphurus*".   {Masculine}

stigmatus, *Phyllogomphoides* (Say, 1839: 17)
[Original designation: *Aeshna stigmata* Say]
    Gr. (+ L.) στίγμα = a prick, puncture, mark (in dragonfly names often used for the pterostigma) + *–atus –a –um* = equipped with.

    The name reflects the large pterostigma: "This species resembles the *fraterna*, but it is much more yellowish, the stigma of the wings is about double the size, the markings differ".
{declinable adjective}

stultus, *Lestes* Hagen, 1861: 67
[as *Lestes stulta* Hagen]
    L. *stultus –a –um* = foolish.

    Perhaps a defect of Hagen's type might have led to the name: "The abdomen is wanting". If not, the allusion is unknown.
{declinable adjective}

Stylogomphus Fraser, 1922: 69
    L. *stylus*: medieval orthography for *stilus* = a stake, a pointed instrument used by the Romans for writing upon wax tablets. The name applies to the anal appendages that formerly were also called '*styli*' + *Gomphus* (q.v.).

    The name refers to the attenuate male cerci: "appendages a little longer than segment 10, the superior curved, at first divaricate and then approximating and with the ends overlapping, the inferior cleft for about half of its length, the two branches parallel"; "Anal appendages unlike any other species of Gomphine that I know of".
{Masculine}

Stylurus Needham, 1897: 166

> Gr. στῦλος = pillar [≠ *stylus* as in the foregoing lemma] + –ουρος –ος –ον (in compounds) –tailed [from οὐρά = tail; in entomology used for abdomen].

> In his publication Needham proposes three new genera from larval characters: "Believing that the immature stages throw much light on the relationship of the imagoes …I propose three new genera …; *Lanthus* …, *Orcus* …, and Stylurus (στυλος and οὐρα), type *plagiatus* Selys." The last genus is based on the elongate ninth segment of larvae, which sets it apart from other gomphids (p.168): "Ninth abdominal segment one half longer than the 8th, its lateral margins nearly parallel".   {Masculine}

subarctica, *Aeshna* Walker, 1908: 385

> L. prefix *sub-* (in compounds) = (*inter alia*), somewhat + *arcticus* –*a* –*um* = northern, arctic [from Gr. Ἄρκτος = the constellation of the Great Bear, under which the arctic region seems to be situated].

> The name reflects the northerly distribution: "Boreal zone, from Anticosti and Nova Scotia to Isle Royale, Mich., and the north shore of Lake Superior."   {declinable adjective}

submedianus, *Arigomphus* (Williamson, 1914: 54)
[Original designation: *Gomphus submedianus* Williamson]

> L. prefix *sub-* (in compounds) = (*inter alia*), lying near to + *medianus* –*a* –*um* = in the middle, middle.

> Whereas not explained in the first description, the name perhaps refers to submedian thoracic stripes.   {declinable adjective}

subornata, *Plathemis* Hagen, 1861: 149
> L. prefix *sub-* (in compounds) = (*inter alia*), under, beneath, below + *ornatus –a –um*: past participle of *orno* = to decorate, adorn.

> The species has yellow stripes on the underside of abdomen: "abdomen with a broad, maculose stripe each side of the dorsum and broader ones on the venter, yellow (in males it is wanting towards the apex)". {declinable adjective}

sulcatum, *Enallagma* Williamson, 1922c: 114
> L. *sulcatus –a –um*: past participle of *sulco* = to cleave.

> The name refers to a feature of the female's mesostigmal lamina: "the posterior and inferior black portion of the lamina grooved (hence the specific name), to receive the dorsal branch of the superior appendage of the male". {declinable past participle}

superbus, *Pseudoleon* (Hagen, 1861: 148)
[Original designation: *Celithemis superba* Hagen]
> L. *superbus –a –um* = *inter alia*, superb, magnificent.

> In his first description Hagen emphasizes: "a peculiar and most beautiful species". Therefore the overall appearance is at the base of the name. {declinable adjective}

susbehcha, *Ophiogomphus* Vogt & Smith, 1993: 503
> The name of the dragonfly in Lakota Sioux

> "Lakota Sioux, n., susbehcha – 'dragonfly'."
> {noun in apposition}

Sympetrum Newman, 1833: 511
> Newman introduces the new taxon: "GENUS. – SYMPETRUM.[d] Newman" and in his footnote d he explains: "Συμπιεζω *comprimo* [= to compress] ητρον abdomen". In his text he continues "The remaining species of Dr. Leach's genus, *Libellula* widely differ from each other in the form of the posterior segments ...; but in none of them are these segments compressed as in the genus *Sympetrum*". {Neuter}

Tachopteryx Uhler in Selys, 1859: 551
    Gr ταχύς –εῖα –ύ = swift + πτέρυξ = wing, winged creature.

Although not explained in the first description, the meaning of the name is self-evident.   {Feminine}

taeniolata, Macromia Rambur, 1842: 139
    L. *taeniola* = a little band or ribbon + suffix *–atus –a –um* = marked with, equipped with.

The name probably refers to the pale mid-lateral thoracic band. A *taenia* was worn around the head normally, but Rambur must not have been aware of this: "vertex triangulaire, bifide velu, d'un bleu verdâtre métallique. Thorax légèrement velu, d'un vert bleuâtre métallique, avec une bande antérieure de chaque côte, commençant très-bas et descendant jusqu'aux pattes, une latérale qui fait le tour du thorax, et deux petites sous sa partie postérieure jaunes." [Vertex triangular, hairy, bifid, metallic greenish-blue. Thorax slightly hairy, of a metallic bluish green, with an anterior band on each side, beginning very low and descending to the legs, one lateral which circles the thorax, and two small under its posterior part, yellow].
                                        {declinable adjective}

talaria, Cordulegaster Tennessen, 2004: 830
    L. *talaria* = the ankles or parts about the ankles.

Tennessen explains his choice of the name: "From *talaria* (Latin) liberally translated meaning 'wings about the ankles,' referring to the habit of males flying low over the shallow water of small seeps in search of females". A philologist would not agree with this liberal translation, but nomenclaturally the name completely meets the requirements.   {noun in apposistion}

Tanypteryx Kennedy, 1917: 507

Kennedy explained in the first description: "The name proposed is from the Greek: τἄνυπτέρυξ = swift-winged. The erection of this genus leaves in *Tachopteryx* Selys only the species *thoreyi* ...". That means Kennedy clearly wanted the name to have the same meaning as *Tachopteryx*, in which *T. hageni* originally was described. But he was mistaken, for τανυπτέρυξ means: with extended wings, long-winged. {Feminine}

tarascana, Argia Calvert, 1902: 90

L. *tarascanus –a –um* = pertaining to the Tarascos.

"The specific name refers to the 'Tarascos,' an Indian tribe of Guerrero." (Free and sovereign State of Guerrero, Mexico).
{declinable adjective}

Tauriphila Kirby, 1889: 268

Gr. ταῦρος = bull + –φιλος –η –ον (in compounds) = loving.

This name might be a reference to feeding near cattle, but nothing about that is mentioned by Kirby. {Feminine}

Telebasis Selys, 1865: 378

Gr. τηλε- (in compounds) = far, far apart + βάσις = (*inter alia*) base, pedestal.

The long petiolation of wings is at the base of the name: "{*Argia*} Différent ... des *Telebasis* (De Selys) par les ailes cessant d'être pétiolées avant la première nervule basale postcostale." [{*Argia*} Different ... from *Telebasis* (De Selys) by the wings ceasing to be petiolated before the first basal postcostal vein]. {Feminine}

tenebrosa, Somatochlora (Say, 1839: 19)

[Original designation: *Libellula tenebrosa* Say]
L. *tenebrosus –a –um* = dark.

The name refers to the overall coloration: "thorax and abdomen greenish-black". {declinable adjective}

tenera, *Perithemis* (Say, 1839: 31)
[Original designation: *Libellula tenera* Say]
    L. *tener –a –um* = delicate, tender.

    The smallness mentioned in the first description might be enough to justify the name: "Length nine tenths of an inch."
                                              {declinable adjective}

tenuatus, *Lestes* Rambur, 1842: 245
[as *Lestes tenuata* Rambur]
    L. *tenuatus –a –um*: past participle of *tenuo* = to make thin, slender.

    The slenderness of the species is explicitly mentioned by Rambur: "De la taille de la *Viridis*, mais plus grêle" [Size of the (old world species *Chalcolestes*) *viridis*, but more slender].
                                          {declinable past participle}

tezpi, *Argia* Calvert, 1902: 77
    "The specific name is derived from the legendary 'Noah' of Michoacan." The Noah of the Mexican cataclysm was Coxcox, called by certain peoples Teocipactli or Tezpi. He had saved himself, together with his wife Xochiquetzal, in a bark, or, according to other traditions, on a raft made of cypress-wood (*Cupressus disticha*).   {noun in apposition}

Tholymis Hagen, 1867b: 221
    As usual Hagen does not explain what made him create this very denomination. It looks Greek, but it is not. It might be something like a composition of parts of Gr. θώραξ, λυγαῖος (= shadowed, murky) and θέμις (see *Celithemis*), as HAGEN (1867b: 219) states, that in the species *T. citrina* (q.v.) the thorax of adult males is dark colored.   {Feminine}

thoreyi, Tachopteryx (Hagen in Selys, 1858: 633)
[Original designation: *Uropetala thoreyi* Hagen in Selys]
"d'après un mâle unique de la collection de M. Hagen, reçu de M. Thorey, de Hambourg, auquel il l'a dédié." [From a single male from M. Hagen's collection, received from M. Thorey [Georg Thorey (1790-1884)] of Hamburg, to whom he dedicated it.]
{noun in the genitive case}

tibialis, Argia (Rambur, 1842: 241)
[Original designation: *Platycnemis tibialis* Rambur]
L. *tibialis –is –e* = concerning the tibia.

This was the only one of Rambur's *Platycnemis* species where the front of the tibiae was black: "les mêmes tibias, noirs à face anterieure" [The same tibiae, with anterior face black]. In the other species of *Platycnemis* in RAMBUR 1842 the front of the tibiae is not black. {declinable adjective}

titia, Hetaerina (Drury, 1773: 83)
[Original designation: *Libellula titia* Drury]
Drury never explains his names, which are almost always female names from Roman antiquity. The name of this species appears to come from a female member of the plebeian Titius family from Rome and might be from a tale concerning Roman antiqity from Drury's own time. That family name is rarely mentioned in the Republican period, and did not rise out of obscurity until much later. The nomen *Titius* is a patronymic surname, based on the praenomen *Titus*, which must have belonged to an ancestor. Titus was roughly the sixth-most common Latin praenomen throughout Roman history. {noun in apposition}

tonto, Argia Calvert, 1902: 89
"Probably worthy of specific distinction, although nearly related to *A. lacrymans* are two males and a female, in alcohol, from Tombstone, Arizona, received from Prof. Needham." "Prof. Needham's express request prevents me from naming this species after himself, and I therefore call it **Argia tonto**, "the 'Tontos' being an Arizonan tribe." {noun in apposition}

townesi, **Stylurus** Gloyd, 1936: 5

"The unique male was sent by Mr. Townes to Mr. E. B. Williamson in January, 1933. At that time it was determined as a new species but was not described immediately in the hopes that more specimens could be obtained. Recently Mr. Townes donated the specimen to the Williamson Collection, and in compliance with his wishes it is here described. I take pleasure in naming the new species in his honor." Henry K. Townes, Jr. (1913-1990), was an American entomologist and collector of the holotype. He and his wife founded the American Entomological Institute in Ann Arbor, Michigan, in 1962 as an independent, nonprofit research institute. {noun in the genitive case}

Tramea Hagen, 1861: 143

As usual, Hagen does not explain his choice of name. Twelve years before (HAGEN 1849, 174) he had foreshadowed the publication of the genus as *Trapezostigma* (Gr. τραπέζιον = trapezium + στίγμα = a prick, puncture, mark, in dragonfly names often used for pterostigma), a name referring to a characteristic described thus in HAGEN 1861, 143: "pterostigma small, trapezoidal". But for the final publication Hagen simplified the unwieldy denomination to *Tramea* with a double effect: *Trapezostigma* would have been neuter and the adjectival names of the species transferred to this genus would have had to be adapted in gender, a change Hagen preferred to avoid (see above *Celithemis*). *Tramea* he could use as feminine and at the same time he could add a pun. For this name seems to allude to L. *trameo* (infinitive *trameare*) = to pass through, which may be taken as a reference to the vagrant behavior of several species of this genus. {Feminine} *translata*, *Argia* Hagen in Selys, 1865: 410

> L. *translatus –a –um*: past participle of *transfero* (a very irregular verb) = to transfer, transform.

The name refers to changes from teneral to adult males: "♂ Très adulte. Les dessins páles disparus. Le thorax noir, même sur les côtés. Les parties qui étaient claires chez le jeune sont saupondrées de bleu-àtre." ["♂. Very adult. The pale markings disappeared. The thorax black, even on the sides. The parts that were clear in the young were sprinkled bluish.]

{declinable past participle}

transversa, *Didymops* (Say, 1839: 19)
[Original designation: *Libellula transversa* Say]

> L. *transversus –a –um* = turned across, lying across.

As Say does not explain his choice of the name, two different features might be at its base: In his first description he says: "thorax with a yellow whitish band at the anterior base of the anterior wings, and a white band between the two pairs of wings, descending obliquely on the pleura, where it is yellow". Almost at the same time BURMEISTER (1839, 845) describes this very species (under the name *Epophthalmia cinnamomea* [from Gr. ἐπ(ι)- (in compounds) – upon + ὀφθαλμός = eye + adjectival suffix –ιος –ια –ιον = concerning ..., a reference to a process at the rear of the eyes in that genus + L. *cinnamomeus –a –um* = cinnamon-colored]. There the features mentioned by Say read: "macula dorsi ante alas, vitta thoracis laterali" [with a dorsal mark before the wings, and a lateral thoracic band], but Burmeister continues: "fasciaque frontis albida" [and a whitish frontal band]. So also this horizontal mark may have led to the name.

{declinable adjective}

traviatum, Enallagma Selys, 1876a: 519
>   *traviatus –a –um*: Latinized from Italian *traviato* = gone astray.

SELYS 1876a describes this species, which he separates from *E. aspersum*, as being very similar to the two species following in the publication on the next pages, *E. divagans* and *E. exsulans*: "Cet *E. traviatum* est in quelque sorte, par rapport à l'*aspersum* type, ce que le *divagans* est à l'*exsulans*. La femelle rapelle bien d'ailleurs a celle de *divagans*." [This *E. traviatum* is in some way, by its relation to the type of *aspersum*, what *divagans* is in relation to *exsulans*. The female (*traviatum*) resembles very much that of *divagans*]. So it is clear that he wants to signify this close relationship by choosing a denomination which is semantically close. {declinable adjective}

Triacanthagyna Selys, 1883: 745
>   Gr. τρι- (in compounds) = three + ἄκανθα = prickle, thorn + γυνή = woman.

The name refers to three spines on the tenth abdominal segment of the females in this genus: "♀. Le 10e segment prolongé en dessous en une plaque procombante armée de trois pointes aiguës assez longues, egales, dont les deux latérales un peu écartées." [The 10th segment, prolonged underneath, into a prominent plate, armed with three sharp, fairly long, equal points, having the two lateral ones slightly apart]. {Feminine}

trifida, Triacanthagyna (Rambur, 1842: 210)
[Original designation: *Gynacantha trifida* Rambur]
>   L. *trifidus –a –um* = split into three, three-forked.

Also for this species name the reference is to the spines on female tenth abdominal segment: "segmento ultimo subtus producto trispino (femina)" [last segment prolonged by three spines beneath (in the female)] "dernier segment chez la femelle, prolongé et saillant en dessous, où il présente trois épines assez fortes, un peu courbées." [Last segment in the female, prolonged and protruding below, where it presents three rather strong, slightly curved spines]. {declinable adjective}

tuberculifera, *Aeshna* Walker, 1908: 385
> L. *tuberculum* = a small swelling, bump, or protuberance + suffix *–fer –fera –ferum* = bearing.

> In this species the males have a tubercle on the base of their cerci: "superior appendages with a prominent inferior basal tubercle". {declinable adjective}

uhleri, *Helocordulia* (Selys, 1871a: 274)
[Original designation: *Cordulia uhleri* Selys]
> "Un mâle de Randal, Maine (coll. Harris, Mus.de Boston); deux femelles (coll. Uhler), de New-Jersey." [A male from Randal, Maine (Harris Collection, Boston Museum); two females (Uhler coll.), from New Jersey.] Philip Reese Uhler (See p. 75) was an American librarian and entomologist who specialised in Heteroptera. {noun in the genitive case}

umbrata, *Erythrodiplax* (Linnaeus, 1758: 545)
[Original designation: *Libellula umbrata* Linnaeus]
> L. *umbratus –a –um* = shady, shaded (from *umbra* = shade).

> Linnaeus' description is a good example of how unsatisfactory such characterizations were at that time: "L. alis planis albis: fascia fusca. *Habitat in* America. *Rolander. Alarum fascia in medio; apices alarum obscuriores.*" [Dragonfly with plain white wings: with a dark band. It lives in America. Rolander (a disciple of Linnaeus as source of information). The band of the wings in the middle; the tips of the wings darker]. So several features might have led to the name: probably the dark band on all wings mentioned by Linnaeus or perhaps the obfuscated tips of the wings; or even the dull brown or black color of the body, not mentioned in that description. {declinable adjective}

umbrosa, Aeshna Walker, 1908: 380
>L. *umbrosus –a –um* = full of shade, rich in shade, shady.

>The species was described in a key for *Aeshna* species so any behaviour which most probably induced the name is not mentioned there. HAROLD WHITE (in litt.) describes it thus: "Walker was quite familiar with this species that often can be found flying in swarms at dusk or along shady woodland streams." Otherwise the name might refer to the dark color: "Face rather dark olivaceous, lateral thoracic bands rather narrow (about 1 mm.), straight, not widening above, nearly surrounded by a margin darker that the ground color of the thorax".
>{declinable adjective}

unguiculatus, Lestes Hagen, 1861: 70
[as *Lestes unguiculata* Hagen]
>L. *unguiculus* = a small claw (diminutive of *unguis*) + suffix *–atus –a –um* = marked with, equipped with.

>The the special form of paraprocts of the the male probably has led to the name: "the inferior appendages long, narrow, cruciate, incurved at the apex". {declinable adjective}

vacillans, Leptobasis Hagen in Selys, 1877: 101
>L. *vacillans*: present participle of *vacillo* = to be in a weak condition, stagger, totter.

>The name perhaps is a reference to the extremely slender abdomen: "stature excessivement grêle" [stature excessively slender] as if it were in a weak condition. {present participle}

vastus, Gomphurus (Walsh, 1862: 391)
[Original designation: *Gomphus vastus* Walsh]
>L. *vastus –a –um* = (*inter alia*) immense, enormous.

>Probably the name refers to the wide abdominal club: "Abdomen black, expanded to an unusual width on segments 7-9".
>{declinable adjective}

velox, *Dythemis* Hagen, 1861: 163
   L. *velox* = swift, quick.

The name sounds as if it pertains to flight, but nothing about that is found in the first description. So it is more probable to have been chosen for reasons of grammar (cf. *fugax*).
{adjective}

ventricosus, *Gomphurus* (Walsh, 1863: 249)
[Original designation: *Gomphus ventricosus* Walsh]
   L. *venter* (stem *ventr-*) = paunch + suffix *–(c)osus* = rich in, remarkable by.

The wide abdominal club probably has induced the name: "Abdomen black, joints 7-9 greatly dilated and widely margined, especially 8, precisely as in *G. vastus*". {declinable adjective}

verna, *Celithemis* Pritchard, 1935: 6
   L. *vernus –a –um* = of or belonging to spring, spring.

The name refers to flight season: "Several days search revealed only the one specimen of *verna*, found in company of these two species {*C. elisa* + *C. fasciata*} and sharing their habits. This was the first part of June; *C. eponina* was making its debut; and *C. verna* its last appearance". The intention of the author seems clear, for if he had had in mind choosing a female first name as in others in the genus *Celithemis* (*Amanda, Elisa, Martha, Bertha*) one would expect there to be some evidence of it.
{declinable adjective}

vernale, *Enallagma* Gloyd, 1943: 1
   L. *vernalis –is –e* = of or belonging to spring, vernal.

The specimens on which the description was based were only captured in the last days of May and the first days of June in different years at different localities. {declinable adjective}

vernalis, Lanthus Carle, 1980: 175
> "*L. vernalis* [*–is –e*]... (L. adj. 'of the springtime', referring to the early season of the species.)" {declinable adjective}

verticalis, Aeschna Hagen, 1861: 122
> L. *vertex* (stem *vertic-*) = (*inter alia*) top or crown of the head, summit + suffix *alis –is –e* = concerning (the modern notion of vertical originates from land survey in antiquity, where a line from the ground to the *vertex* is perpendicular). Hagen does not explain how he wants the name to be understood. So the allusion is unknown. {declinable adjective}

verticalis, Ischnura (Say, 1839: 37)
[Original designation: *Agrion verticalis* Say]
> L. *verticalis –is –e* = vertical, concerning the vertex.

The name probably refers to the black color of the male's vertex: "frontal projection black above, sometimes connected by this color with the vertex". {declinable adjective}

vesiculosa, Erythemis (Fabricius, 1775: 421)
[Original designation: *Libellula vesiculosa* Fabricius]
> L. *vesicula* = a little blister + *–osus –a –um* = full of, abounding in, remarkable by.

In the first description Fabricius says twice: "Fronte elevata, vesiculosa" [with an elevated frons, spectacular by vesicular structures]. Therefore he thought this information to be highly relevant. These structures seem to be the ocelli, which in some photographs can be seen protruding near the bases of the antennae. The explanation in FLIEDNER, 2006, 17 [p. 83, endnote 13], which does not consider the first description, therefore is wrong.

{declinable adjective}

vesperum, Enallagma Calvert, 1919: 380
> L. *vesperus –a –um* = of or belonging to the evening.
>
> p. 384: "The name *vesperum* is suggested for this species for its habit of flying after sunset to a degree greater than in most of its allies". {declinable adjective}"

vibrans, Libellula Fabricius, 1793: 380
> L. *vibrans*: present participle of *vibro* = to brandish, shake, flash, glitter.
>
> As there is no explanation in the first description, the allusion remains unknown. {present participle}

vicinum, Sympetrum (Hagen, 1861: 175)
[Original designation: *Diplax vicina* Hagen]
> L. *vicinus –a –um* = near, neighboring; nearly resembling.
>
> The name refers to the similarity to *S. costiferum* described just before it: "similar to *D costifera*, ... Is it distinct? May it not be a variety?" {declinable adjective}

vidua, Lestes Hagen, 1861: 69
> L. *vidua* = widow.
>
> Perhaps the overall impression, which is described as "brassy-black", might have appeared like a sign of mourning.
> {noun in apposition}

vigilax, Lestes Hagen in Selys, 1862: 306
> L. *vigilax* = watchful.
>
> As there is no explanation in the first description, the allusion is unknown (cf. *fugax*). {adjective}

villosipes, Arigomphus (Selys, 1854: 53)
[Original designation: *Gomphus villosipes* Selys]
>L. *villosus –a –um* = shaggy, hairy + *–pes* (in compounds) = –footed.

>The name describes the femora: "fémurs (qui sont finement velus)" [femora (which are pubescent)]. {declinable adjective}

vinosa, Boyeria (Say, 1839: 13)
[Original designation: *Aeshna vinosa* Say]
>L. *vinosus –a –um* = fond of wine, full of wine.

>As Say does not explain his choice of the name it remains enigmatic. There are two possibilities. One meaning of the L. word, dating from 1834, is 'having a wine-colored tinge', perhaps alluding to the brown color of the species. Alternatively, the males' typical flight behavior as described by WILLIAMSON (1907b: 144) may have led to the name: "its tendency to examine critically every object projecting above the water often makes its capture an embarrassing matter to the collector. More than once as I waited for an approaching male that insect suddenly left the line of flight I had mapped out for it, flew to within an inch of my legs, circled around one leg a time or two, then the other, then about both, and then quietly resumed its flight along the stream, oblivious of the net which had frantically fanned all around it". This behaviour may have reminded Say of the erratic movements caused by drunkenness.   {declinable adjective}

virginiensis, Neurocordulia Davis, 1927: 156
>From the type locality + *–ensis –is –e* = adjectival suffix indicating place of origin.

>"Type, female. Buckingham County, Virginia, June 21, 1919."
{declinable adjective}

viridifrons, Hylogomphus (Hine, 1901: 60)
[Original designation: *Gomphus viridifrons* Hine]
>L. *viridis –is –e* = green + *–frons* (in compounds) = –fronted.

>The original description includes "face and occiput green".
{adjective}

viriditas, *Coryphaeschna* Calvert, 1952: 264
[Syn. *Coryphaeschna virens* (Rambur, 1842)]
> L. *viriditas* = greenness.

The name refers to the overall coloration of the species. By this denomination Calvert replaced the pre-occupied name of *Aeschna virens* Rambur which had been described as "toute verte" [totally green]. The name *Aeschna virens* Rambur 1842 was proccupied by *Aeschna virens* Charpentier 1840, which was a younger synonym of *Aeschna viridis* Eversmann 1836, a Eurasian species. {noun in apposition}

vivida, *Argia* Hagen in Selys, 1865: 406
> L. *vividus –a –um* = lively, vivid.

Presumably because of bright color the species was given its name: "♂... le fond d'un bleu de ciel très clair" [♂ ... the background of a very bright sky-blue]. {declinable adjective}

vulnerata, *Hetaerina* Hagen in Selys, 1853: 40
> L. *vulneratus –a –um*: past participle of *vulnero* = to wound.

In the genus *Hetaerina* one typical feature of the males is the red spot at the base of all four wings. (SELYS 1853: 30): "♂ ... Ailes ... la base de quatre a tache rouge" [♂ ... The wings ... the base of all four with a red spot]. This has led to species names like *sanguinea* (= bloody), *sanguinolenta* (= full of blood), *mortua* (= dead), *laesa* (= wounded), *carnifex* (= executioner), *cruentata* (= stained with blood), *moribunda* (= about to die) or *occisa* (= slayed). The name *vulnerata* fits very well in this semantic field, and also might refer to other red elements of coloration, for instance that of the sides of the thorax: "le rest de côtes roussatre" [the rest of the sides russet]. {declinable past participle}

walkeri, Aeshna Kennedy, 1917: 588
>"This remarkable *Aeshna*, which is probably one of the last to be described from north of Mexico, I take pleasure in naming for Dr. E. M. Walker, who in his beautiful monograph of the North American species of this group has opened the way for future students." Edmund Murton Walker (See p. 76) was Professor of entomology University of Toronto. He founded the invertebrate collection at the Royal Ontario Museum and also had many published works, including the three volume *Odonata of Canada and Alaska*, considered a definitive textbook on the topic. He was editor of the *Canadian Entomologist* journal from 1910 to 1920. {noun in the genitive case}

walshii, Somatochlora (Scudder, 1866: 217)
[Original designation: *Cordulia walshii* Scudder]
>The species is named after Benjamin D. Walsh (See p. 77), American entomologist. {noun in the genitive case}

walsinghami, Anax McLachlan, 1883: 127
>"Several examples were captured by Lord Walsingham, and the description has been made from a pair which have long borne the above name in my collection, but the species was never described." Thomas de Grey, Sixth Baron of Walsingham (1843-1919) was an English lepidopterist. {noun in the genitive case}

weewa, Enallagma Byers, 1927: 385
>"Holotype: one male Chipola Lake Wewahitchiky, Gulf Co., Fla." "*Enallagma weewa*, named after Wewahitchika, Florida, the type locality ..." {noun in apposition}

westfalli, Phanogomphus (Carle & May, 1987: 68)
[Original designation: *Gomphus westfalli* Carle & May]
>"We name the new species in honor of Minter J. Westfall, Jr in light of his many contributions to the odonatological community."

>Minter J. Westfall, Jr. (See p. 78) was an American odonatologist who wrote the definitive works on "*Dragonflies of North America*" and "*Damselflies of North America*" co-authored with fellow entomologist, Mike May. {noun in the genitive case}

westfalli, Ophiogomphus Cook & Daigle, 1985: 90
"We take pleasure in naming this beautiful species for Professor Minter J. Westfall, Jr. [See p. 78], in recognition of his outstanding contributions to the knowledge of American gomphids." {noun in the genitive case}

whitehousei, Somatochlora Walker, 1925: 154
"Dedicated to Mr. F. C. Whitehouse, from whom I received my first pair of specimens." Francis C. Whitehouse (1879-1959), Canadian odonatologist. {noun in the genitive case}

williamsoni, Aphylla (Gloyd, 1936: 9)
[Original designation: *Gomphoides williamsoni* Gloyd]
"With feelings of sincere admiration and respect and in appreciation of his intense interest in the genus Gomphoides and in a form which he took so much joy in collecting in his last field trip, I name this species in honor of Mr. E. B. Williamson." Edward Bruce Williamson (See p. 80) was a noted entomologist and botanist in the early part of the 20th century. He spent most of his career as an amateur, but active and well-respected, scholar of Odonata and served as the curator of Odonata for the University of Michigan Museum of Zoology from 1916 to his retirement in 1933. {noun in the genitive case}

williamsoni, Somatochlora Walker, 1907: 69
"I take pleasure in naming this insect after Mr. E.B.Williamson, who has shown me many favours of late and given me a great deal of valuable advice and assistance in my studies of dragon-fly life."
{noun in the genitive case}

Williamsonia Davis, 1913b: 95
"I would propose the name *Williamsonia*, after Mr. Edward Bruce Williamson of Bluffton, Indiana, the well-known student of dragonflies." (See p. 80) {Feminine}

xanthosoma, *Neurocordulia* (Williamson, 1908b: 432)
[Original designation: *Platycordulia xanthosoma* Williamson]

> Gr. ξανθός –ή –όν = yellow (frequently with a shade of red) + σῶμα = body. In Greek there is an adjectival suffix –σωμος –η –ον = -bodied; but the –a of σῶμα shows that it would be Latinized and therefore to be treated as a declinable adjective. It is preferable that the name be considered as a noun. That is in accordance with Charpentier, who coined the first generic dragonfly names in –*soma* (i.e. *Cyrtosoma* {junior synonym of *Anax*}, *Chlorosoma* {preoccupied, now *Somatochlora*} and *Pyrrhosoma*). The name refers to the coloration: "Entire insect yellow or yellowish".

{noun in apposition}

yamaskanensis, *Neurocordulia* (Provancher, 1875: 248)
[Original designation: *Aeschna yamaskanensis* Provancher]

> Yamaska = a river in southern Quebec, Canada + –*ensis* –*is* –*e* = adjectival suffix indicating place of origin.

> The name is a reference to the type locality: "Prisé à St. Hyacinthe" (city on the Yamaska river).   {declinable adjective}

Zoniagrion Kennedy, 1917: 488

> Gr. ζώνιον: diminutive of ζώνη = girdle, (also) stripes on a fish + *Agrion* (see: *Acanthagrion*).

> "The name proposed is suggested by the heavily banded caudal gills of the nymph. Ζώνιον = a little girdle; ἄγριον = living in the fields, wild, savage – the name of a genus of dragonflies."

{Neuter}

References

Resources used in eliciting etymologies.

AHRENS, G. 1988. *Medizinisches und naturwissenschaftliches Latein: mit latinisiertem griech. Wortschatz.* Verlag Enzyklopädie: Leipzig. 353 pp.

GENAUST, H. 1996. *Etymologisches Wörterbuch der botanischen Pflanzennamen.* 3rd ed. Basel, Birkhäuser (reprinted 2005 Hamburg, Nikol). 701 pp.

HÄMÄLÄINEN, M. 2016. Catalogue of individuals commemorated in the scientific names of extant dragonflies, including lists of all available eponymous species-group and genus-group names – Revised edition. *International Dragonfly Fund Report* 92. 132 pp. (also: http://www.dragonflyfund.org/images/reports/IDF_Report_92_H%C3%A4m%C3%A4l%C3%A4inen_2016.pdf)

HENTSCHEL, E. & WAGNER, G. 1993. *Zoologisches Wörterbuch.* 5. durchgesehene Auflage. Gustav Fischer: Jena (UTB 367). 576 pp.

LEWIS, C.T. & SHORT, C. 1963. *Latin Dictionary Based on Andrews's edition of Freund's Latin Dictionary.* Oxford University Press: New York

LIDDELL, H.G & SCOTT, R. 1996. *A Greek Lexicon-English. 9th ed with a revised supplement.* Clarendon Press: Oxford

PAPE, W. 1911. *Wörterbuch der griechischen Eigennamen. 3. Aufl., neu bearbeitet von Dr. G. Benseler. 4. Abdruck.* Viewg & Sohn: Braunschweig

WERNER, F.C. 1972. *Wortelemente lateinisch-griechischer Fachausdrücke in den biologischen Wissenschaften.* Suhrkamp: Frankfurt/M. (Suhrkamp Taschenbuch 64). 475 pp.

References containing original descriptions or explanatory matter.

ABBOTT, J. C., & HIBBITTS. T. D. 2011. *Cordulegaster sarracenia* , n. sp. (Odonata: Cordulegastridae) from east Texas and western Louisiana, with a key to adult Cordulegastridae of the New World. *Zootaxa* 2899: 60–68.

BANKS, N. 1896. A new species of *Gomphus*. *Journal of the New York Entomological Society* 4: 193–195.

BELLE, J. 1970. Studies on South American Gomphidae (Odonata) with special reference to the species from Surinam. *Studies on the Fauna of Suriname and other Guyanas* 11(55): 1–158.

BELLE, J. 1975. Two new species of *Phyllocycla* Calvert, 1948 from Central America (Anisoptera: Gomphidae). *Odonatologica* 4: 65–71.

BELLE, J. 1987. *Phyllogomphoides nayaritensis*, eine neue Libellenart aus Mexico (Odonata: Gomphidae). *Entomologische Zeitschrift mit Insektenbörse* 97: 11–13.

BIRD, R. D. 1933. *Somatochlora ozarkensis*, a new species from Oklahoma (Odonata–Cordulinae). *Occasional papers of the Museum of Zoology, University of Michigan* No. 261: 1–7.

BRAUER, F. M. 1865. Dritter Bericht über die auf der Weltfahrt der kais. Fregatte Novara gesammelten Neuropteren. *Verhandlungen der kaiserlich-königlichen zoologisch-botanischen Gesellschaft Wien* 8: 501–512.

BRAUER, F. M. 1868. Verzeichnis der bis jetzt bekannten Neuropteren im Sinne Linné's. *Verhandlungen der Zoologisch-Botanischen Gesellschaft in Wien* 18: 359–416; 711-742.

Brauer, F. M. 1900. Odonates décrits en 1900 par le Brauer. In: Von ihrer Königl. Hoheit der Prinzessin Therese von Bayern auf einer Reise in Süd-Amerika gesammelte Insekten. *Berliner Entomologische Zeitschrift* 45: 253–268.

Brittinger, C. 1850. Die Libelluliden des Kaiserreichs Österreich. *Sitzungsberichte Akademie der Wissenschaften in Wien* 4: 328–336.

Bromley, S. W. 1924. A new *Ophiogomphus* (Aeschnidae: Odonata) from Massachusetts. *Entomological News* 35: 343–334.

Brunelle, P.-M. 2000. A new species of *Neurocordulia* (Odonata: Anisoptera: Corduliidae) from eastern North America. *Canadian Entomologist* 132: 39–48.

Burmeister, H. 1839. *Handbuch der Entomologie.* T. C. Friedr. Enslin: Berlin. pp. 757–1050.

Byers, C. F. 1927. *Enallagma* and *Telagrion* from western Florida, with a description of a new species. *Annals of the Entomological Society of America* 20: 385–392.

Byers, C. F. 1939. A study of the dragonflies of the genus *Progomphus* (Gomphoides) with a description of a new species. *Proceedings of the Florida Academy of Sciences* 4: 19–85.

Calvert, P. P. 1890. Notes on some North American Odonata with descriptions of three new species. *Transactions of the American Entomological Society* 17: 33–40.

Calvert, P. P. 1895. The Odonata of Baja California, Mexico. *Proceedings of the California Academy of Sciences* (2nd Series) 4: 463–558.

Calvert, P. P. 1898. The odonate genus *Macrothemis* and its allies. *Proceedings of the Boston Society of Natural History* 28: 301–332.

Calvert, P. P. 1899. Odonata from Tepic, Mexico, with supplementary notes on those of Baja California. *Proceedings of the California Academy of Sciences* (3rd Series) 1: 371–418.

Calvert, P. P. 1901–1908. *Biologia Centrali-Americana, Odonata.* London, R. H. Porter & Dulau & Co.

Calvert, P. P. 1903. Additions to the Odonata of New Jersey, with descriptions of two species: *Entomological News* 14: 33-40, pl. 3.

CALVERT, P. P. 1907. The differentials of three North American species of *Libellula*. *Entomological News* 18: 201–204.

CALVERT, P. P. 1913a. The species of *Nehalennia* (Odonata). *Entomological News* 24: 310–316.

CALVERT, P. P. 1913b. The true male of *Nehalennia integricollis* and *N. pallidula*, n. sp. (Odon.). *Entomological News* 24: 373–374.

CALVERT, P. P. 1919. Gundlach's work on the Odonata of Cuba: a critical study. *Transactions of the American Entomological Society* 45: 335–396.

CALVERT, P. P. 1921. *Gomphus dilatatus*, *vastus*, and a new species, *lineatifrons* (Odonata). *Transactions of the American Entomological Society* 47: 221–232.

CALVERT, P. P. 1931. The generic characters and the species of *Palaemnema* (Odonata: Agrionidae). *Transactions of the American Entomological Society* 57: 1-111, 21 pl.

CALVERT, P. P. 1947. *Aeshna psilus*, a new species of the group of *Ae. cornigera* Brauer (Odonata: Aeshnidae). *Notulae Naturae* 194: 1–11.

CALVERT, P. P. 1948. Odonata (dragonflies) of Kartabo, Bartica District, British Guiana. *Zoologica* 33: 47–87.

CALVERT, P. P. 1952. New taxonomic entities in Neotropical Aeshnas (Odonata: Aeshnidae). *Entomological News* 63: 253–264.

CANNINGS, R. A. & GARRISON, R. W. 1991. *Sympetrum signiferum*, a new species of dragonfly (Odonata: Libellulidae) from western Mexico and Arizona. *Annals of the Entomological Society of America*. 84: 474–479.

CARLE, F. L. 1979. Two new *Gomphus* (Odonata: Gomphidae) from eastern North America with adult keys to the subgenus *Hylogomphus*. *Annals of the Entomological Society of America* 72: 418–426.

CARLE, F. L. 1980. A new *Lanthus* (Odonata: Gomphidae) from eastern North America with adult and nymphal keys to American Octogomphines. *Annals of the Entomological Society of America* 73: 172–179.

CARLE, F. L. 1981. A new species of *Ophiogomphus* from eastern North America, with a key to the regional species (Anisoptera: Gomphidae). *Odonatologica* 10: 271–278.

CARLE, F. L. 1982. *Ophiogomphus incurvatus*: a new name for *Ophiogomphus carolinus* Hagen (Odonata: Gomphidae). *Annals of the Entomological Society of America* 75: 335–339.

CARLE, F. L. 1983. A new *Zoraena* (Odonata: Cordulegastridae) from eastern North America, with a key to the adult Cordulegastridae of America. *Annals of the Entomological Society of America* 76: 61–68.

CARLE, F.C. 1986 The classification, phylogeny and biogeography of the Gomphidae (Anisoptera). I. Classification. *Odonatologica*, 15: 275–326.

Carle, F. L. 1992. *Ophiogomphus* (*Ophionurus*) *australis* spec. nov. from the Gulf coast of Louisiana, with larval and adult keys to American *Ophiogomphus* (Anisoptera: Gomphidae). *Odonatologica* 21: 141–152.

CARLE, F. L. & MAY, M. L. 1987. *Gomphus* (*Phanogomphus*) *westfalli* spec. nov. from the gulf coast of Florida (Anisoptera: Gomphidae). *Odonatologica* 16: 67–75.

CHARPENTIER, T. de. 1840. *Libellulinae Europaeae Descriptae et Depictae*. Lipsiae, Voss. 180pp. LXVIII pl.

COOK, C. & DAIGLE, J. J. 1985. *Ophiogomphus westfalli* spec. nov. from the Ozark region of Arkansas and Missouri, with a key to the *Ophiogomphus* species of eastern North America (Anisoptera: Gomphidae). *Odonatologica* 14: 89–99.

COOK, C. & LAUDERMILK, E. L. 2004. *Stylogomphus sigmastylus* sp. nov., a new North American dragonfly previously confused with *S. albistylus* (Odonata: Gomphidae). *International Journal of Odonatology* 7: 3–24.

COWLEY, J. 1934. Notes on some generic names of Odonata. *Entomologist's Monthly Magazine* . 70: 240–247.

CURRIE, B. P. 1917. *Gomphus parvidens*, a new species of dragonfly from Maryland. *Proceedings of the United States National Museum* 53: 223–226.

CURRIE. R. P. 1903. The Odonata collected by Messrs. Schwarz and Barber in Arizona and New Mexico. *Proceedings of the Entomological Society of Washington* 5: 298–303.

DAIGLE, J. J. 1995. *Argia carlcooki* spec. nov. from Mexico (Zygoptera: Coenagrionidae). *Odonatologica* 24: 467–471.

DAVIS, W. T. 1913a. Dragonflies of the vicinity of New York City with a description of a new species. *Journal of the New York Entomological Society* 21: 11–29.

DAVIS, W. T. 1913b. *Williamsonia*, a new genus of dragonflies from North America. *Bulletin of the Brooklyn Entomological Society* 8: 93–96.

DAVIS, W. T. 1921. A new dragonfly from Florida. *Bulletin of the Brooklyn Entomological Society* 16: 109–111.

DAVIS, W. T. 1927. A new dragonfly from Virginia. *Bulletin of the Brooklyn Entomological Society* 22: 155–156.

DONNELLY, T. W. 1961. *Aeshna persephone*, a new species of dragonfly from Arizona, with notes on *Aeshna arida* Kennedy. *Proceedings of the Entomological Society of Washington* 63: 193–202.

DONNELLY, T. W. 1962. *Somatochlora margarita*, a new species of dragonfly from eastern Texas. *Proceedings of the Entomological Society of Washington* 64: 235–240.

DONNELLY, T. W. 1966. A new gomphine dragonfly from eastern Texas (Odonata: Gomphidae). *Proceedings of the Entomological Society of Washington* 68: 102–105.

DONNELLY, T. W. 1967. The discovery of *Chrysobasis* in Central America, with the description of a new species (Odonata: Coenagrionidae). *Florida Entomologist* 50: 47–52.

DUNKLE, S. W. 1992. *Gomphus* (*Gomphurus*) *gonzalezi* spec. nov., a new dragonfly from Texas and Mexico. *Odonatologica* 21: 79–84.

DRURY, D. 1770. *Illustrations of Natural History* 1. London, White.

DRURY, D. 1773. *Illustrations of Natural History* 2. London, White.

ERICHSON, W. F. 1848. Die Insecta. Pp. 533–617 in: SCHOMBURGK, Reisen in British Guiana. Leipzig, Weber.

FABRICIUS, J. C. 1775. *Systema Entomologiae*. Flensburg and Leipzig, Libraria Korte.

FABRICIUS, J. C. 1793. *Entomologia systematica, Emendata et Aucta*. Vol. 2. Copenhagen, C. G. Proft.

FABRICIUS, J. C. 1798. *Entomologia systematica, Emendata et Aucta. Supplement*. Copenhagen, C. G. Proft.

FERGUSON, A. 1950. *Gomphus maxwelli*, a new species of dragonfly from Texas (Odonata: Gomphinae, group *Arigomphus*). *Field & Laboratory* 18: 93–96.

FÖRSTER, F. 1900. Odonaten aus New-Guinea. *Természetrajzi Füzetek kiadja a Magyar nemzeti Muzeum* 23: 81–108.

FÖRSTER, F. 1909. Beiträge zu den Gattungen und Arten der Libellen. *Nassauischer Verein für Naturkunde, Wiesbaden*, 62: 211–235.

FRASER, F. C. 1922. New and rare Indian Odonata in the Pusa Collection. *Memoirs of the Department of Agriculture in India* (*Entomological Series*) 7: 1–81.

GARRISON, R. W. 1986. The genus *Aphylla* in Mexico and Central America, with a description of a new species, *Aphylla angustifolia* (Odonata: Gomphidae). *Annals of the Entomological Society of America* 79: 938–944.

GARRISON, R. W. 1994a. A revision of the New World genus *Erpetogomphus* Hagen in Selys (Odonata: Gomphidae). *Tijdschrift voor Entomologie* 137: 173–269.

GARRISON, R. W. 1994b. A synopsis of the genus *Argia* of the United States with keys and descriptions of new species, *Argia sabino, A. leonorae and A. pima* (Odonata Coenagrionidae). *Transactions of the American Entomological Society* 120: 287-368.

GARRISON, R. W. 1996. A synopsis of the *Argia fissa* group, with descriptions of two new species, *A.* anceps sp.n.and *A. westfalli* sp.n. (Zygoptera: Coenagrionidae). *Odonatologica* 25: 31-47.

GLOYD, L. K. 1933. A new Corduline dragonfly, *Tetragoneuria sepia*, from Florida (Odonata). *Occasional papers of the Museum of Zoology, University of Michigan* No. 274: 1–5.

GLOYD, L. K. 1936. Three new North American species of Gomphinae (Odonata). *Occasional papers of the Museum of Zoology, University of Michigan* No. 326: 1–18.

GLOYD, L. K. 1938. A new species of the genus *Libellula* from Yucatan. *Occasional papers of the Museum of Zoology, University of Michigan* No. 377: 1–4.

GLOYD, L. K. 1943. *Enallagma vernale*, a new species of Odonata from Michigan. *Occasional papers of the Museum of Zoology, University of Michigan* No. 479: 1–8.

GONZÁLEZ SORIANO, E. 2002. *Leptobasis melinogaster* spec. nov., a new species from Mexico (Zygoptera: Coenagrionidae). *Odonatologica* 31: 181–185.

GUNDLACH, J. 1888. *Contribucion á la entomologia Cubana. Neurópteros, Tomo* 2: 189–281.

HÄMÄLÄINEN, M. 2016a. Dragonflies and the Ill-fated Arctic Explorer Sir John Franklin (1786-1847). *Argia* 28(4): 15-19.

HAGEN, H. 1856. Die Odonaten-Fauna des russischen Reichs. *Stettiner Entomologische Zeitung* 17: 363–381.

HAGEN, H. 1861. *Synopsis of the Neuroptera of North America, with a list of the South American species.* Washington, D. C., Smithsonian Institute: vi-xx, 1-347.

HAGEN, H. 1867a. Revision der von Herrn Uhler beschriebenen Odonaten. *Stettiner Entomologische Zeitung* 28: 87–95.

HAGEN, H. 1867b. Die Neuroptera der Insel Cuba. *Stettiner Entomologische Zeitung* 28: 215–232.

HAGEN, H. 1868a. Odonaten Cubas. *Stettiner Entomologische Zeitung* 29: 274–287.

HAGEN, H. A. 1868b. The Odonat-Fauna of the Island of Cuba. *Proceedings of the Boston Society of Natural History* 11: 289-294.

HAGEN, H. 1869. Zur Odonaten-Fauna von Neu-Granada nach Lindig's Sammlungen. *Stettiner Entomologische Zeitung* 30: 256–263.

HAGEN, H. A. 1873a. Report on the Pseudoneuroptera and Neuroptera of North America in the Collection of the late Th.W. Harris. *Proceedings of the Boston Society of Natural History* 15: 263-301.

HAGEN, H. 1873b. Odonata from the Yellowstone. *Report of the U.S. Geological and Geographical Survey of the Territories* 6: 727–729.

HAGEN, H. A. 1874a. Report on the Pseudo-Neuroptera and Neuroptera collected by Lieut. W. L. Carpenter in 1873 in Colorado. *Report of the U.S. Geological and Geographical Survey of the Territories* 7: 571–606.

HAGEN, H. A. 1874b. The odonate fauna of Georgia, from original drawings now in possession of Dr. J. LeConte, and in the British Museum. *Proceedings of the Boston Society of Natural History* 16: 349–365.

HAGEN, H. A. 1875. Synopsis of the Odonata of America. *Proceedings of the Boston Society of Natural History* 18: 20–96.

HAGEN, H. A. 1888. On the genus *Sympetrum* Newman. *Entomologica Americana* 4: 31-34.

HAGEN, H. A. 1889. Synopsis of the Odonata of North America. *Psyche* 5: 241–250.

HAGEN, H. A. 1890a. A synopsis of the Odonat genus *Leucorhinia* Britt. *Transactions of the American Entomological Society* 17: 229–236.

HAGEN, H. A. 1890b. Descriptions of some North American Cordulina. *Psyche* 5: 366-373.

HARVEY, F. L. 1898. Contributions to the Odonata of Maine. III. *Entomological News.* 9: 59–64, 85–88.

HINE, J. S. 1901. A new species of *Gomphus* and its near relatives. *Ohio Naturalist* 1: 60–61.

ILLIGER, K. 1802. Namen der Insektengattungen, ihr Genitiv, ihr grammatisches Geschlecht, ihr Silbenmaß, ihre Herleitung; zugleich mit den Deutschen Bezeichnungen. *Magazin für Insektenkunde* 1: 125-155.

KARSCH, F. 1890. Beiträge zur Kenntniss der Arten und Gattungen der Libellulinen. *Berliner Entomologische Zeitschrift* 33: 347–392.

KELLICOTT, D. S. 1895. Odonata—a note and a description. *Entomological News* 6: 239.

KENNEDY, C. H. 1915. Notes on the life history and ecology of the dragonflies (Odonata) of Washington and Oregon. *Proceedings of the United States National Museum* 49: 259–345.

KENNEDY, C. H. 1917. Notes on the life history and ecology of the dragonflies (Odonata) of Central California and Nevada. *Proceedings of the United States National Museum.* 52: 483–635.

KENNEDY, C. H. 1918a. New species of Odonata from the southwestern United States. Part I. Three new Argias. *Canadian Entomologist* 50: 256–260.

KENNEDY, C. H. 1918b. New species of Odonata from the southwestern United States. Part II. *Canadian Entomologist.* 50: 297–299.

KENNEDY, C. H. 1920. Forty-two hitherto unrecognized genera and subgenera of Zygoptera. *Ohio Journal of Science* 21: 83–88.

KIRBY, W. F. 1889. A revision of the subfamily Libellulinae, with descriptions of new genera and species. *Transactions of the Zoological Society of London* 12: 249–348.

KIRBY, W. F. 1890. *A synonymic catalogue of Neuroptera Odonata or dragonflies, with an appendix of fossil species.* London, Gurney & Jackson. 202 pp.

KIRBY, W. F. 1894. On some small collections of Odonata (dragonflies) recently received from the West Indies. *Annals & Magazine of Natural History* 14: 261–269.

KNOPF, K. W. & TENNESSEN, K. J. 1980. A new species of *Progomphus* Selys, 1854 from North America (Anisoptera: Gomphidae). *Odonatologica* 9: 247–252.

LEACH, W. E. 1815. *Entomology.* In Brewster, D., *The Edinburgh Encyclopedia* 9: 57–172

LINNAEUS, C. 1758. *Systema naturae per regna tria naturae, secundum classes, ordines, genera, species, cum characteribus, differentiis, synonymis, locis.* (Edition 10) 1 (Animalia). Holmiae, Laurentii Salvii.

LINNAEUS, C. 1763. Centuria insectorum. Proposuit Boas Johansson. *Amoenitates Academicæ* 6: 384–415.

MARTIN, R. (1907) Cordulines. In: *Collections zoologiques du baron Edm. de Selys Longchamps: Catalogue systématique et descriptif* Fasc. 17: 1–94.

McLachlan, R. 1883. Two new species of *Anax*, with notes on other dragonflies of the same genus. *Entomologist's Monthly Magazine* 20: 127–131.

McLachlan, R. 1886. Two new species of *Cordulina*. *Entomologist's Monthly Magazine* 23: 104–105.

McLachlan, R. 1895. Some new species of Odonata of the "Légion" *Lestes*, with notes. *Annals & Magazine of Natural History* (6) 16: 19–28.

McLachlan, R. 1896. On some Odonata of the subfamily Aeschnina. *Annals & Magazine of Natural History* (6) 17: 409–425.

Montgomery, B. E. 1943. *Sympetrum internum*, new name for *Sympetrum decisum* auct., nec Hagen (Odonata, Libellulidae). *Canadian Entomologist* 75: 57–58.

Morse, A. P. 1895. New North American Odonata. *Psyche* 7: 207–211.

Muttkowski, R. A. 1910. Catalogue of the Odonata of North America. *Bulletin of the Public Museum of the City of Milwaukee* 1: 1–207.

Muttkowski, R. A. 1911. Studies in *Tetragoneuria* (Odonata). *Bulletin of the Wisconsin Natural History Society* 9: 91–134.

Navás, R. P. L. 1911. Neuropteros do Brasil. *Revista do Museu Paulista* 8: 476–481.

Needham, J. G. 1897. Preliminary studies of N. American Gomphinæ. *Canadian Entomologist* 29: 144–146, 164–168, 182–186.

Needham, J. G. 1902. Three new Gomphines. *Canadian Entomologist* 34: 275–278.

Needham, J. G. 1903. Life histories of Odonata, suborder Zygoptera. Part 3. In: Aquatic insects of New York state, E. P. Felt, ed. *Bulletin of the New York State Museum* 68: 218–278.

Needham, J. G. 1942. Two new species of dragonflies collected by Mrs. Alice L. Dietrich in Mississippi. *Canadian Entomologist* 74: 71–73.

Needham, J. G. 1950. Three new species of North American dragonflies with notes on related species. *Transactions of the American Entomological Society* 76: 1–12.

NEEDHAM, J. G. 1951. A new species of *Ophiogomphus* (Odonata). *Entomological News* 62: 41–43.

NEEDHAM, J. G. & BETTEN, C. 1901. Aquatic insects in the Adirondacks. *Bulletin of the New York State Museum* 47: 383–612.

NEEDHAM, J. G. & WESTFALL, M. J., JR. 1955. *A manual of the dragonflies of North America (Anisoptera) including the Greater Antilles and the provinces of the Mexican border.* Berkeley: University of California Press.

NEEDHAM, J. G., WESTFALL, M. J. & M. L. MAY. 2000. *Dragonflies of North America.* Revised edition. Gainesville, FL: Scientific Publishers:

NEWMAN, E. 1833. Entomological Notes. Class.–Neuroptera. Natural Order.-Libellulites, ined. *The Entomological Magazine* 1: 511-514.

PALISOT DE BEAUVOIS, A. 1805. *Insectes recuellis en Afrique et en Amérique dans les royaumes d'Oware, a Saint-Dominque et dans les États-Unis pendant les années 1781–1797.* Paris, Levrault.

PAULSON, D. R. 1983. A new species of dragonfly, *Gomphus (Gomphurus) lynnae* spec. nov., from the Yakima River, Washington, with notes on pruinosity in Gomphidae (Anisoptera). *Odonatologica* 12: 59–70.

PAULSON, D.R. 1994. Two new species of *Coryphaeshna* from Middle America, and a discussion of the red species of the genus (Anisoptera: Aeshnidae). *Odonatologica* 23: 379–398.

Paulson, D. R. & Dunkle, S.W. 2012. *A Checklist of North American Odonata Including English Name, Etymology, Type Locality, and Distribution.*

Paulson, D. R. & Dunkle, S.W. 2018. *A Checklist of North American Odonata Including English Name, Etymology, Type Locality, and Distribution.*

PRITCHARD, A. E. 1935. Two new dragonflies from Oklahoma. *Occasional papers of the Museum of Zoology, University of Michigan* No. 319: 1–10.

PROVANCHER, L. 1875. Description de plusiers insectes nouveaux. *Naturaliste Canadien* 7: 247–251.

RAMBUR, J. P. 1842. *Histoire naturelle des insectes. Névropteres.* Paris: Roret

REID, M. & RICKARD, M. 2018. *Coryphaeschna apeora* (Icarus Darner) in Texas: a new species for the United States. *Argia* 30 (3): 12-14.

ROBERT, A. 1954. Un (!) nouveau *Somatochlora* subarctique (Odonates, Corduliidae). *Canadian Entomologist* 86: 419–422.

ROOT, F. M. 1923. Notes on Zygoptera (Odonata) from Maryland, with a description of *Enallagma pallidum*, n. sp. *Entomological News* 34: 200–204.

ROOT, F. M. 1924. Notes on dragonflies (Odonata) from Lee County, Georgia, with a description of *Enallagma dubium*, new species. *Entomological News* 35: 317–324.

SAY, T. 1839. Descriptions of new North American neuropterous insects, and observations on some already described. *Journal of the Academy of Natural Sciences of Philadelphia* 8: 9–46.

SCUDDER, S. H. 1866. Notes on some Odonata from the White Mountains of New Hampshire. *Proceedings of the Boston Society of Natural History* 10: 211–222.

SCUDDER, S. H. 1866. Notes upon some Odonata from the Isle of Pines. *Proceedings of the Boston Society of Natural History* 10: 187–198.

SELYS-LONGCHAMPS, M. E. DE 1850. Revue des odonates ou libellules d'Europe. *Mémoires de la Société Royale des Sciences de Liége* 6: xxii 408 pp.

SELYS-LONGCHAMPS, M. E. DE 1853. Synopsis des Caloptérygines. *Bulletins de l'Académie Royale des Sciences, des Lettres, et des Beaux-Arts de Belgique* 20, Annexe: 1–73.

SELYS-LONGCHAMPS, M. E. DE 1854. Synopsis des Gomphines. *Bulletins de l'Académie Royale des Sciences, des Lettres, et des Beaux-Arts de Belgique* 21: 23–112.

SELYS-LONGCHAMPS, M. E. DE 1857. Neuroptéres de l'isle de Cuba. In: R. DE LA SAGRA, *Histoire physique, politique, et naturelle de l'Ile de Cuba. Animaux articulés* 7: 435–473.

SELYS-LONGCHAMPS, M. E. DE- 1858. Monographie des Gomphines. *Mémoires de la Société Royale des Sciences de Liége* 11: 257–720.

Selys-Longchamps, M. E. de 1859. Additions au synopsis des Gomphines. *Bulletins de l'Académie Royale des Sciences, des Lettres, et des Beaux-Arts de Belgique* (2) 7: 530–552.

Selys-Longchamps, M. E. de 1860. Synopsis des Agrionines, Dernière légion: Protonevra. *Bulletins de l'Académie Royale des Sciences, des Lettres, et des Beaux-Arts de Belgique* (2) 10: 431–462.

Selys-Longchamps, M. E. de. 1862. Synopsis des Agrionines, Seconde légion: *Lestes. Bulletins de l'Académie Royale des Sciences, des Lettres, et des Beaux-Arts de Belgique* (2) 13: 288–338.

Selys-Longchamps, M. E. de 1865. Synopsis des Agrionines, 5me légion: *Agrion. Bulletins de l'Académie Royale des Sciences, des Lettres, et des Beaux-Arts de Belgique* (2) 20: 375–417.

Selys-Longchamps, M. E. de 1868. Communication sur quelques Odonates du Mexique. *Comptes-rendus des séances de la Société entomologique de Belgique* 11: 66-71.

Selys-Longchamps, M. E. de 1871a. Synopsis des Cordulines. *Bulletins de l'Académie Royale des Sciences, des Lettres, et des Beaux-Arts de Belgique* (2) 31: 238–316, 519–565.

Selys-Longchamps, M. E. de 1871b. Aperçu statistique sur les Névroptères Odonates. *Transactions of the Entomological Society of London* 19: 409–416.

Selys-Longchamps, M. E. de 1873a. Troisiemes additions au synopsis des Gomphines. *Bulletins de l'Académie Royale des Sciences, des Lettres, et des Beaux-Arts de Belgique* (2) 35: 732–774.

Selys-Longchamps, M. E. de 1873b. Appendices aux troisiemes additions et liste des Gomphines, décrites dans le synopsis et ses trois additions. *Bulletins de l'Académie Royale des Sciences, des Lettres, et des Beaux-Arts de Belgique* (2) 36: 492–531.

Selys-Longchamps, M. E. de 1874. Additions au synopsis des Cordulines. *Bulletins de l'Académie Royale des Sciences, des Lettres, et des Beaux-Arts de Belgique* (2) 37: 16–34.

Selys-Longchamps, M. E. de 1875. Notes on Odonata from Newfoundland, collected in 1874 by Mr. John Milne. *Entomologist's Monthly Magazine* 11: 241–243.

SELYS-LONGCHAMPS, M. E. DE 1876a. Synopsis des Agrionines, 5me légion: *Agrion* (suite). Le genre *Agrion*. *Bulletins de l'Académie Royale des Sciences, des Lettres, et des Beaux-Arts de Belgique* (2) 41: 247–322, 496–539, 1233–1309.

SELYS-LONGCHAMPS, M. E. DE 1876b. Synopsis des Agrionines, 5me légion: Agrion (suite). Le genre *Agrion*. *Bulletins de l'Académie Royale des Sciences, des Lettres, et des Beaux-Arts de Belgique* (2) 42: 490-531, 952-991.

SELYS-LONGCHAMPS, M. E. DE 1877. Synopsis des Agrionines, 5me legion: *Agrion* (suite et fin). Les genres *Telebasis, Argiocnemis* et *Hemiphlebia*. *Bulletins de l'Académie Royale des Sciences, des Lettres, et des Beaux-Arts de Belgique* (2) 43: 97-159.

SELYS-LONGCHAMPS, M. E. DE 1878a. Secondes additions au synopsis des Cordulines. *Bulletins de l'Académie Royale des Sciences, des Lettres, et des Beaux-Arts de Belgique* (2) 45: 183–222.

SELYS-LONGCHAMPS, M. E. DE 1878b. Quatriemes additions au synopsis des Gomphines. *Bulletins de l'Académie Royale des Sciences, des Lettres, et des Beaux-Arts de Belgique* (2) 46: 408–471.

SELYS-LONGCHAMPS, M. E. DE 1879. Revision des *Ophiogomphus* et descriptions de quatre nouvelle Gomphines américaines. *Comptes-rendus des séances de la Société entomologique de Belgique* 22: 62–70.

SELYS-LONGCHAMPS, M. E. DE 1883. Synopsis des Aeschnines, Première partie: Classification. *Bulletins de l'Académie Royale des Sciences, des Lettres, et des Beaux-Arts de Belgique.* (3) 5: 712–748.

SULZER, J. H. 1776. *Abgekürzte Geschichte der Insekten nach dem Linnaeischen System.* 1. Winterthur, H. Steiner & Co.

TENNESSEN, K. J. 1983. A new species of *Gomphus* from Tennessee (Odonata: Gomphidae). *Annals of the Entomological Society of America* 76: 743–746.

TENNESSEN, K. J. 2004. *Cordulegaster talaria*, n. sp. (Odonata: Cordulegastridae) from west-central Arkansas. *Proceedings of the Entomological Society of Washington* 106: 830–839.

TENNESSEN, K. J. & VOGT, T. E. 2004. *Ophiogomphus smithi* n. sp. (Odonata: Gomphidae) from Wisconsin and Iowa. *Proceedings of the Entomological Society of Washington* 106: 540–546.

Tough, J. 1900. A new species of *Gomphus*. *Occasional Memoirs of the Chicago Entomological Society* 1: 17–18.

Trybom, F. 1889. Trollsländer (Odonater) insamlade under Svenska expeditionen till Jenisei, 1876. *Bihang till Kunglia Svenska vetenskapsakademiens handlingar* 15: 1–21.

Uhler, P. R. 1857. Contributions to the neuropterology of the United States. (Libellula). *Proceedings of the Academy of Natural Sciences of Philadelphia* 9: 87–88.

Vogt, T. E. & Smith, W. A. 1993. *Ophiogomphus susbehcha* spec. nov. from north central United States. *Odonatologica* 22: 503–509.

Walker, E. M. 1907. A new *Somatochlora*, with a note on the species known from Ontario. *Canadian Entomologist* 39: 69–74.

Walker, E. M. 1908. A key to the North American species of *Aeshna* found north of Mexico. *Canadian Entomologist* 40: 377–391, 450–451.

Walker, E. M. 1912. The Odonata of the prairie provinces of Canada. *Canadian Entomologist* 44: 253–266.

Walker, E. M. 1918. On the American representatives of *Somatochlora arctica* with descriptions of two new species (Odonata). *Canadian Entomologist* 50: 365–375.

Walker, E. M. 1925. The North American dragonflies of the genus *Somatochlora*. *University of Toronto Studies, Biological Series* 26: 1–202.

Walker, E. M. 1940. Odonata from the Patricia portion of the Kenora District of Ontario with description of a new species of *Leucorrhinia*. *Canadian Entomologist* 72: 4–15.

Walker, E. M. 1952. The *Lestes disjunctus* and *forcipatus* complex (Odonata: Lestidae). *Transactions of the American Entomological Society* 78: 59–74.

Walsh, B. D. 1862. List of the Pseudoneuroptera of Illinois contained in the cabinet of the writer, with descriptions of over forty new species, and notes on their structural affinities. *Proceedings of the Academy of Natural Sciences of Philadelphia* 14: 361–402.

WALSH, B. D. 1863. Notes on Odonata. Pp. 207–271 In: Observations on certain N. A. Neuroptera, by H. HAGEN, M.D., of Koenigsberg, Prussia; translated from the original French MS., and published by permission of the author, with notes and descriptions of about twenty new N. A. species of Pseudoneuroptera. *Proceedings of the Entomological Society of Philadelphia* 2: 167–272.

WARE, J. L., PILGRIM, E., MAY, M. L., DONNELLY, T. W. & TENNESSEN, K. 2016. Phylogenetic relationships of North American Gomphidae and their close relatives. *Systematic Entomology* 42: 347-358.

WESTFALL, M. J., JR. 1943a. *Enallagma davisi*, a new species from Florida (Odonata). *Entomological News* 54: 103–108.

WESTFALL, M. J., JR. 1943b. The synonymy of *Libellula auripennis* Burmeister and *Libellula jesseana* Williamson, and a description of a new species, *Libellula needhami* (Odonata). *Transactions of the American Entomological Society* 69: 17–31.

WESTFALL, M. J., JR. 1947. A new *Macromia* from North Carolina. *Journal of the Elisha Mitchell Scientific Society* 63: 32–36.

WESTFALL, M. J., JR. 1956. A new species of *Gomphus* from Alabama (Odonata). *Quarterly Journal of the Florida Academy of Sciences* 19: 251–258

WESTFALL, M. J., JR. 1957. A new species of *Telebasis* from Florida (Odonata: Zygoptera). *Florida Entomologist* 40: 19–27.

WESTFALL, M. J., JR. 1975. A new species of *Gomphus* from Arkansas (Odonata: Gomphidae). *Florida Entomologist* 58: 91–95.

WESTWOOD, J. O. 1837. *Illustrations of exotic entomology by Dru Drury. A new edition brought down to the present state of the science.* London.

WHITE III, H. B. 2016. R. Heber Howe Jr.: New England Odonatologist. *Argia* 28 (1): 25-27.

WHITE III, H. B. & CALHOUN, J.C. 2009. Miss Mattie Wadsworth (1862-1943): Early Woman Author in *Entomological News*. *Transactions of the American Entomological Society* 135(4) 413-429.

WHITE III, H. B. & O'BRIEN, M. 2017. Naming an Undescribed Dragonfly: Williamson's *Williamsonia* and the Travails of R. Heber Howe, Jr. *Northeastern Naturalist* 24, Monograph 14, 1-43.

WILLIAMSON, E. B. 1898. A new species of *Ischnura* (Order Odonata). *Entomological News* 9: 209–211.

WILLIAMSON, E. B. 1900. Notes on a few Wyoming dragonflies (Order Odonata). *Entomological News* 11: 453–458.

WILLIAMSON, E. B. 1902. A new species of *Gomphus* (Odonata) related to *G. fraternus*. *Entomological News* 13: 47–49.

WILLIAMSON, E. B. 1903. A proposed new genus of Odonata (dragonflies) of the subfamily Aeschninae, group *Aeschna*. *Entomological News* 14: 2–8.

WILLIAMSON, E. B. 1907a. Two new North American dragonflies. *Entomological News* 18: 1–7.

WILLIAMSON, E. B. 1907b. A collecting trip north of Sault Ste. Marie, Ontario. *Ohio Naturalist* 7: 129-148.

WILLIAMSON, E. B. 1908a. Three related American species of Aeshna. *Entomological News* 19: 264-272; 301-308.

WILLIAMSON, E. B. 1908b. A new dragonfly (Odonata) belonging to the Cordulinae, and a revision of the classification of the subfamily. *Entomological News* 19: 428–434.

WILLIAMSON, E. B. 1909. The North American dragonflies (Odonata) of the genus *Macromia*. *Proceedings of the United States National Museum* 37: 369–398.

WILLIAMSON, E. B. 1914. *Gomphus pallidus* and two new related species. *Entomological News* 25: 49–58.

WILLIAMSON, E. B. 1922a. Libellulas collected in Florida by Jesse H. Williamson, with description of a new species (Odonata). *Entomological News* 33: 13–19

WILLIAMSON, E. B. 1922b. Notes on *Celithemis* with descriptions of two new species (Odonata). *Occasional papers of the Museum of Zoology, University of Michigan*. No. 108: 1–22.

WILLIAMSON, E. B. 1922c. Enallagmas collected in Florida and South Carolina by Jesse H. Williamson with descriptions of two new species (Odonata, Agrionidae). *Entomological News* 33: 114–118, 138–144.

WILLIAMSON, E. B. 1923a. A new species of *Williamsonia* (Odonata–Corduliinae). *Canadian Entomologist* 55: 96–98.

WILLIAMSON, E. B. 1923b. Notes on American species of *Triacanthagyna* and *Gynacantha*. *University of Michigan Museum of Zoology, Miscellaneous Publications* No. 9: 1–80.

WILLIAMSON, E. B. 1931. A new North American *Somatochlora* (Odonata–Cordulinae). *Occasional papers of the Museum of Zoology, University of Michigan*. No. 225: 1–8.

WILLIAMSON, E. B. 1932. Two new species of *Stylurus* (Odonata–Gomphinae). *Occasional papers of the Museum of Zoology, University of Michigan* No. 247: 1–18.

WILLIAMSON, E. B. & GLOYD, L. K. 1933. A new *Somatochlora* from Florida (Odonata–Cordulinae). *Occasional papers of the Museum of Zoology, University of Michigan* No. 262: 1–7.

Appendix

Categorisation of roots of the names of genera and species

Within each category relevant roots are in *italics*.

People
From antiquity or literature

*Amphi*agrion	*Argia*	Celi*themis*	Croco*themis*
Ery*themis*	Macro*themis*	Nanno*themis*	*Nehalennia*
Palto*themis*	Peri*themis*	Pla*themis*	
amazili	*attala*	*berenice*	*danae*
domitia	*dryas*	*eponina*	*irene*
julia	*junius*	*lais*	*lydia*
marcella	*persephone*	*servilia*	*tezpi*
titia			

Female denominations

domina	*septima*	*vidua*

Friends/ Relatives/ Colleagues

Boyeria	Hagenius	Palaemnema	Remartinia
Williamsonia		aaroni	alberta
albrighti	amelia	anna	barberi
baretti	bellei	bertha	byersi
calverti	carlcooki	daeckii	davisi
doubledayi	dugesi	edmundo	eiseni
elisa	emma	fletcheri	franklini
gaigei	gonzalezi	grafiana	graslinellus
hageni	hagenii	harknessi	hineana
hinei	hodgesi	howei	ivae
jesseana	kellicotti	kennedyi	laurae
leonorae	lintneri	lynnae	margarita
martha	maxwelli	michaeli	morrisoni
needhami	ramburii	rhoadsi	rogersi
sahlbergi	sandrius	sayi	scudderi
selysii	septima	shurtleffi	smithi
stella	thoreyi	townesi	uhleri
walkeri	walshii	walsinghami	westfalli
whitehousei	williamsoni	williamsoni	

Professions

Anax	Lestes	Archilestes	Hetaerina
heros	princeps		

Appendix

Places

Geographical Provenance

*Neo*erythromma	*alabamensis*	*alachuensis*	*alleghaniensis*
americana	*arizonicus*	*azteca*	*californica*
californicus	*canadensis*	*cardenium*	*caribbea*
carolina	*comanche*	*cubensis*	*eremita*
extranea	*floridensis*	*georgiana*	*hudsonica*
illinoiensis	*insularis*	*insularis*	*internum*
kurilis	*mainensis*	*maya*	*mexicana*
nahuana	*nayaritensis*	*novaehispaniae*	*oklahomensis*
ozarkensis	*pacifica*	*patricia*	*peruviana*
pima	*potulentus*	*resolutum*	*rupinsulensis*
sabino	*sitchensis*	*susbehcha*	*weewa*
tarascana	*tonto*	*virginiensis*	*weewa*
yamaskanensis			

North/South/East/West

*Hesper*agrion		*australis*	*boreale*
borealis	*eurinus*	*frigida*	*glacialis*
hudsonica	*occidentis*	*septentrionalis*	*subarctica*

Environment/habitat

Acanth*agrion*	Amphi*agrion*	Apanis*agrion*	Canna*phila*
Amphi*agrion*	Chrom*agrion*	*Helo*cordulia	Hesper*agrion*
Idiataphe	Hesper*agrion*	Zoni*agrion*	*amnicola*
frigida	*glacialis*	*juncea*	*sarracenia*

Appearance
Morphology

*Acanth*agrion	*Aphylla*	*Basi*aeschna	*Brachymesia*
Brechmorhoga	*Cordulegaster*	*Calo*pteryx	*Cordulia*
*Coryph*aeshna	*Didymops*	*Doro*cordulia	*Dromogomphus*
Dythemis	*Epitheca*	*Erpeto*gomphus	*Erythrodiplax*
Gomphus	*Gynacantha*	*Ischnura*	*Leptobasis*
Leucorrhinia	*Macromia*	*Miathyria*	*Micrathyria*
*Nasi*aeschna	*Neoerythromma*	*Neoneura*	*Neurocordulia*
Octogomphus	*Oplon*aeschna	*Orthemis*	*Pachydiplax*
*Palto*themis	*Perithemis*	*Phyllocycla*	*Phyllogomph*oides
Planiplax	*Plathemis*	*Progomphus*	*Protoneura*
*Rhion*aeschna	*Somato*chlora	*Stylogomphus*	*Stylurus*
Sympetrum	*Tanypteryx*	*Telebasis*	*Tacho*pteryx
Tramea	*Triacanthagyna*	abbreviatum	acuminatus
aequabilis	aequalis	albi*stylus*	angulatum
angusti*folia*	angusti*pennis*	antennatum	antilope
armata	armatus	auri*pennis*	axilena
basidens	bison	brevi*phylla*	brevi*stylus*
canis	carunculatum	cervula	clausum
clepshydra	concisum	constricta	cornutus
costi*ferum*	crassus	crocei*pennis*	cultellatum
cynosura	damula	demorsa	denticollis
deplanata	diastatops	digiticollis	dilatatus
dimidiata	dissocians	dorsalis	elongata
ensigera	exilis	forcipata	forcipatus
forficula	fumi*pennis*	furcata	furcifer
furcillata	gracilis	gravida	heterodon
heterodoxum	inacuta	inaequalis	incurvata

incurvatus	*inequiunguis*	*integricollis*	*intensa*
linearis	lineati*frons*	lineati*pes*	longi*pennis*
longi*pes*	lutei*pennis*	melino*gaster*	*nervosa*
*nodi*sticta	pall*ipes*	*palmata*	*palmata*
parvidens	*pentacantha*	*plana*	*protracta*
psilus	*rectangularis*	*recurvatum*	sanguini*ventris*
semicircularis	*sigma*	*sigmastylus*	*simplicicollis*
spicatus	*spiniceps*	*spinigera*	*spinosa*
spinosus	*spumarius*	*sulcatum*	*tenera*
tenuatus	*tibialis*	*trifida*	*tuberculifera*
unguiculatus	*vacillans*	*ventricosus*	*verticalis*
vesiculosa	*villosipes*	viridi*frons*	xantho*soma*

Color

*Chrom*agrion	*Croco*themis	*Eryth*emis	*Erythro*diplax
*Leuco*rrhinia	Neo*erythro*mma		Somato*chlora*
*albi*cincta	*albi*stylus	*auri*pennis	basi*fusca*
citrina	*concolor*	*crocei*pennis	*cuprea*
cyanea	*discolor*	*exusta*	*ferruginea*
fervida	*flavescens*	*flavida*	*fumi*pennis
funerea	*fusca*	*herbida*	*immunda*
lividus	*lucifer*	*luctuosa*	*lugens*
*lutei*pennis	*melino*gaster	*moesta*	*multicolor*
nigrescens	*obscurus*	*oenea*	*olivaceus*
pallens	*pallidula*	*pallidum*	*pallidus*
*palli*pes	*pictum*	*quadricolor*	*rubicundulum*
sanguini*ventris*	*sepia*	*tenebrosa*	*umbrata*
umbrosa	*vinosa*	viridi*frons*	*viriditas*
vivida	*vulnerata*	*xantho*soma	

The Scientific Names of North American Dragonflies

		Pattern	
Celithemis	*Zoniagrion*		*abdominalis*
albicincta	*annulata*	*apicalis*	*aspersum*
aspersus	*balteata*	*basifusca*	*bilineata*
binotata	*bipunctata*	*brevicincta*	*cingulata*
costalis	*designatus*	*diadema*	*didyma*
dimidiata	*exclamationis*	*fasciata*	*filosa*
geminatus	*hastata*	*hymenaea*	*interrupta*
lacerata	*lacrimans*	*laterale*	*lineatifrons*
lineatipes	*luteipennis*	*maculata*	*maculata*
nodisticta	*notatus*	*obliqua*	*obsoleta*
onusta	*ornata*	*petechialis*	*plagiatus*
quadratum	*quadrimaculata*	*saturata*	*saucium*
semiaquea	*semicinctum*	*semifasciata*	*signatum*
signiferum	*spoliatus*	*stigmatus*	*submedianus*
subornata	*taeniolata*	*transversa*	*verticalis*

		Size	
Macrodiplax	*Macromia*	*Micrathyria*	*Nannothemis*
abbreviatus	*angustifolia*	*angustipennis*	*brevicincta*
breviphylla	*brevistylus*	*crassus*	*diminutus*
grandis	*heros*	*ingens*	*intensa*
longipennis	*longipes*	*magnifica*	*minor*
minuscula	*minusculum*	*minuta*	*minutus*
parvulus	*perparva*	*princeps*	*vastus*

Appendix

From typical species

*Amphi*agrion   *Ophio*gomphus   *Oplon*aeschna

Beauty, Wonder

*Cal*opteryx

amanda	*amata*	*bella*	*cara*
lepida	*magnifica*	*pulchella*	*superbus*

Similarities to other taxa

*Apanis*agrion	*Argia*	*Arigomphus*	*Enallagma*
*Erpeto*gomphus	*Gomphaeschna*	*Libellula*	Macro*diplax*
Macrothemis	*Ophiogomphus*	*Phyllogomphoides*	*Pseudo*leon
adelphus	*adnexa*	*agrioides*	*anceps*
annexum	*anomalus*	*antilope*	*bison*
canis	*cervula*	*collocata*	*composita*
compositus	*conditum*	*congener*	*consanguis*
cynosura	*damula*	*disjunctus*	*divagans*
erratica	*fraternus*	*gemina*	*geminatum*
graslinellus	*hybridus*	*imitans*	*mithroides*
munda	*potulentus*	*pseudimitans*	*translata*
traviatum	*vicinum*		

The Scientific Names of North American Dragonflies

Other			
Behaviour			
Cannaphila	*Coenagrion*	*Pantala*	*Tachopteryx*
Tauriphila	*Tramea*	*alacer*	*apeora*
apomyius	*divagans*	*ebrium*	*erratica*
exsulans	*fugax*	*lentulus*	*madidum*
pertinax	*praecox*	*potulentus*	*provocans*
secreta	*sedula*	*severus*	*stultus*
talaria	*traviatum*	*umbrata*	*vernale*
velox	*vernalis*	*vernalis*	*vesperum*
vibrans	*vigilax*	*vinosa*	*vivida*
Evolution			
Archilestes	*Neoneura*	*Progomphus*	*Protoneura*
Frequency			
Coenagrion	*plebeja*		
Semantic similarities			
adelphus	*colubrinus*	*exsulans*	*illotum*
consanguis	*crotalinus*	*erronea*	*incesta*
fraternus	*elaps*	*divagans*	*pollutum*
	eutainia	*traviatum*	*immunda*
	lampropeltis		

Appendix

Doubt

ambiguum	*dubium*	*interrogatum*	*intricatus*
mendax	*molesta*	*specularis*	

Conservation status of specimen

demorsa	*intacta* ?	*salva*	*stulta* ?

Incertae sedis

From the Latin for "of uncertain placement" this term is used to label a group when its taxonomic position is unclear. We use it loosely for those taxa for which we are unable to deduce a meaning.

*Aes*hna	*Basi*aeschna	*Coryph*aeshna	*Epi*aeschna
*Gomph*aeschna	*Ladona*	*Libellula*	*Nasi*aeschna
*Oplon*aeschna	*Rhion*aeschna	*Tholymis*	
argo	*carolus*	*cavillaris*	*civile*
corruptum	*descriptus*	*durum*	*exsulans*
forensis	*incesta*	*intacta*	*janata*
lentulus	*libera*	*madidum*	*modestus*
munda	*mutata*	*obtrusum*	*pertinax*
pollutum	*posita*	*praecox*	*praevarum*
prognata	*proxima*	*severus*	*specularis*
stultus	*verticalis*	*vibrans*	

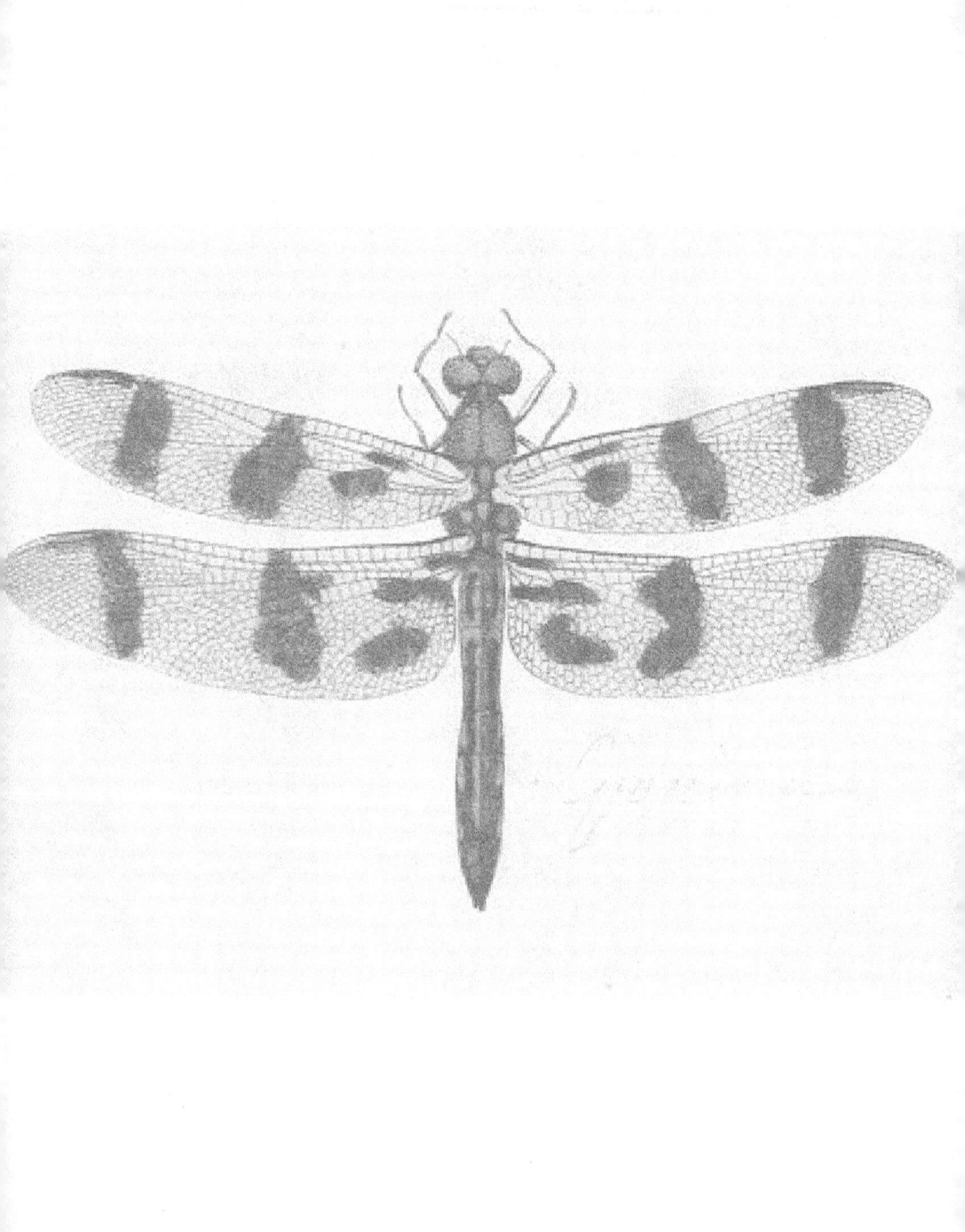

www.ingramcontent.com/pod-product-compliance
Lightning Source LLC
Chambersburg PA
CBHW031143020426
42333CB00013B/493